Philip Johnson
Writings

Foreword by
Vincent Scully

Introduction by
Peter Eisenman

Commentary by
Robert A. M. Stern

Philip Johnson
Writings

New York
Oxford University Press
1979

Frontispiece: Andy Warhol, *Philip Johnson.* 1972.
Acrylic and silkscreen enamel on canvas, 96 x 96 inches.

Grateful acknowledgment is made to the following
for permission to quote from copyright material:
Architectural Review, Architectural Press, Ltd., for "The Frontiersman,"
"House at New Canaan, Connecticut," and "Where Are We At?"
ARTnews, 122 East 42nd Street, New York, N.Y., for "Correct and Magnificent Play,"
copyright © 1953 *ARTnews,* and "Is Sullivan the Father of Functionalism," copyright © 1956 *ARTnews*
George Braziller, Inc., for "Letter to Dr. Jürgen Joedicke"
Mount Holyoke Alumnae Quarterly, for "Our Ugly Cities"
The New York Times, for "In Berlin: Comment on Building Exposition"
Perspecta: Yale Architectural Journal, for "Johnson," "The Seven Crutches of Modern Architecture,"
and "Whence and Whither"
Program, Graduate School of Architecture and Planning, Columbia University, for "Schinkel and Mies"

Library of Congress Cataloging in Publication Data:
Johnson, Philip Cortelyou, 1906–
Writings.
Bibliography: p. 276
1. Architecture, Modern—20th century—Collected works. 2. Architecture—
Collected works. I. Scully, Vincent. II. Stern, Robert A. M. III. Eisenman, Peter.
NA 680.J63   724.9   77-17482
ISBN 0-19-502378-1
ISBN 0-19-502573-3 (signed copies boxed)

Coordinating Editor: Helen M. Franc
Design: Massimo Vignelli
Design Assistant: Lorraine Wild
Printed in the United States of America

Contents

Foreword
Vincent Scully

This anthology of Philip Johnson's critical essays is long overdue. Johnson has occupied a special position in American architecture for more than a generation—one is tempted to say since the publication of his and Hitchcock's The International Style *in 1932. His analysis in that book of what modern architecture was supposed to be must be counted among this century's most influential writings on architectural form. The text was indeed prescriptive rather than simply descriptive in character, and its more doctrinaire aspects have been acknowledged by Johnson as being his rather than Hitchcock's.*

Since that time, Johnson's brilliant and highly entertaining lectures, some of the best of which are represented in the selections here, have been uniquely influential in keeping the interest of architects and laymen alike focused upon architecture as physical form—that is, upon real buildings whose social functions have to be resolved, considered, and experienced in terms of form. In that process, Johnson's tastes and methods, despite some disarming eclecticisms, have remained fundamentally classicizing in character. The excellent seventeenth-century version of Poussin's Landscape with the Burial of Phocion *that is so prominently displayed in his Glass House is not there for nothing. Its geometric structure and calm, aristocratic theme represent the heart of Johnson's artistic aspirations, though his anarchic modern wit and Ezra Pound-like Americanism prevent him from sustaining the high seriousness of that classic mode for very long. "When Neimee gives you the Cartee Blanchee," he said in a lecture of 1977 about working in Texas, "by God, you know you've arrived." In his lectures of thirty years ago his most famous aphorism had been "I'd rather sleep in the nave of Chartres Cathedral with the nearest john six blocks down the street than I would in a Harvard house with back-to-back bathrooms." There is clearly a difference in the critical value of the two remarks, but each represents a perception, at once realistic and ironic, of what architecture is all about: namely, its effect on human emotions, and getting it built. Each statement shocked its hearers a little at the time, but the later one less than the earlier, probably because the younger generation had begun to grow up to Johnson's ironies, had indeed begun to learn from him, as from events in general, to value style and intelligence in human beings, and to loathe hypocrisy, sentimentality, and cant. Those vices, which were once all too conspicuous in the teaching and criticism of modern architecture, have indeed always been the primary targets of Johnson's wit. Contempt for them has occasionally led him into some extreme social and philosophical positions and, more permanently, into a kind of impatience which has sometimes seemed a flaw in his intellectual processes. But it has also directed his major perception, noted above: that Architecture is Form, and that intentions in architecture usually count for very little unless alchemized into form. Here Johnson reminds us of Geoffrey Scott, who in* The Architecture of Humanism *of 1914 ridiculed what he regarded as the major anti-formal fallacies of architectural criticism. Consequently, when Johnson had a choice of masters during the thirties, he passed over Gropius and seized hold of Mies van der Rohe; and events have proved him right to have done so, since Mies still remains the classic shaper of most of our contemporary architectural types, from apartment, office, and government buildings to schools and airports. He has created this century's most pervasive academic architecture. Johnson apparently understood Mies's special and academically viable union of universal concept with materialistic particularity long before most other people did, and he has more or less held on to the resultant shapes in his own work. Not always: he traveled toward Rome, for example, during the early fifties, at about the same time as Kahn, but Johnson never probed as systematically as Kahn into Roman structure and space, so that his "Roman" buildings remain essentially scenographic in character.*

But Johnson has always supplemented his historical interests with a rich experience of directly contemporary painting and sculpture, and the growth of his distinguished collection in later years has not only coincided with his design of some outstanding museums but also with the general return of his work toward basically Miesian forms. Yet we might argue that Johnson's lectures (in which medium most of the ideas in his writings originally took shape) have on the whole been even more effective and influential than his buildings. The latter, it is true, have some special qualities, essentially humanistic ones: moderate scale and a general air that can only be described as taut and tasteful. The lectures, though much in the same clear and deceptively brittle mode, have more body and bite to them. They are, perhaps paradoxically, more physical than the buildings; they project the kind of primitive architectural dance that the buildings tend to lack. They can, for example, make an audience experience architecture's spatial physicality by situating its members in space with an intense physical awareness of familiar lecture halls that they never had before. I can vividly remember Johnson doing exactly that in malevolent old Room 100 at Yale in 1947. Now, in the 1970's, he is still the only lecturer who can make Rudolph's terrifying Hastings Hall behave. He stands right in the middle of the deadly perspective and at once sanctions and controls it. Taking up something equivalent to the fourth ballet position in which Rigaud painted Louis XIV, he forces the concrete masses back and keeps them there. He invokes architecture by his presence even more than by his words. He is so good at controlling an audience that he can be a shameless demagogue when the mood takes him. (The same with clients: his job on Hines in the multi-screen, commercial, designed-to-rent space in Pennzoil Place is an outrageous classic in the extensive literature deriving from the flattery of patrons by artists. Perhaps only Wright was better at it, though his style was of a different era.) But there is always a kind of existential truth in even Johnson's most outrageous attitudinizings, because the larger principles behind them tend in fact to be truly existential in character. Now is now for Johnson. He deals with what is and enjoys it and doesn't expect any special favors from fate because of it. History, in his view, shapes but can hardly comfort or guide us, and since the future belongs to the young simply because they are young, then (Johnson's most endearing attitude of all) they are probably right today; and, at his best, he has systematically tried to understand, encourage, and employ their force.

Is there, however, no building by Johnson that is as significant and architecturally inspirational as his lectures have been? Of course there is: the Glass House itself—of all Johnson's works at once the most personal and universal, a single living unit plugged directly into the going sources of power and totally opened to nature thereby. If those sources were to dry up, the shape of the problem would change, but the fundamental humanist challenge would remain: how to use technology in order to be free; how to shake off conceptual limitations in order to be released to all the choices of life and the magnificent rhythm of the natural world. Johnson is fond of saying that he couldn't live in the Glass House without the Brick one, but this is typical ironic self-deprecation, because the Glass House is the heart of what Johnson believes in, which is nothing less than the ageless humanist dream stated in contemporary terms and embodied in a contemporary form. The Glass House almost escapes from matter into pure Idea, which the humanists would have regarded as its fundamental strength. And in its proximity to intellectual concept it is perhaps not so different from Johnson's bright, impatient words. It is at least all of a piece with them and—since it is *a building—it remains for architects the most solid moral sanction for those words. In it, for nearly thirty years, Johnson has held what amounts to an open seminar for those who care about architecture. The benefit that American architecture as a whole has gained from that ongoing conversation is incalculable. It began at a time when the American criticism of architecture by architects was at an extremely low ebb, and when the architectural profession itself was all too largely sunk in its habitual, sullen, anti-intellectualism. Johnson more than anyone else turned all that around, and for a while he was quite venomously hated for it. Yet, however different they were and became—and this itself is essential to the liberating point—it is hard to imagine Kahn, Venturi, Moore, and many others (including Eisenman and Stern) without that critical conversation, and indeed without Johnson before them. In the larger sense, Johnson revived the great literate tradition of Sullivan and Wright, and, transforming it into a more contemporaneous, ironic mode, transmitted it to the younger men. He spoke and wrote, with unflagging wit and occasional daring, the words reproduced in this book. Through them he played a central part in opening up the minds of two whole and very effective generations of architects and critics, and he showed them a little something about classy defiance as well.*

From that point of view, the contributions of Eisenman and Stern to this volume seem to me especially interesting and even moving. Stern, it is true, at times uses his comments to tick off some inveterate enemies, and Eisenman projects a rather cabalistic aura of cultural crisis and secret doom. But Stern's paragraphs are full of precise information and on-the-spot memories of old wars (in which he played a role no less honorable than Johnson's), while Eisenman's essay seems to me quite the most thoughtful and challenging that has yet been written about Johnson's writings and buildings. It endows Johnson with—or perceives in him—a complexity and ambiguity of character that has not been sufficiently appreciated before, and it suggests some tragic dimensions not previously recognized. Johnson himself might well be secretly pleased at such recognition (as who would not be), but he will certainly pooh-pooh it. That, too, is part of what this volume may now help us all to recognize better as a structure of thought and character in a Johnson not so simple, and not simply perceptive and amusing, but increasingly multi-leveled, shadowed, and complex.

Introduction[1]
Peter Eisenman

"In architectural works, man's pride, man's triumph over gravitation, man's will to power assume visible form. Architecture is a veritable oratory of power made by form." Friedrich Nietzsche, quoted by Philip Johnson, "The Seven Crutches of Modern Architecture," 1954.

Philip Johnson may be the last architect of the Enlightenment.

"Words tend to become tools of knowledge . . . tend to increase interest in the values of the description of things and not in things themselves . . . words are for the mind, not the eye. Words . . . deny us the mysterious communication by the eye." Johnson, "Why We Want Our Cities Ugly," 1967.

Philip Johnson is an essayist, an anti-*philosophe*. After days of reading all that he has written, and after seeing much of it compacted into one volume, one has a sense of having been inundated with an erudition rather than confronted with a body of theory. His writings are a monument, perhaps more so than his buildings, to an education and culture that are no longer with us. The essays, while admittedly not of the belles-lettres tradition, nevertheless possess wit, charm, and devilish insight. What on first glance appears to be somewhat casual writing, tending in fact toward the facile, conceals a rapier-like fineness which, without drawing blood, slices the world into slabs of his measured content. For Johnson words are thought, and art is feeling. His writing is a constant struggle to have beauty triumph over idea.

"Ideas keep us from the agony of art." Johnson, "Beyond Monuments," 1973.

This is not intended to be a discussion of the complete writings of Philip Johnson. It is based on a selection that attempts to place his widely dispersed written *oeuvre* into some understandable framework, and thus for the first time tries not only to see the range of ideas inherent in Johnson's writings but also to give them their intellectual due; to demonstrate that they are not, as he himself would have us believe, merely the exotic banter of an elite connoisseur.

And, although Johnson would profess to the contrary, would disclaim all manner of knowing, it will be my contention that in this tremendous outpouring of words there is a highly selective attitude that subtly suggests another Johnson: the ideologue.

"Words mean what you want them to mean." Johnson, paraphrasing Through the Looking Glass, *Informal Talk, Architectural Association, 1960.*

The writings discussed here are intended to isolate and position his ideology. In doing so, the usual classification of writings according to chronology or according to the building types or individual architects discussed in them is eschewed for a litmus of another kind. Thus, the subject matter here is not necessarily all of Johnson's best or even most important writing; some is not "vintage" Johnson. But insofar as any text contributes to our understanding of the ideological mind, it is worth considering.

As a young architect who holds Johnson in great esteem, I must say at the outset that this introduction is not an apologia for his activity. Nor is it merely a gesture to one of the few architects who from the 1930's to the present has stood against the philistinism of conventional practice, who created a climate for serious discussion of architecture, and who fostered a generation of young architects as few others in his position have. It is rather an attempt to make Johnson stand up and be counted, to be seen, despite himself, for the impact he has had on our architecture (not that we necessarily believe him, nor does he want us to), and to bring the force of his consciousness to the public domain. That consciousness must be seen for the seriousness of its discourse.

On the other hand, it is perhaps a little ironic to expose what turns out to be Johnson's self-made myth of himself as a counter-intellectual gadfly. Yet it is necessary to do so in order to allow history to write its own myths. Moreover, in a time of diffusion, a time of what many people would call post-modernism, the sensibility that is Johnson's needs to be identified.

"The word kills art." Johnson, "Style and the International Style," Barnard College, 1955.

On Functionalism

"All architecture is more interested in design than in plumbing." Johnson, "Where Are We At?," 1960.

"You can embellish architecture by putting toilets in." Johnson, "The Seven Crutches of Modern Architecture," 1954.

There can be little doubt that by the late 1920's Johnson, the young philosophy student out of Harvard traveling in Germany, understood and distinguished two intersecting currents in modern architecture: one, the moral sanction given to the forms of the machine aesthetic; the other, the political sanction given to the polemics of the machine society. These intersected and had a common root in the doctrine that was known generally as functionalism.

It is clear from his first published essay on architecture that Johnson recognized the potential for such a dual practice to have a certain paralyzing effect on any form of aesthetic idealism,[2] and it is this idealism that must be seen as the underpinning of his conception of architecture. Thus, in the brief period from 1931 to 1933 Johnson used his writings to construct a very intricate counterposition to functionalism. Careful, clever, moving among people and ideas in the half-light of the euphoria of the late twenties and early thirties, he cut quietly and subtly at the moral and political roots of the dual doctrine of modern architecture. He did so not with theory or polemic, but by infiltration—by developing a fifth column that paraded as the standard-bearer of that dual doctrine, seemingly marching alongside the cadre of architectural modernists who carried the enthusiasm of those early years.

It is only when one examines, with almost forty years of hindsight, the disintegration of that movement that one can see mirrored in the American context the cunning and efficacy of his activity. The substance of this activity and the tactics he employed can be pieced together from the texts in this book. Johnson's reasons for writing them, however, are more elusive; yet it will be argued that it is precisely these reasons that remain the key to understanding the essential Johnson. In short, why should anyone seek to erode the basis of his own activity? That is, why should someone who is overtly propagandizing modern architecture at the same time be covertly eroding its basic tenets? This essay can only begin to probe the surface of such a phenomenon. It will remain for scholars and historians to elaborate the full implications of the paradox: the narrow distinction between ideologue and anti-ideologue, between artist and connoisseur. To see Johnson's position vis-à-vis functionalism is the first step in unraveling this riddle.

For Johnson, architecture in 1931 had three attributes: first, it was progressive; second, it stood for originality and individual genius; and finally, it represented the practical expression of solutions to American building problems.[3] Now, while we can read "progressive" and "practical expression" as two aspects of functionalism, the second attribute, concerning originality and individual genius, seems to contradict the other two. Moreover, when the architect said, "Can I make this building serve its purpose?" Johnson meant, "Can I make it look as if it is serving its purpose?" This sotto voce contradiction of functionalism belies a real desire for a return to some *Gesamtkunstwerk* conception of architecture.

"Beautiful workmanship of the machine . . . rather than imitation by the machine."

"Beyond the practical advantages, modern architecture is beautiful. For while the modern architect accepts the machine age, he also transcends it." Johnson, Built To Live In, *1931.*

Time and again, Johnson's technique is to drive a wedge into an apparently monolithic phenomenon. This technique is articulated for the first time in the two different versions of his review of the Berlin Building Exposition (see p. 49).[4] Here he distinguishes between the empiricism and the positivism of the Anglo-German classical functionalism of Walter Gropius and the essentially Neo-classical idealism of Mies van der Rohe. Describing the house by Mies at the exhibition, Johnson says that it is not, as so many American architects then preferred to think, *purely functional.* This he said at a time when the polemic that accompanied this building of Mies's and many others like it was couched in strict functional dogma. For Johnson to recognize and expose the incipient hegemony of functionalism is not only characteristic of his personal style but also serves his own ideological biases very well.

From this essay on, Johnson never loses an opportunity to use Mies as a cudgel against functionalism. His talk in 1961 honoring Mies is no exception.[5] In it he calls the functionalists "literal-minded believers in . . . *die neue Sachlichkeit*" who felt that "architecture was now at last purely functional."

The second architect Johnson uses to erode the underpinnings of functionalism is Karl Friedrich Schinkel. Johnson's identification with Schinkel is no mere stylistic affinity. His elevation of Schinkel to a position of primacy among all architects of the Western tradition suggests more than questions of historical accuracy or personal preference. At first glance, in Johnson's giving Schinkel priority over Soane, and Mies over Le Corbusier, there is the suggestion of a desire to create a Germanic hegemony, raised simultaneously over the Anglo-Saxon and Latin worlds. But there are subtler implications in this association. For Schinkel has been considered by many to be the first modern architect; he was the first great eclectic. Following the historical sequence of the Renaissance, the Baroque, and the Rococo, styles with a formal consistency and an ideological imprint, Schinkel broke with both the sequence and the consistency. Yet in precisely the sense that Schinkel was modern he was also decidedly un-modern, for he was a Neo-classicist. And Neo-classicism in its concern not only for backs and fronts but also for sides of buildings, and thus for isolated blocks, was ideally suited to the romantic vistas of German nineteenth-century landscape. And it is in the context of this Germanic Neo-classicism that many of the German architects of the twenties and thirties invoked Schinkel's name *against* the specter of modernism in Germany. This fact was not lost on Johnson. So while the selective and analytic eclecticism of Schinkel was in his own time modern, Johnson's invocation of Schinkel the Neo-classicist, as a representative of a sensibility which in a contemporary sense is decidedly anti-modern, is quite a paradoxical confection. Eclecticism was, for Johnson, anti-ideological. It represented an alternative to the first truly synthetic and consistent *Weltanschauung* since the Rococo—that of the International architecture of the Bauhaus. Thus it is with the term "eclectic" that Johnson begins to subvert modernism's hydra-headed ideology.

Now, having said all this, how are we to interpret Johnson's self-proclaimed image of himself, admittedly of a later date, as not merely an eclectic, but a "functional eclectic"?[6]

It is obvious in retrospect that "functionalist" was a vague characterization applied as an ethical balm to objects that might more appropriately have been called either expressionist or rationalist. Yet it is also true that functionalism with its moral imperative seems to deny anything that could be considered eclectic. Conversely, eclecticism by its own definition abjures those principles of "fit-to-form" that are the underpinnings of functionalism. Thus, Johnson's self-invocation of the term "functional"—which he also rejects—must be seen to have several purposes. First, the pairing of the term "functional" with the term "eclectic" cuts the former's ideological edge. (It is no accident that Alfred Barr called Hannes Meyer a "fanatical functionalist," by which he really meant fanatical Marxist).[7] Second, the term "functional" is useful to Johnson in that it identifies him with main-line modernism. But the operative term in the pair is in fact "eclectic," for it gave Johnson room to move.

Since eclectic architecture is an architecture of connoisseurs and not of purists, it serves to protect architectural borrowings from questions of principle. Thus, we see one of the effects of Johnson's multiple inversion. Eclecticism allows him to choose from history whatever forms, shapes, or directions he wants. In both his architecture and his writings it allows him the freedom of a first leap from the mainstream. And if one is as knowledgeable as Johnson, who knows his sources better than anyone, then one can create new images from little-known references. Hence the scalloped, cylindrical pastiche on the tower of the Kline Geology Laboratory at New Haven may be seen to derive from Hans Poelzig's drawing for a bank in Dresden, published in an obscure monograph by Theodore Heuss in 1939. The term "eclecticism" in this way provides a context that has no rules, for rules allow everyone to play; it makes for an elitist fantasy masquerading as a populist game.

Johnson's self-proclaimed pairing of functional/eclectic will be seen to be cooperative with his linking of the terms "international" and "style." In the former pairing, "functional" is drained of its morality and "eclectic" seems to deny the ideology inherent in style. In the latter pairing, the ideology is taken from the term "international," and "style" is given a certain morality. These two pairs when taken together have a devastating impact on modernism.

On Style

"We might even question whether words like value or morals are applicable to an architectural style." Johnson, "Whence and Whither," 1965.

A discussion of style in itself, even without the ramifications of "international," is not entirely innocent. To many, it is not merely a search for beauty, as Johnson would have us believe, but often involves a modification of the architectural language itself. But when it comes to Johnson's use of the term "international" in his pairing of the terms "international" and "style," there is an elision, which is an even more elaborate ideological confection than "functional eclectic." For the combination is more complex, less obvious, and more intrinsically loaded. Like the pairing of "functional" and "eclectic," it combines what might have been thought at the time to be mutually exclusive terms.

Since the mid-nineteenth century, the discussion of style has exhibited two parallel tendencies. The one that became the central tradition of German art history since Gottfried Semper was concerned with classification and typologies. The other, coincidental with the rise of the German state, was tinged with a latent nationalism—with the idea that Gothic and Baroque were German in their essence. Johnson should have been aware of this latter interpretation of style.

Nevertheless, as early as his first writings on architecture, Johnson used the term "modern style" to refer to the new architecture which up to then had been referred to in the European context as the "Modern Movement" or "Modern Architecture."[8] And at the same time, Johnson acknowledged its "international" character.[9] But, in fact, its principles as articulated hardly had anything international about them. They were a mix of aesthetics and pragmatics—steel frame, glass wall, and flat roof; standardized construction made possible by mass production; the façade as a reflection of the more important plan. One year later, in 1932, Johnson along with Henry-Russell Hitchcock and Alfred Barr, using similar principles, replaced the term "modern style" with the uncomfortable liaison of "international" and "style." This was the ultimate reduction. From "Modern Movement" to "Modern Architecture" to "Modern Style" to "International Style":[10] in the first transformation, the ideological content implied by the word "movement" was neutralized by the word "architecture"; in the second transformation, the neutrality of "architecture" gave way to the non-ideological implications of "style"; and in the last transformation, the politically explosive term "international" became attached as merely an adjectival appendage to the notion of style.[11] Moreover, the final incarnation of the term did not even include the notion of "modern."[12] As will be seen, this sequence of subtle linguistic transformations holds a further key to Johnson's intellectual position.

"The International Style, for example, needs no one to say it was good or it was bad. The International Style is its own justification." Johnson, "Where Are We At?," 1960.

In most of Johnson's definitions, the International Style is seen as containing the same ingredients as the Modern Movement; and it is no mere accident that on first reading its principles seem to square with those of main-line modernism. In the catalogue *Modern Architecture* which accompanied the 1932 exhibition, the principles of the International Style, as first elaborated by Alfred Barr, are volume, regularity, flexibility, and a fourth principle comprehending technical perfection, proportion, composition, and lack of ornament. In the book *The International Style* of the same year, the principles are reduced to three: emphasis on volume; regularity as opposed to symmetry; and dependence on the intrinsic elegance of materials, technical perfection, and fine proportions, as opposed to applied ornament. The elaboration of principles in these terms conveniently allows Johnson and Hitchcock to elide modernism with the International Style and to group Mies, Gropius, and Le Corbusier together. But how, for example, does the principle of volume square with Johnson's own description of Mies? Volume is "space enclosed by planes or surfaces," says Johnson, a definition which really only befits Le Corbusier's early work; Mies, according to Johnson, thought of his houses as anything but volumes, as screens connecting inside and outside. Thus, even though the work of these two architects might have looked similar, both making use of a stripped-down, unembellished set of white planes, only the concerns of Le Corbusier seem parallel to other modernist activity. By grouping these two together, Johnson negates the unique significance and impact of modernism, namely the potential change in the nature and meaning of the architectural object and the radical change proposed in the relationship of viewer to object.

Secondly, for Johnson to reduce "modernism" to a style is one thing, but to attempt the same tactic with the term "international" is quite another matter. For the word has a very complex currency. It had already been used by Walter Gropius, in his book *Internationale Architektur* of three years previous, to signal the ascendancy of Bauhaus influence beyond the boundaries of Weimar culture. In another sense, the term was obviously imbued with the aspirations of the Left. Thus, when "international" was put together with "style," the two had a corrosive effect on one another. The moral and political force of "international" became compressed—its pulse was lost. It was now the term "style" and not the term "international" which was injected with ideological content—not too surprisingly, in view of Johnson's particular sensitivity to the term "style," which he had put forward in the first place.

This transformation of the Modern Movement into the International Style—the linguistic transformation marking the actual transformation—was to characterize American architecture until the late sixties. Furthermore, what can be seen in retrospect to have been a clever manipulation of the ideology of the Modern Movement in Europe transformed a pluralistic conception of the good society into an individualistic model of the good life and thus reduced a cultural alternative to a stylistic nicety.

This reduction of modernism to a discussion of style drained out the ideological implications of the European architecture of the twenties and packaged them neatly into a consumable fashion that was to burst rampant onto the American scene after World War II. Corporate imagery in the guise of modern architecture inevitably became an object for consumption. Considering the ultimately left-wing ideology implicit in much of what was in the twenties the mainstream Modern Movement in Europe, it is not surprising that Johnson would have attempted to subvert these implications. Whether this transformation was a conscious endeavor is not at issue; the fact remains that in Johnson's writing this ideology is reduced to style.

It is in this context that style becomes architecture for art's sake. Style allows Johnson to break from the implicit ideology of modernism to his own iconoclastic eclecticism. But to situate modernism in a modern style—and thus to remove its ideological content—implicitly transforms his own latent eclecticism into an ideology. Paradoxically, the International Style must then be defined by Johnson as a counter to the confusion of a continuing eclecticism.[13]

The circle has closed. One is left with no opening, whether we opt for Johnson on style or Johnson on eclecticism. For, in fact, his attack is on the ideology of "modernism" and not on the politics of "international." Again he is clearing ground for himself, and the International Style is the cover for the operation. The International Style thus becomes both the label and the sanction for his own latent ideological beliefs. Often in such games of hide-and-seek the smoke screens become confused with the reality. One often falls into intellectual traps that in fact were set for others. But in Johnson's case, the strategy places him outside the modern canon not only functionally, but also formally. Again this is Johnson the iconoclast driving holes into the bottom of the ship of modernism, rocking it, and then jumping before anyone realizes that the boat is sinking.

On Architects

"Architecture, one would think, has its own validity. It needs no reference to any other discipline to make it 'viable' or to 'justify' its value." Johnson, "Where Are We At?," 1960.

If we were to leave Johnson on functionalism, and on style, we would be leaving the paradox he has introduced into these terms without a plausible explanation with respect to his own architecture. However, a third category of discussion, on architects, while it presumably leaves the world of ideas for the world of people, exposes a set of ideas on architecture that are perhaps more easily accessible to us. For much of what Johnson says about other architects will, in reality, reveal more about his own architecture and in turn will begin to create the lens that we must inevitably focus on him. For, in fact, when Johnson is speaking about the work of other architects, he is often speaking about himself. This produces a kind of reversal of historical roles, whereby it is "Boswell" who becomes a surrogate for Johnson, the biographer who becomes autobiographer. Therefore, while this body of writing seems to be yet another attempt to distance himself not only from his own architecture but also from himself, in fact it brings us closer to him. And it is through this surrogate of other architects that another inversion in Johnson's writings can be noticed. For example, when speaking of "functionalism" or "style," terms which are supposedly laden with idea content, he seems to be trying to undermine their principles. But when he is speaking of other architects, supposedly a more subjective category, he appears to be consciously elaborating his own principles. Taken separately, there is nothing unusual in either of these activities. But what is rather incongruous—and perhaps unconscious on Johnson's part—is the combination of the two: the simultaneous urge to reduce the idea content in terms that are generally thought to contain ideas and, conversely, to infuse ideas into the context of personalities. For example, the set of recurring themes that appear in Johnson's architecture, which would most appropriately be discussed in the context of the International Style, are not; instead, when he turns to another architect such as Buckminster Fuller, one of Johnson's favorite targets in the post-World War II period, the first of these themes—the problem of entry and approach—becomes a primary issue. How does one put a door in a dome, he repeatedly asks. Let's not call Fuller's work architecture but sculpture, he says. (Again he makes a distinction that on other occasions he refutes.) Sculpture is not architecture precisely because it does not have the problem of how one gets in and out. Entry—the problem of the door in the wall and the approach to the wall—is fundamental to the nature of Johnson's architecture.

"Let Fuller put together the dymaxion dwellings of the people so long as we architects can design their tombs and their monuments." Johnson, "Where Are We At?," 1960.

While the same irony and superficial disdain are also manifest when Johnson speaks of Le Corbusier and Frank Lloyd Wright, his discussion of these architects again reveals several of his own preferences. Johnson seems at his most elusive in dealing with Le Corbusier, giving and taking away simultaneously, seeming to reduce ideas to personalities. For example, in his talk at Yale about the postwar work of Le Corbusier,[14] he begins by implying that some people would call Le Corbusier's work "sculpture" in the pejorative sense of the word; he then opines that the difference between architecture and sculpture is purely semantic, and then he goes on to call Le Corbusier's work "space sculpture." Continuing in the same vein, he observes, "People who do not like Le Corbusier would say . . ."; and then he will parenthetically remark that he, of course, likes Le Corbusier, sometimes.

His discussion of Le Corbusier, however, also reveals a second pervasive and obsessive theme, that of ideal form. In one such text Johnson will speak of the pilotis of the Villa Savoye as a means for Le Corbusier to expose the sixth and most difficult side of his *prisme pur*;[15] in the same text he will speak of the oversized pilotis of the *prisme pur* of the Marseilles Unité d'Habitation as a play of fantasy versus discipline—the pilotis are like the hands of vaudeville weight lifters, which by their oversized straining give one the intense feeling of mass; and in a third instance, looking at the Law Courts at Chandigarh, he says the *prisme pur* is turned inside out like a glove—the tricks of the Marseilles roof and the pilotis are now put inside the volume. Here in a flurry of words is a history that has never been written, a capacity to see that cannot be taught, and a sense of his own architecture that has never been elaborated.

When Johnson turns to Frank Lloyd Wright he is somewhat more direct. Typically, his remarks will begin with what seems to be a profound compliment, but delivered in such an offhand manner as to give one pause. He will then follow with something like, "and he is also a great nineteenth-century architect" or "he belongs to another generation." If the meaning of this was lost on Johnson's audiences, it certainly was not lost on Wright. Johnson's writings are scored by allusions to the continuing antagonism between himself and Wright.

These examples are merely a hint of a method of operation that is relentless in its constancy, which at every repetition diminishes and distances its subject. But it is Mies van der Rohe who provides the key to the essential Johnson. Of all architects it is Mies to whom Johnson refers without any of his customary irony. Yet it is not a simple connection that can be made, for while there are obvious similarities in the work of the two men, these are used by Johnson as a foil for their less obvious differences. For example, when Johnson talks about Mies's Seagram Building he again reveals one of his own major preoccupations—the problem of the corner. There are three important corners, says Johnson: the corner against the corner, the corner against the sky, the corner against the ground. This attitude toward the corner distinguishes his concept of the *prisme pur* from that implied by the taut frontal surfaces of Le Corbusier. For Le Corbusier, the notion of the skin neutralizes the corner as it wraps around it and, in its suggestion of containment, gives character to the space inside and creates a dialogue between the internal spaces and the surface; whereas for Johnson, the concern for the corner reduces this dialogue and concentrates its energy in the intersection of the four planes rather than in the planes themselves. For Mies, on the other hand, as for Johnson, the articulation of the corner is primary; yet again there is a difference. While for Mies the corner reveals both structure and connection, for Johnson the corner involves a detachment of the form from its structural function and an isolation of the form from the internal and external volume of which it is traditionally an integral part. Thus, to see the kind of Neo-classicism he creates at Lincoln Center as having anything to do with Mies, or for that matter with his disaffection with the International Style, is to miss his idea of the surrogate, which now is also in the form itself. Therefore, while at first glance Johnson's corner seems to mean "Mies" or "Schinkel," in fact it means something which is quite the opposite. This duplicity in the form is, of course, completely parallel to the technique of duplicity in the writing. One has only to see the hanging columns of the Founders Room in his addition to The Museum of Modern Art to understand that the attempt to detach the structure from the form—to take the supporting function from the column—is not mere wit or capricious mannerism, but rather a way to signal a different attitude to the form "column." For here the form becomes its own *Ding an sich:* this is Johnson the product of

German nineteenth-century philosophy playing a modernist theme.

"How long ago it was that Goethe said the pilaster is a lie! One would answer him today—yes, but what a delightfully useful one." Johnson, "Johnson," 1961.

On Johnson

But in the end, it is not the reality of columns or corners but the metaphor of glass which gives us Johnson on Johnson. Yet is it the transparency of surface or the reflection of mirrored depth that permits us to understand that the cracks in the surface may ultimately be closed by pulling them farther apart? Are we seeing the transparency of Hegelian idealism or the "opacity" of a reflecting mirror telling us something about ourselves at the same time that it conceals something about itself?

"I am a historian first and an architect only by accident and it seems to me that there are no forms to cling to, but there is history." Johnson, Informal Talk, Architectural Association, 1960.

Johnson is at his most opaque when he is speaking of himself—the historian speaking of the architect, the critic reviewing his own book, the architect presenting his house. It is Johnson as a surrogate for Johnson.

One finds the often repeated cadence, particularly in his presentations to university audiences, of Johnson taking off on Johnson, of Johnson being flippant at his own expense. For example, his apparently innocuous introduction to a lecture at Barnard College[16] becomes a key to understanding much of what would seem to be Johnson's wit. His words, seemingly casually chosen, are diabolical mirrors. Not only do they mask his intentions, they also strip and fracture his audience. They beam yet another multiple inversion. Words and audience: first, belief; second, irony and disbelief. So far this is obvious. It is the third mirror that is crucial. It penetrates beneath his own façade. It is his own attempt to make himself believe what he is saying—to suspend his own disbelief. For in this final turn, words attempt to cover the fragility of Johnson's own uncertainty about himself and his own art. Whether he can deceive us or not, he can never wholly deceive himself. He alone lives locked within the reality of his works—they reveal to him what his words attempt to hide.

Thus, for Johnson, the text is a critical instrument. It is the script that distances the performer from his audience. The text forbids the audience access to the reality of the person who is behind the character they are confronting on the stage. But further, it does not allow the actor to know himself. It distances what he says from what he is. For it is from his center—from his own private self—to a periphery of detachment that Johnson must move to make his most incisive contributions. The text provides that generative impulse.

It is Johnson's nature to be always one step ahead, astride every situation while others are off balance. And it is this capacity to understand and pinpoint where that balance is at any given time that gives Johnson the opportunity to remove himself from the center, to be on the edge, and to be able to jump aside to yet another delicate periphery when the center has caught up to his former position. Thus, it is not only the ideology of an anti-ideologue, but perhaps also, and even more importantly, a temperament and an insight that make him impatient with the status quo. His iconoclasm is rooted less in political, social, or any particular aesthetic belief than in the "Prince" inherent in him—the aristocrat who serves neither ideological principles nor historical events.

"How often dislikes and personal preferences of aesthetic form can engender meaningless rationalistic criticism—an attempt to confirm personal taste through generalized logic." Johnson, "Correct and Magnificent Play," 1953.

Johnson is never trapped by such personal rationalizing. For he remains always away from his own center. In his writings he is never caught in the web of his own conceits. He is detached, almost distant from himself. So acutely aware of this separation of his own person from himself is he that he often cites it in others: "the publicist Le Corbusier writing for the architect Le Corbusier."[17] Perhaps he has to be two Johnsons—one the cultural critic, the other the architect—to survive. Perhaps it is this Janus-like capacity that affords him such an unerring view of the cultural landscape as it exists at every moment of its being.

"I consider my own house not so much as a home (though it is that to me) as a clearing house of ideas *which can filter down later, through my own work or that of others." Johnson, quoted by Selden Rodman,* Conversations with Artists, *1957.*

Johnson is at his most transparent—the lucid ideologue—when speaking of his own house. Certainly his 1950 presentation of the Glass House at New Canaan in the *Architectural Review*[18] is an architect's way of presenting his own architecture. It is at once modest, straightforward, and telling. It is obviously the model used by James Stirling in his article "Stirling Connexions,"[19] which consists of parallel photos showing historical precedents and examples of his own work. But while Stirling seems interested in acknowledging what has preceded him, Johnson seems interested in the reverse, in creating a patrimony. It is now Johnson who, while following these precedents in time, by his particular use of them makes them seem as if he were the originator of their use.[20]

Here again Johnson deploys some of what have been his continuing themes about the nature of architecture. For example, in his linking of ideal form to the intellectual revolution of the late eighteenth century, he places himself in a lineage of humanist abstraction, yet in his concern for the oblique angle of approach to a frontalized building and the play of asymmetric rectangles he forges an eclectic union that places his work even before the precedent of Schinkel's work. This essay on the Glass

House is the first instance in which Johnson talks seriously, without his usually self-deprecating irony, the first time that he talks directly about the nature of his *own* architecture.

In 1965, in his article "Whence and Whither,"[21] Johnson further reveals this architectural paternity. He says, with his typically casual iconoclasm, that architecture is not the design of space, but rather the organization of procession; it exists in time. If one takes these two themes, space and procession, as the "brackets" of his words, then the Glass House in New Canaan and Pennzoil Place in Houston can be seen as the two poles of his work. They are in fact both preoccupied with the processional: the one pedestrian, the other vehicular. They are both glazed volumes of non-space, the one transparent glass, the other opaque glass.

From the Parthenon through Schinkel, Choisy, and the Beaux-Arts, architecture was concerned with corners, not fronts; with perspective, not axonometric views. In linking the oblique processional approach to the frontal appearance of the Glass House, Johnson is also countering one of the classical canons of the orthodox modernism of Le Corbusier and Cubism: in the modern canon, the façade was to be frontal, space was layered vertically and understood stereometrically, stress was at the periphery. The Glass House layers space horizontally, and its conception is from the diagonal.

In the traditional sense both Pennzoil and the Glass House are a-spatial; the latter is a void, and the former is a solid. But both lack the traditional energies—tension, compression, and so forth—that mark architectural space. They represent the beginning and the end of modern architecture. The Glass House is transparent and the carrier of metaphoric imagery; Pennzoil is opaque, not metaphoric, not a polemic of the machine-made aesthetic, but rather the mute, unrelenting object itself.

It is only the steel wainscot line on the Glass House that violates this principle of a-spatiality. It turns the glass into a membrane—a container of interior space and not a void. But in none of Johnson's writings on his house can one find a discussion of this very crucial and untypical architectonic gesture, which differentiates him from the Mies van der Rohe of the Barcelona Pavilion and the Farnsworth House.[22]

But ultimately, it is not in the context of his patrimony that one must finally return to Johnson's presentation of his own house.[23] For me, it is in the context of something much more profound that this article and this house are fascinating. For it is here that text, building, and person fuse to shatter the paradox. And it is the casual text caption Johnson gives for his figure 17 in this article (see p. 223) that places the house and Johnson once and for all in a new context:

"The cylinder made of the same brick as the platform from which it springs, forming the main motif of the house, was not derived from Mies but rather from a burnt wooden village I saw once where nothing was left but the foundations and

chimneys of brick." Johnson, "House at New Canaan, Connecticut," 1950.

How are we to interpret such a metaphor? Who builds a house as a metaphoric ruin? Why the burnt-out village as a symbol of one's own house? But further, that Johnson should reveal the source of his imagery seems the most telling of all: the Glass House is Johnson's own monument to the horrors of war. It is at once a ruin and also an ideal model of a more perfect society; it is the nothingness of glass and the wholeness of abstract form. How potent this image will remain long after all of us have gone, as a fitting requiem for both a man's life and his career as an architect! I know of no other architect's house that answers so many questions, has such a symbiotic relationship with personal atonement and rebirth as an individual.

In a more general context, the Glass House prefigures for me the parallel anxiety of post-World War II architecture. It remains the last pure form, the final gesture of a belief in a humanism so debilitated by the events of 1945. And at the same time it contains, in the image of that ruin, the seeds of a new conception of an architecture that is not for the reification of an anthropocentric man, but exhibits a more relativistic condition, a parity between man and his object world.

A successful monument, Johnson has said, should partake of the past and of the time in which it is built.

"A glass box may be of our time, but it has no history." Johnson, Statement concerning the Franklin Delano Roosevelt Memorial, 1962.

Johnson's writings, like his glass box, have the transparency of our time. It will remain for history to reveal their opacity.

Notes to the Introduction

1. *The original intention of my participation in this book was that it be a series of commentaries related to the individual texts by Philip Johnson. These commentaries were to be paired with those of Robert Stern in an effort to suggest two points of view, often contrary, for each of Johnson's texts. However, when it came to deciding which articles were to be included and how they were to be classified, a certain unresolvable opposition between Stern and myself developed. Therefore, it was decided that Stern would make the outline, select the articles, and write the commentaries, and I would write an introduction.*

What follows is an essay developed according to my classification of Johnson's writing. It presents his writings not in any historical sequence or context, but rather as a series of ideas, grouped under these headings: On Functionalism, On Style, On Architects, and On Johnson; it attempts a view of Johnson which has often been obscured by personalities and events. While most of the references are to articles and talks presented in the book, some refer to articles which the reader will have to find in their original sources, a chore made easier by David Whitney and David White's comprehensive bibliography, pp. 276–84.

2. Built To Live In, *a pamphlet prepared for The Museum of Modern Art, March, 1931 (see pp. 29–31). It is interesting to note that in his description of the forthcoming "Modern Architects" exhibition (omitted here), Johnson says that Mies van der Rohe was to plan its installation.*

3. *Ibid.*

4. *"The Berlin Building Exposition of 1931,"* T-Square, *January, 1932; and "In Berlin: Comment on Building Exposition,"* New York Times, *August 9, 1931 (see pp. 49–51).*

5. *"Speech Honoring Mies van der Rohe on His Seventy-Fifth Birthday," Chicago, February 7, 1961 (see pp. 207–8).*

6. *The term was first used by Johnson in his talk to students at the Architectural Association in London in 1960 (see pp. 106–16).*

7. *See his introduction to Henry-Russell Hitchcock and Philip Johnson,* The International Style *(New York: Norton, 1932), p. 14.*

8. Built To Live In, *op. cit.*

9. *Ibid. While it is obvious that Barr, Hitchcock, and Johnson were all working in close collaboration during the period of 1931–1932, the important point in this context is that at the time of the publication of this article Johnson still uses the term "modern style" and not its imminent transformation to "international style."*

10. *Although Alfred Barr is the author of the preface to The Museum of Modern Art's catalogue for "Modern Architecture: International Exhibition," 1932, in which the principles of the International Style were supposedly elaborated for the first time, Johnson had put forward principles of the modern or new style on at least two occasions: in the exhibition prospectus* Built To Live In *and in the article "The Architecture of the New School" (see pp. 33–36). Barr was in fact responsible for changing "Modern Style" to "International Style," but he did so for the latter's overtones of sixteenth-century Mannerism and not for the reasons stated above.*

11. *The term "international" is "explosive" in the context of its use as a code word for "Marxist." In many cases, it carried no such connotations (e.g., the Rockefellers' funding of the International House for students, the existence of the Carnegie-backed Institute of International Education, etc.).*

12. *While initially there might have been a more considerable confusion concerning these terms than the sequential substitution of one for the other that I have suggested above, my main intent here is not so much to establish patrimony for the designation "International Style" as to describe the process for bringing to consciousness a term that would then prove both ideologically useful to Johnson and well suited to his patrons.*

It is interesting to note how by 1966, in Johnson's review of the book by Robin Boyd, The Puzzle of Architecture *(see pp. 129–33), the principles of the International Style have become structural honesty; repetitive, modular rhythms; clarity, expressed by oceans of glass; the flat roof; the box as the perfect container; no ornament.*

13. *"Retreat from the International Style to the Present Scene," lecture at Yale University, May 9, 1958 (see pp. 85–97).*

14. *"Post-War Frank Lloyd Wright and Le Corbusier," lecture at Yale University, May 2, 1958.*

15. *"Correct and Magnificent Play," review of Le Corbusier's* Complete Works, *Vol. V (see pp. 201–5).*

16. *"Style and the International Style," speech at Barnard College, April 30, 1955 (see pp. 73–79).*

17. *"Correct and Magnificent Play," op. cit.*

18. *"House at New Canaan, Connecticut" (see pp. 213–25).*

19. Architectural Review, *CLVII* (*May, 1975*), *pp. 273–76.*

20. *This is similar to the concept of swerving articulated by Harold Bloom in his book* The Anxiety of Influence *(New York: Oxford University Press, 1973) and later by Vincent Scully in his lecture on "The Shingle Style Today" at Columbia University, 1973.*

21. *See pp. 151–55.*

22. *This idea was first expressed by Johnson publicly in the three-part television series with Rosamond Bernier for CBS's Camera Three in 1976.*

23. *"House at New Canaan, Connecticut," op cit.*

Philip Johnson
Writings

Commentary by
Robert A. M. Stern

Where Are We At?

Built To Live In

From a pamphlet issued by The Museum of Modern Art, March, 1931.

A little-known curiosity, this pamphlet was intended as a "fund-raising sales pitch" for The Museum of Modern Art's forthcoming "Modern Architecture: International Exhibition." What was being promoted was not only this particular show, but the very idea of having an architecture exhibition in an "art" museum—a radical concept at the time, carried still further when in 1932 the museum established, coequal with its Department of Painting and Sculpture, a Department of Architecture, with Johnson as its chairman.

Aside from the style of writing, which seems rather more indebted to Le Corbusier sifted through Bruce Barton than to anything Johnson might have picked up from either of his mentors, Henry-Russell Hitchcock or Mies van der Rohe, the text is notable for its emphasis on technological progress as the primary cause of "a revolution in architecture" and for the ingenuous quality of its faith in such shibboleths as "mass production—low cost" and "the plan is the thing." Johnson comes down hard on revivalist styles and what is now called Art Deco but makes it very clear that he is not against the idea of style itself; his concern for the issue of aesthetics is rationalized in terms of issues of functionalism and technological determinism.

"Can I make this building serve its purpose?" The architect has asked this question since the beginning of time. Today technical knowledge, new materials and a fresh outlook have made his answer an emphatic "Yes." Progressive architects all over the world have struck out vigorously along new paths.

Early Beginnings: As far back as 1851 Joseph Paxton gave the first prophecy of the new style when he built the Crystal Palace, an amazing structure of iron and glass, for the London Exposition. The next half century saw striking advances in the technique of building with iron and steel. The great bridges, railroad stations and factories were regarded first as unheard of feats and then as commonplaces. Meanwhile architecture kept tranquilly to its copy-book tradition of designing in styles borrowed from the past, indifferent to the progress being made in its sister art of engineering.

A Revolution in Architecture: Nevertheless, at the same time, a few independent men, one of whom was Richardson in America, refused to continue imitating past greatness. Their number gradually increased. At the turn of the century, Berlage in Holland, Behrens in Germany and Perret in France and above all Frank Lloyd Wright in America, made a definite stand for originality. Such progress laid the foundation for a complete revolution in building. The revolution was based on a full realization of the possibilities inherent in the new materials—steel and reinforced concrete. The promise of the Crystal Palace was fulfilled.

All the discoveries made by the engineers while architecture had remained stagnant were now at the disposal of the architects. Examples of American grain elevators and factories furnished immediate inspiration. Engineering and architecture were united once more. A new style of architecture had been invented.

Activity in America and Abroad: Today the style has passed beyond the experimental stage. In almost every civilized country in the world it is reaching its full stride. In America the houses of Frank Lloyd Wright, the skyscrapers of Raymond Hood, the buildings of Howe & Lescaze, the work of Richard J. Neutra in Los Angeles and the Bowman Brothers in Chicago, to name the most outstanding examples, bear witness to the widespread nature of the movement in our country. Le Corbusier is famous as a leader of modern architecture in France. In Germany, to build in any other manner would be an anachronism. Russia has "gone modern." She has borrowed the energetic planners and builders of Frankfort and has directed them to build fourteen cities in five years! The Dutch have been prominent in the field from the beginning. Moreover, new buildings in Switzerland, Austria, Czechoslovakia, Sweden, Finland and Japan indicate that the style is international in character.

What Is Modern Architecture?

Modern architecture was born and exists in an era of applied science. Modern architecture does not fight the machine age but accepts it. The architect is solving anew the old problems presented by the home, factory, school, railroad station, civic building and church. Heavy walls of stone or brick with small windows were formerly a necessity. Now steel posts carry the load, converting the outer wall into a mere curtain. This has made possible walls of glass framed with steel, light walls of metal or tile and, in some cases, no walls at all. Flat roofs have become practical.

Mass Production—Low Cost: The building is composed of standardized construction units economically made in mass production. When the units are thus standardized and the houses designed purposely for middle class homes or workers' dwellings, no competitor can enter the field with the modern architect. On the other hand, if the house is custom built for the rich man and the materials are expensive, the cost will be in proportion, but relatively much lower than that of a building done in the old way.

The Plan Is the Thing: Modern architecture is *based* on planning. The architect builds to keep the plan inviolate. He does not allow a traditional style to interfere with the logic of his original interior arrangement. His façade reflects the plan. The needs of the building determine the exterior and interior design.

Planning the City: The logic of the new planning reaches beyond the conception of a building as an isolated problem. Numerous buildings are grouped together according to their corporate functions. Communities, like buildings, are planned from the point of view of serving function. Formal gridiron plans, like that of New York, or radial planning, like that of Paris and Washington, D.C., are superseded by planning of streets according to the districts which they connect. The immense waste caused by New York's congestion is estimated by Mr. McAneny, President of the Regional Plan Association, to be as high as $1,000,000 a day. A thorough study of functions both of skyscrapers and streets would eliminate such waste.

Flexibility of Modern Architecture: Since planning is the guiding spirit of the modern architect, his building becomes a flexible instrument. In temperate climates extensive wall areas are made of glass. In cold climates the north walls have small windows. For light and warmth the southern exposure has large windows of double glass. Thick curtains insure privacy and control the light. The window area toward the noisy street side is reduced. Houses in the country may be open on all sides. Sun porches, gardens or gymnasiums utilize the flat roof space. The size and shape of the site is carefully considered. There may be a long thin house on a thin lot or a square house on a square lot.

A New Style: The new style adapts itself to every kind of structure, whether it be a factory, church or home. In every instance, the building will be modern architecture without a single change in principle. It will not be a Greek temple made into a bank, a Gothic church become an office tower, or, worst of all, a "modernistic" hodge-podge of half-hidden construction and fantastic detail.

Art in Modern Architecture: Beyond the practical advantages, modern architecture is beautiful. For while the modern architect accepts the machine age, he also transcends it. The building can serve every function of structure and utility and at the same time have elegance and refinement of proportion. The architect works consciously to create flat surfaces where he can apply sheets of metal and glass, and panels of wood and marble. Beautiful workmanship of the machine is striven for rather than imitation by the machine of what was originally hand-made ornament. The modern architect builds to reveal beauty of construction, plan and materials.

An Architectural Exhibition

The Museum of Modern Art's Exhibition and the Future of Building: The Museum of Modern Art in New York has followed closely this international activity in architecture. The Museum was founded in the summer of 1929 by a group of American art patrons, principally New Yorkers but including trustees from Boston, Chicago and Washington. They believed the art of our time was not receiving adequate presentation in existing institutions. Since the fall of the same year exhibitions have regularly been held at the Museum's quarters in the Heckscher Building, 730 Fifth Avenue. During the first year of its services approximately 200,000 people have visited the galleries.

Although the Museum has until now exhibited only works of painting and sculpture, it has long felt the need for a comprehensive exhibition of modern architecture. Never in this country or abroad has such an exhibition been held. Obviously, an exhibition is by far the best way of presenting effectively to the public every aspect of the new movement. The hope of developing intelligent criticism and discussion depends upon furnishing the public a knowledge of contemporary accomplishments in the field. Our present limited vision in this respect is caused by the very lack of those examples which the exhibition will supply. An introduction to an integrated and rational mode of building is sorely needed. The stimulation and direction which an exhibition of this type can give to contemporary architectural thought and practice is incalculable. It is desirable that we view and ponder the new mode of building which fits so decidedly into our methods of standardized construction, our economics and our life.

31

The Architecture of the New School

From Arts, *XVII (March, 1931),*
393–98.

An a priori conception of what a Modern or International Style building must be almost causes Johnson to miss the virtues of this quite extraordinary building for the New School for Social Research, with its bold, horizontally banded façade, its polychromy, its sure sense of materials. It is interesting to note his use of the term "International Style" as early as 1931, and to note also that the three "elements" of the new style that he describes are not only different from those which he and Hitchcock would enunciate together in their book, The International Style, *published a year later, but are also rather less clearly articulated—leaving more to individual talent and aesthetic judgment. One can only speculate on the leavening role Hitchcock brought to bear on that collaborative work; certainly, his published retrospective glances at the book have suggested that the zeal to "categorize" was not necessarily his own.* [1]

1. *"The International Style Twenty Years After,"* Architectural Record, *CX (August, 1951), pp. 89–98, included as an appendix in paperback reprint of* The International Style *(New York: Norton, 1966); "Modern Architecture—A Memoir,"* Journal of the Society of Architectural Historians, *XXVII (December, 1968), pp. 229, 233.*

The New School for Social Research deserves critical comparison with modern architecture in Europe. Very few American buildings reveal any influence of the International Style, with which the names of Le Corbusier, Oud, Gropius, and Miës van der Rohe are associated. The work of Neutra in Los Angeles and Howe & Lescaze in Philadelphia are other isolated indications that the International Style is gradually taking root in America. Most of the architecture, however, which passes for modern in our country has combined earlier manners, such as Viennese or Paris, 1925, with the mania for verticalism so predominant in our skyscrapers. Not in any sense can these works be considered a part of the style which is finding vigorous expression especially in Germany, France, Holland, Russia, and Japan.

What may reasonably be considered the elements of the new style? (1) The purpose or function of the building as restricted by the exigencies of purely structural requirements is the major factor in the creation of the plan. The architect employs this plan as a starting point for the ultimate design of the whole building, which thus develops rationally from within. The interior arrangement inevitably determines the general formation of the façade. (2) The building relies chiefly on this functional and structural arrangement for its decorative effect. Ornament is not employed. (3) The genius of the architect coordinates the practical needs in such a way that fine proportion and simple design create the beauty of the building.

Viewed in its location on Twelfth Street, the New School, at first glance, gives the impression that many of these elements have been embodied here. But a closer inspection suggests that the architect has produced the illusion of a building in the International Style rather than a building resulting from a genuine application of the new principles.

The most noticeable feature of the façade is the central section with broad alternating bands of ornamental brick and windows which project from the plain brick walls on either side. This central portion extends three feet beyond the normal wall supports, concealing them and at the same time making possible the uninterrupted ribbon windows and brick bands. Cantilevering cannot justify itself if the space which the projection creates cannot be utilized. Between the supporting posts thus standing free and the outer windows, an inner set of windows has been placed at a distance which prevents even a thin person from passing between post and window. Had the architect been guided by functional requirements and the building allowed to grow from within out, the posts would have been placed in the outer wall.

Furthermore, it is difficult to find the reason for cantilevering the central portion and not the whole façade. One would naturally assume that such a device reflected an interior arrangement that called for reduced light and space on the sides. The plan shows that this is not the case for this recession of the façade cuts what would have been a normal room into a large rectangle and a small one. This space has been used as one room, however, not as two, and that as a classroom giving the students ample space and light but compelling the instructor to speak from a darkened niche.

The façade, moreover, is not devoid of ornament. The brick bands which alternate with the ribbon windows are composed of horizontal black and white stripes produced by raised lines of white brick set in a background of black brick. The window areas are cut horizontally by slender bars and again vertically by mullions at points corresponding to the hidden supports, obviously for effect. Here again we are confronted with the illusion of the modern style which persists throughout the building. Superficially, the ornament of the façade appears to derive from structural considerations. But in modern architecture the structural details are as plain as structure will permit, whereas here they have been worked upon in order to provide ornament. The architect has been timid of aesthetic economy.

These ornamental features mar the façade as a piece of design. They produce a sense of heaviness in the building. Modern architecture strives to be as light as plane surfaces and slender frames will make it. This type of ornament is similar to that of Erich Mendelsohn, who has extensively employed projecting courses of brick and thick window frames.

The conception of the façade as a whole also contributes to the feeling of massiveness. The central cantilevered portion is held vise-like by the flanking dark brick walls. In other words, the central section gives the feeling of a cube which has been inserted in the façade. This block-like technique shows the influence of Dutch constructivism.

The symmetry of the façade suggests the monumental architecture of the past obtained at the expense of convenient planning. Had the architect allowed the inner arrangement to reflect itself in the façade, the asymmetrical result would have been much more interesting.

Before passing from the exterior to the interior one more feature of the façade might be mentioned. The central portion slants away from the building line, the top story being one foot farther back than the first story. This batter, the architect argues, corrects the optical illusion that the building leans over the street. The expense of this refinement is hardly consistent with economy of construction, which is a major concern of modern building in general.

Such is the façade. It was not generated by pursuing to a rational conclusion the fundamental needs. The real procedure of modern architecture was reversed; the façade design arbitrarily controls the interior.

When the School for Social Research planned its new building, the directors presumably knew what interior arrangement would best suit their purposes. It is, therefore, not pertinent to criticize their solution of functional problems. Attention should be called, however, to two of these solutions in the plan. The two large lecture rooms slope toward the windows, following the contour of the auditorium dome below. Hence, the audience must face the light during the daytime, the most impractical illumination for a lecture. Even more unusual is the location of the recreational hall at the head of the stairway which has not been shut off from the library directly below—a room ordinarily requiring seclusion.

The design of the auditorium is as arbitrary as that of the façade. Its egg shape is not determined by acoustical requirements, for after the original design had been completed it was found necessary to specify perforations in the concrete dome for this very purpose. Nor would the regular steel construction of such a building suggest the domical shape. Nor does an egg-shape plan best economize space in a rectangular building. In other words, the architect has imposed on an auditorium a preconceived form in much the same way as the Beaux-Arts designers have done for a hundred years.

The monumental stairway which leads from the library to the recreation hall is likewise baffling. A double flight of stairs leading directly into the reading room seems unreasonable. Function would demand but one flight, and that more inconspicuously placed. In the center of this composition, symmetrically flanked by stairs and pyramidal bookshelves, is a great niche. Instead of containing a commemorative statue, the space is empty. On close examination of the walls the inquisitive will find three concealed doors which lead into the stacks. Monumentality of this sort is out of place in a modern building.

The decorative detail throughout is inconsistent. The architect has used doorframes of the American hospital type, wisely avoiding the more common imitation-wood steel frames. In the mouldings of the bookcases and the ornamental treatment of the railing, Urban is working in his own Viennese tradition. The ceiling moulding around the foyer is in the Neo-Rococo style of Oskar Kaufmann. One wonders if the unpleasant checkerboard effect of the double front windows, caused by the horizontality of the outer window frames and the verticality of the inner ones, was intentional. The color is for the most part excellent. The practice of painting different walls different colors is typical of early work of the group de Stijl in Holland and Bauhaus work in Germany. The color schemes in some rooms are identical with those of the Bauhaus, though in others quite original.

In the New School we have the anomaly of a building supposed to be in a style of architecture based on the development of the plan from function and façade from plan but which is as formally and pretentiously conceived as a Renaissance palace. Urban's admiration for the New Style is more complete than his understanding. But the very fact that the School can be subjected to analysis from the point of view of the new elements of building shows how far the architect has been influenced by the New

Style. His work is an outstanding piece of pioneering in New York. Although it diverges, as has been shown, in many respects from the best work that has already been done here and abroad, it is on the whole a most important evidence that the International Style is creating an increasingly prominent place for itself in America. The use of ribbon windows to emphasize the horizontality of the façade, the fundamental simplicity of design, and the successful use of color in the interior are all features that are real contributions to better architecture. The New School for Social Research is an encouraging sign that soon there will be many more buildings in this country similar in spirit but which will come closer to a true mastery of the International Style.

The Skyscraper School
of Modern Architecture

From Arts, XVII (May, 1931), 569–75.

In his recent work at Minneapolis and especially at Houston, Johnson the architect has come round pretty much full circle from Johnson the International Style polemicist. Consider in relationship to the Pennzoil building the outraged cry of the romantic minimalist of forty-five years earlier as he lambasts as "ridiculous" the "slanted roof" of Arthur Loomis Harmon's Shelton Hotel. In this over-zealous essay, Johnson's obsessive search for aesthetic principles by which to define the new style focuses on details of buildings while blinding him to those very splendors of size and sculptural invention that characterize the Shelton and other great towers of the American twenties and that now inspire him in his own work, as they then did the work of Le Corbusier and Mies.

Interestingly, in this regard, Johnson's tall buildings of the 1970's seem to represent in part a conscious revival of those ideas deemed appropriate to the "tall building" by Mies and some lesser figures of the Modern Movement in its expressionist phase during the late teens and early twenties. His I.D.S. Center can be viewed as the realization of Mies's experiments with the crystalline properties of glass as seen in the Polygonal Glass Skyscraper project of 1920–21; Pennzoil is an evocation of the jagged profile of Mies's Prismatic Glass Skyscraper project of 1919; and the Post Oak Central building is a quite literal homage to R. G. and W. M. Cory's Starrett-Lehigh Building, which Hitchcock and Johnson featured in the "Modern Architecture: International Exhibition." Of course, one can look at any of these examples of Johnson's late commercial phase, as well as at some of his important monumental commissions of the 1960's, such as the John F. Kennedy Memorial in Dallas, and see at work as well the powerful influence of the minimalist sculpture of Donald Judd and Robert Morris, which Johnson admires and collects.

"The skyscraper is far and away the most important architectural achievement of America, her great gift to the art of building." T. E. Tallmadge in *Architecture in America* has written an opinion shared by professors and public, architects and laymen. Indeed so characteristic of current architectural criticism is Tallmadge's statement, that there may be said to exist a school of opinion which believes the skyscraper has founded a new style of architecture.

It is instructive to consider what elements of a new style the critics find in our skyscrapers. Unanimously, they appear awed by the sheer size of the buildings. "Above the waters stands the magic mountain of steel and stone, shining and glorious, as one of the crowns of human endeavor." This reaction of Fiske Kimball's in *American Architecture* is typical of many lyric outbursts of admiration that can be multiplied indefinitely by a glance through their works. Tallmadge says of the skyscraper: "Its eyes gaze down from immeasurable heights on a welter of humanity and machinery. Its shining flanks are dappled with shadows of aeroplanes that 'laugh as they pass in thunder.'" Comparisons to nature are frequent. "We seem to be in the presence of some titanic results of the forces of nature," writes Dean Edgell referring to the Shelton Hotel, "rather than a building by the hand of man. The mass seen at dusk is as impressive as Gibraltar." One may object that this romantic enthusiasm is not architectural criticism but it must be reckoned with because it permeates their writings.

From the fundamental love of the colossal is derived their subsidiary criteria of the "skyscraper style." Cheney praises the "integrity and expressive 'drive' and 'lift'" as virtues of skyscraper design. Since the main feature of the skyscraper is height, the vertical lines should be emphasized. Buttressing and vertical striping heighten the "majestic effect." Hugh Ferriss, who is not an architect, has had, as Cheney rightly points out, more influence on architecture than the architects. His falsely lighted renderings that picture fantastic crags rising high above dark caverns have made popular a type of building which only the artist's brush can construct. Nevertheless, it is apparent that they have moved the architect to attempted simulation.

Our critics claim honesty of construction. The idea is not new. Even before Louis Sullivan enunciated his now platitudinous "Form follows function," the principle that the building must honestly express the construction was generally accepted. To-day it is common knowledge that the walls of skyscrapers do not support it and are but curtains hung on a steel framework. Any pedestrian on Park Avenue may see the two-inch gap between the sidewalk and the wall of the apartment buildings. True expression of this hanging phenomenon would require a wall designed to look as light as it is without giving the feeling of masonry construction. The critics believe modern skyscraper walls answer the problem satisfactorily, not realizing perhaps that in verticalism are the remnants of masonry pier-buttressing. The walls should deny *plainly* that they rest on the ground since actually they do not.

Another conviction of our critics is that the Zoning Law helped to create a new architecture. They have been excited by the prospect of a statute that can produce style. While it is true that the Zoning Law had an effect on architecture quite beside its original intention of mere limitation, this effect has been very different from what most people have supposed it to be. That the set-back was a feature of architecture prior to the Law is not generally realized. The Woolworth Tower, built four years before the Law was passed, has more set-back feeling than the Empire State, built fourteen years after the regulation was established. The Empire State Building, except for the incongruous mooring mast, is essentially a smooth, solid mass arising from a low base; the Woolworth Tower is a series of graduated blocks. This shows that the legislative ruling had little to do with creating an architectural style.

The Law did, however, hasten a tendency toward piling of masses and pyramiding implicit in the architects' striving for the colossal. From the Woolworth Tower to the Telephone Building, the line of development has been straight. After the Gothic spires of Cass Gilbert, asymmetrical stepping came into fashion, bringing even more romantic compositions. Sheer "crags" are broken by terraces which only accentuate the perpendicularity. Raymond Hood was among the first to revolt from this romanticism. His latest skyscraper, the McGraw-Hill Building, has avoided the set-backs, keeping to the absolute minimum which the Law requires. The two set-backs on the front only hamper the architectural effect. Since the sides have not been stepped, there is no pyramidal impression.

Another tenet of our critics is that restrained ornament fits properly into the grand scheme of the skyscraper. The style of ornament does not seem important to them. Italian Romanesque on the Shelton, the crisply-cut "modernistic" of Ely Kahn or even Ralph Walker's flat wriggly panels on the Telephone Building are all equally acceptable. Yet, for a "new style" of architecture to possess many styles of ornament is an anomaly. While the critics feast their eyes on the grandiose bulk, they are annoyed not at all by the miles of machine-made ornament clamped to the structure. Fiske Kimball says of the Shelton Hotel: "Faint touches of Italian Romanesque detail are insignificant in the essential freshness of conception." Examining the Telephone Building, Edgell finds "there is scarcely ornament on the building in the historic sense." In fact, our critics are really happiest when ornament is not a part of the picture. The enchantment of distance and enveloping haze is a constantly recommended setting. They squint at the skyline from Brooklyn, safe from the intrusion of ornament, enraptured by the vastness of it all. From the exhilaration of such moments much of their romantic phraseology must derive: Tallmadge—of the Telephone Building—"crazy pinnacles"; Cheney, "jutting crags and receding terraces"; Edgell—of the Shelton Hotel—"The boldness of the scheme frightens and awes"; Kimball, "rhythmic heights."

The emphasis is on mass. One might conclude that our critics would favor no ornament. Such an assumption is false. Though not concerned with ornament, they cannot do without it. Let them but catch a glimpse of a building by Le Corbusier, some fine exterior without ornamentation, and their reactions will at once reveal how inbred is their feeling that decoration is a necessary adjunct to architecture.

The Shelton Hotel will serve to make concrete some of these points. I shall contrast it with the Monadnock Building, an early example of the skyscraper which has not been equalled for straightforward honesty.

Since the lyricism of our critics which deals with hazy vistas and "Gibraltars" is unanswerable, I shall turn to more definite matters. Edgell specifically maintains that the Shelton reveals its steel construction, an assertion made invalid by comparison with the Monadnock Building which is constructed of masonry. The heavy brick walls supporting the building make the windows of necessity narrow, producing logically the vertical support lines. But the verticality of the Shelton has no structural basis. Its walls are hung on an interior steel framework, making the potential size of the windows the height and width of the whole wall. Yet its windows are smaller and comparatively less in number than those of the Monadnock. In short, the Shelton, though built of steel, looks more like a masonry building than does the Monadnock which actually is masonry.

The lower stories of both buildings are battered. In the one the batter is legitimate, since the walls must be fifteen feet thick to support the weight above. In the other, its use is indefensible. The walls need not exist so far as support is concerned. The projecting bays of windows in the earlier building are necessary to let in light where otherwise flat thick walls would substantially curtail it. But the vertical projections on the Shelton are an unnecessary expense, violate the regularity of the steel framework and bar the light from the rooms flanked by these projections. The roof of the Monadnock is flat in accordance with the practice of modern roof construction. The slanted roof of the Shelton is ridiculous. Although Italian Romanesque construction called for such roofs, their use to-day is unnecessary and merely imitative. The earlier building carries a rudimentary cornice, but the Shelton, hailed because of its lack of cornice, has corbel tables which are far more offensive.

The Monadnock has no ornament. The Shelton is encrusted with it. The batter is ornamental. The arcade, the corbel tables, the gargoyles, the Romanesque windows—all are ornament. The observer who regards these trappings as "insignificant" must indeed be at a great distance.

It is strange that no matter how much our skyscraper designers preach that the only way to build is purely functionally, in practice they continue to use ornament. And ornament to-day is created in an office with a soft pencil. In some cases, the plan and elevation, even the window arrangement, are worked out before "architecture" is applied to the building. There is little wonder that Le Corbusier remarks, pointing to a skyscraper: *"Écoutons les conseils des ingénieurs américains. Mais craignons les architectes américains."*

The story of American skyscraper design is not the story of revolt and founding of a new architecture. A new scale in engineering, perhaps, but not a new aesthetic style. A style must have a consistent attitude on the question of ornament. If a fundamentally new method of construction is introduced, that construction should receive adequate expression. In addition, a style must be worthy of continuing at least a decade; yet already an essentially new kind of skyscraper is emerging.

American megalomania is largely responsible for the growth of the Skyscraper School. In the past, the pyramids and High Gothic cathedrals were colossal. They were architecture as well. By analogy it may seem that our giant engineering achievements should also represent a new architectural triumph. That we build a thousand feet high as easily as other civilizations have built a hundred is a source of national pride. So strong in the minds of our more intelligent citizens is the faith in our culture and so fixed in the hearts of the majority of our populace is the faith in bigness, that there has naturally arisen the cult of the skyscraper—"the great American gift to the art of building."

Rejected Architects

From Creative Art, VIII (June, 1931), 433–35.

The "Rejected Architects" show was a protest on the part of the young International Style architects against the important and establishmentarian exhibitions of the Architectural League of New York which were held, as a rule, in the cavernous gloom of the Grand Central Palace. The League's exhibition for 1931 was especially ambitious in conception because it was the fiftieth anniversary show. In 1965 Johnson was to recall the exhibition in a speech to the Architectural League. He reminisced that the selection committee:

in its wisdom had refused a great many modern designs, had refused works by people who were well known to all of us at one time, but were especially protégés of George Howe in Philadelphia. Actually, the PSFS was included in the exhibition, but so many were left out that George Howe and Bill Lescaze came to the defense of the younger, omitted men. It seems humorous now, but it was deadly serious at that time . . . so angry did we get at this, that some of us, Alfred Barr of The Museum of Modern Art, and I, the Director-to-be of the Department of Architecture, set up an exhibition in a storefront on Sixth Avenue which we called "Rejected Architects," after the famous Salon des Refusés of Paris a hundred years ago. We showed men like Alfred Clauss and Oscar Stonorov, who are now such well-known Philadelphia architects, and we made a lot of noise by having sandwichmen parade up and down Lexington Avenue in front of the Grand Central Palace, to call attention to the unfairness of the League. The League was to us the Establishment that needed doing away with.[1]

A year later, concurrent with the New York showing of the "Modern Architecture: International Exhibition," which Hitchcock and Johnson organized for The Museum of Modern Art, Howe and Lescaze quit the Architectural League and, with help from Messrs. Johnson, Barr, and Howe's publicist, Edward L. Bernays, this move caught the public's attention in a way that the exhibition itself was unable to. The League had mounted yet another of its mammoth shows, tastelessly installed and belligerently mediocre. Howe and Lescaze submitted three works, none of which was accepted for display. Miffed, and assuming that the League's rejection of new work was a gesture of retaliation for their participation in the previous year's "Rejected Architects" show, Howe and Lescaze decided to make the most of the situation. The League's action, as Johnson recalled in 1965, was just the opportunity he and his colleagues had been waiting for to strike a blow against reaction! Howe resigned from the League on February 25, 1932, Lescaze two days later. Bernays succeeded in having the event reported on the front page of the New York Times on Sunday, February 28, 1932, and the item received wide coverage in other American cities as well as abroad. The victory-less battle continued in the pages of the Times and other newspapers through the end of March but, not too surprisingly, little of immediate consequence came out of it.[2] The realities of economic depression tended to trivialize issues of style, and in 1934 Johnson quit the Museum to enter on a strange political and journalistic career, returning to architecture only in 1940.[3]

1. Dinner speech at the annual meeting of the Architectural League of New York, May 26, 1965, printed in the League's News Bulletin (ca. September, 1965), pp. 1–4.
2. For a more extensive discussion, see Robert A. M. Stern, George Howe, Toward a Modern American Architecture (New Haven: Yale University Press, 1975, pp. 151–53.
3. Johnson's political career has recently been discussed in Calvin Tomkins's Profile, "Forms under Light" (New Yorker, May 23, 1977), pp. 48–50.

The day after the Rejected Architects opened their Salon des Refusés, Mr. Ely Jacques Kahn stated to the press that no models had been refused by the League because they were too modern. This is quite true. The Grand Central Palace contained work as modern as that displayed in the Fifty-Seventh Street Show. The official explanation, however, smacks too much of the smug rejection slip: "The number of exhibits submitted was so much greater than could be accommodated that the Committee selected what they considered the best work." Nevertheless, it is more than mere well-grounded rumor, that the officials believed these rejected models unqualifiedly bad—not architecture but unrealizable dreams.

One may, therefore, question the critical ability of Mr. Kahn and his Committee. If the nine rejected models are to them bad architecture, how could this jury in all conscience accept Bel Geddes' project for the Kharkow Theatre Competition, which appears to be very similar, indeed, in the opinion of those versed in the latest work of the International Style, to Alfred Clauss's model for the same competition which was among the exhibits in the rival Show. Moreover, if the Committee could accept Mr. Kocher's fine model for the Darien Art Guild, how could they place it next to Philip Goodwin's pseudo-modern house? The Committee may be competent to choose among English houses, but the conclusion is unavoidable that, not understanding it, they have a positive prejudice against the International Style. Howe & Lescaze's excellent model of the Philadelphia Bank, though admitted, was tucked away in a corner. The disillusionment of one League member was painful when he was finally convinced that Kocher's Aluminum House was actually a part of the Exhibition sponsored by the League. On the other hand, the reasoning behind the juxtaposition of this house and the colossal Rome Academy Zeus is baffling to many more than to the conservative Leaguers.

The public found a new thrill in the Rejected Architects. Here was the chance to witness an unusual fight. Not every day does the orderly profession of architecture dramatize itself in a blaze of controversy. The hullabaloo was initiated by the critics who, bored with the eternal monotony of the League's offerings, jumped at the chance to support a rival group. Mr. Edward Alden Jewell of the *New York Times* and Mrs. Helen Appleton Read of the *Brooklyn Eagle* waxed enthusiastic. So universal today is the romantic love for youth in revolt, especially in the realm of art, that one by one the other writers climbed on the Rejected Architects' bandwagon.

Mr. Deems Taylor, for example, who dubs himself an "ultra-modernist," in architecture is shocked by these "fishbowls and factories." He falls into the common error of assuming that the modern house must be an expression of functionalism absolute, without concern for design. Yet consider the front of the Pinehurst house by Clauss & Daub. Instead of being placed every sixteen feet on the façade, the posts are set back within the living room, an arrangement that decreases the interior circulation and increases the cost of construction. But this non-functional cantilever does give a unified expanse of glass necessary to the design, which would be spoiled if heavy verticals interrupted the façade. But Mr. Taylor draws, in common with the other critics, the false conclusion that modern architecture is a glass architecture. Glass is no more an essential element of this style than of any other. It is only true that glass is often desirable to the modern architect or his client. There are, however, a great number of works in a variety of materials from marble to wood. And the windowless factory, for example, is a direct contradiction of the statement that the style always admits sunlight in the greatest quantities possible.

Miss Bauer's refreshing article in the *New Republic* is unique among the reviews. She has sensed the "subtle balance" by which Clauss & Daub have avoided monotony in their series of small houses. She does not allow her ideal of a non-individualistic architecture to stand in the way of her appreciating the very individual excellence of Clauss's arrangement of this series.

Mr. Douglas Haskell, unlike Miss Bauer, is troubled by the "monotony." He would have more texture of surfaces, more ornamental freedom. It is admittedly a shortcoming of the models that they do give the impression of paucity of materials. They are mostly white, unavoidably suggesting stucco, because models are most easily made of papier-maché painted white. There is, however, an endless number of surfacing materials the modern architect can use: metal (as in Mr. Kocher's aluminum house), brick or glazed tile (as on the McGraw-Hill Building), wood, stone, or even marble. The wish for more individual, more varied, more "interesting" exterior treatment savors of the romantic love of the Cape Cod Cottage or Norman Farmhouse because they fit into the landscape or are made from stones gathered from the very soil of the countryside, or because they are "homey."

The critics of both the Rejected Architects and the League Show have been uncritical. None considered the Salon des Refusés as representing a new style of architecture, ignoring the catalogue which listed the elements of the International Style. Not only have they not recognized the style but they have not even remarked on the chaos in contemporary building. There is a general feeling prevalent that modern architecture is functional (a much misunderstood and abused word) or is somehow synonymous with glass, steel and concrete. Hence, the architect frames his ideas in steel and glass and concrete, and lo! he ends up with a piece of modern architecture. One indication that the style is not to be summed up in terms of construction material alone could have been plainly seen by the critics in William Muschenheim's beach houses, one of the few executed works illustrated at the Rejected Architects. These houses are built of wood. The fact that they are in the International Style, as they very decidedly are, must therefore be dependent on characteristics other than construction materials.

There might have been general criticism of the effect of the setback on the beauty of high buildings. No notice was taken, however, of how the setback complicates the otherwise good design of William Muschenheim's model of a skyscraper, or of how the imposing use of simple bands is vitiated by the law-abiding pyramidal set-back in Raymond Hood's recently constructed McGraw-Hill Building. There might also have been discussion of foreign influences on the young architects. How independent and original are the designs? The very obvious influence of Le Corbusier apparent in the wind shelters and circular staircases of Stonorov was not remarked.

The League fared no better with the critics than did the Rejected Architects. It is hard to follow their sweeping approval of the Swedish display, as though the work were all by one man in one style. And yet we find work as different as Østberg's eclectic Town Hall and the disciplined Exposition buildings of Asplund or the Club House of Sven Markelius and Uno Åhren in the International Style. Surely an alert critic would have compared the unequivocal presentation by the Rejected Architects of the International Style with those examples of the same style in the Swedish section.

So, a Salon des Refusés has again served to announce a new departure. The International Style comes to New York. Of course, there have been pioneers. Mr. George Howe's courageous decision to leave a conventional practice to join with the young Lescaze; Lawrence Kocher's and Lönberg-Holm's impressive work on the *Architectural Record* have started the ball rolling. The trips of Norman Bel Geddes and Joseph Urban to Europe have made ribbon windows the mode, even if these men themselves have never fully understood the new architecture. But it remained for the Rejected Architects to give the International Style what might be called its first formal introduction to this country.

In Berlin:
Comment on
Building Exposition

From the New York Times, August 9, 1931.

This article precedes the somewhat better-known account that Johnson published in T-Square.[1] *Though the* T-Square *article has been made reasonably accessible to students by virtue of its having been reprinted in* Oppositions, *the* Times *version has a sense of polemical urgency that the other lacks and thereby seems worthy of inclusion here.*

The contrast between the Berlin Exposition and the Architectural League's annual exhibition affords Johnson numerous opportunities to go beyond the customary conventions of reportage. In this article he explicitly states personal biases, including his belief in the idea of architecture as art, and explores complex issues such as differences between modernist and modernistic design. (The latter type, which we now call Art Deco, continues to irritate Johnson, who insists it is not a style.)

As this article confirms, from the very outset of his career Johnson established himself not only as a polemicist for the International Style, but also as an outspoken apologist for the work of Mies van der Rohe. His discussion of Mies is broad in its scope, including political issues alongside more conventionally architectural ones. Touching on Mies's role as an arbiter of taste and an organizer of the Modern Movement, Johnson goes to some length to point out, though never satisfactorily to explain, that better-known and more commercially successful architects (such as Erich Mendelsohn) are excluded from its inner circle.

Johnson's emphasis on Mies as a "post-functionalist" not only represents an early, and possibly first, use of the term, but it also raises some questions about the generally accepted claim that it was Johnson, together with Hitchcock, who in presenting the Modern Movement to the American public undermined its high moral purposes and reduced it merely to an issue of style in order to make it more palatable. As Johnson presents Mies's situation, it seems clear that a schism between ideology and style or aesthetics was already deeply cleft within the Modern Movement as it was developing in Europe, and that Johnson from the beginning had firmly aligned himself with the aesthetic point of view. Surely, it was that point of view that he presented to the American public to the virtual exclusion of the other, not to mention the virtual exclusion of those modern architects who did not choose to be (or were not invited to be) included in the Congrès Internationaux d'Architecture Moderne (C.I.A.M.), since 1928 the official organization of the Modern Movement.

1. *"The Berlin Building Exposition of 1931,"* T-Square, *11 (January, 1932), pp. 17–19, 36–37. Reprinted in* Oppositions *2 (January, 1974), pp. 83–85.*

Berlin

Mies van der Rohe's name will become synonymous with the Berlin Building Exposition of 1931. Although Mies was made director of only one section, it is by this section that the exposition will be remembered. Only here has architecture been handled as an art. With the exception of the Mies section, the enormous exposition is devoted to city planning, garden planning, use of construction materials, garages—all conceived in so different a spirit that critical justice could be done only by a separate treatment.

That the city of Berlin should hold such an ambitious exposition at all when its inhabitants are daily expecting complete bankruptcy is a wonder. That the city should at the same time pick its best modern architect to direct the architectural section is a second wonder. One shudders to contemplate whom the city officials of New York would choose for a like position. Mies has had complete charge of this section; his was not only the selection of the architects, but the decision as to what and where to build. All the objects shown had first to meet the approval of the director; no industry could dictate what of its work should be exhibited. Consequently, the crowded confusion, typical of the second floor of the League show in New York last spring, is absent. The advantage to the firm of having a strict esthetic judgment applied before its object is displayed is many times greater than carte blanche to a three-thousand-dollar-a-week niche at the Grand Central Palace. German industries learned this lesson slowly, and it was not until the success of the German exhibits at Barcelona in 1929 also arranged by Mies, that they were finally convinced that submission to an artistic dictator is better than an anarchy of selfish personal opinion. America, which can make changes so quickly, must also one day wake up.

Another advantage of this system to the exhibitor is the artistic unity of the whole arrangement. The art of exhibiting is a branch of architecture and should be practiced as such. Mies has designed the entire hall, containing houses and apartments by the various architects, as itself one piece of architecture. The result is a clear arrangement inviting inspection, instead of the usual long central hall, with exhibits placed side by side.

As in the Werkbund Exposition of 1927, Mies van der Rohe selected only those architects to build who work in the international style—a type of architecture which in America can as yet be seen only in the shops of the rejected architects. The "modernistic" style, as we know it in America, has never really been prevalent here; the Paris 1925 mode has not swept Germany. The equivalent is the Kunstgewerblich, the kind of thing that is known best in America in the work of Bruno Paul or in the Wiener Werkstätten. At least in Berlin the modern has triumphed over the Kunstgewerblich.

Among the houses the one-story single house of Mies stands out above the others. The walls are mainly of glass, with one solid wall facing the street. In spite of the use of glass and the fact that there are no interior doors except the ones that lead to the kitchen, privacy is not lacking. The walls of the bedroom, for instance, separate it not only from the living quarters, but, extending beyond the house into the garden, cut off the bedroom from all but a small portion of the garden. Thus the bedroom, with only glass walls on the outdoors side, is as large as the space inclosed by the solid walls.

The esthetic appearance of the house differs from the box effect of four visible surfaces broken by windows and doors and is rather a three-dimensional space intersected by planes—the thin roof slab and the partition walls.

The house is not, as so many architects here and in America would prefer to have it, purely functional. That is, it could have been built at a lesser cost and have been more economical of space and still have served equally as well its function of living quarters for a married couple. But Mies has long since passed the stage where the house is regarded by the architect as the cheapest, best-planned expression of the needs of the family. The Mies home is admittedly luxurious. For this reason Mies is disliked by many architects and critics, especially the Communists. On the other hand, the public still apparently wants beauty in its everyday surroundings.

There is in the house none of that arbitrariness which Germans call "Spielerei." Functionalism has at least a negative force in modern architecture. In defense of each element of a building the architect must be able to answer the question: "Why?" This basis of modern architecture in function, Mies and the post-functionalists freely admit. The exaggeration of functionalism into a theory of building where esthetic considerations do not enter at all is the attitude they oppose.

Ornament is absent in the Mies house, nor is any needed. The richness of the beautiful woods, the sheets of plate glass and the gleaming chrome steel posts suffice. The essential beauty of the house lies in handling the walls as planes and not as supporting elements. Mies has so placed these planes that space seems to open up in every direction, giving the feeling of openness that, perhaps more than anything else, is the prime characteristic of modern architecture.

Walter Gropius, founder and builder of the Bauhaus, is the second great name in the exposition. His exhibit, however, is much the same as his last year's work at the Paris Salon des Artistes Décorateurs. The development of Gropius through constructivism and Bauhaus Sachlichkeit is evident in his preference for painted wood and artificial materials like oilcloth, linoleum, rubber, and Trolit.

Two among the other architects deserve mention. Otto Haesler, who has the reputation of being the most economic planner and builder among the modern architects of the world, has contributed a section of a great housing project. Of the younger men, Jan Ruhtenberg is the most gifted and original. The work of the also-ran is good, but the genius of Mies depresses the general level.

Architecture
in the Third Reich

From Hound & Horn, *VII*
(October—December, 1933),
137—39.

This is one of Johnson's most important essays, and one of the few to comment on a political issue. By virtue of the subject and Johnson's on-the-scene expertise, it is an invaluable document of the period. Because the essay originally appeared in a now-suspended "little magazine," until its recent republication in Oppositions *it remained quite inaccessible to all except scholar-sleuths.*

Johnson brings to American readers a clear assessment of the German artistic climate viewed in relation to the political climate of the newly formed Third Reich. In many ways, the essay was the most important account of the period until the publication of Barbara Miller Lane's book in 1968.[1]

Because of his curious speculation about Mies's chances for significant commissions and an official position in the new regime, Johnson's views remain especially provocative; only at such time as Mies's career in Germany during the 1930's is fully documented will the emotionally charged issues, rather sketchily suggested by Johnson, be properly aired.

1. Architecture and Politics in Germany 1918—1945 *(Cambridge: Harvard University Press, 1968).*

It would be false to speak of the architectural situation in national socialist Germany. The new state is faced with such tremendous problems of reorganization that a program of art and architecture has not been worked out. Only a few points are certain. First, *Die Neue Sachlichkeit* is over. Houses that look like hospitals and factories are taboo. But also, the row houses which have become almost the distinguishing feature of German cities are doomed. They all look too much alike, stifling individualism. Second, architecture will be monumental. That is, instead of bathhouses, Siedlungen, employment offices and the like, there will be official railroad stations, memorial museums, monuments. The present regime is more intent on leaving a visible mark of its greatness than in providing sanitary equipment for workers.

But what these new buildings will look like is as yet completely unknown. Germany as the birthplace of modern architecture can hardly go back to Revivalism since there exist no architects who could or would design in styles. Nor is it possible that they will adopt the Bauhaus style. It is not monumental enough and it has irretrievably the stamp of Communism and Marxism, Internationalism, all the "isms" not in vogue in Germany today. Somewhere between the extremes is the key; and within the Party are three distinct movements each of which may win out.

First and up till recently the strongest are the forces of reaction, with Paul Schulze-Naumburg at the head. He is the enemy of anything which has happened in the last thirty years. His book *Art and Race,* contains the most stupid attacks on modern art which he considers mere interest in the abnormal, a point of view which he defends by showing juxtaposed clinical photographs of physical abnormalities and modern paintings. In architecture, he approves of nothing since the War, and is himself the architect of many simplified but Baroque country houses including the Crown Prince's Palace in Potsdam. As a personal friend of the leaders of the party he is strongly entrenched.

Paul Erwin Troost, best known to Americans as the designer of the interiors on the S.S. Europa, is a friend of Hitler's and is also a strong conservative. (That some Americans might consider the Europa modern merely shows that "modern" with us has hardly caught up with reaction in Germany.) The strongest single factor in favor of this group in the new state is that Hitler himself is an amateur architect. Before he entered politics he earned his living as a draughtsman and renderer in Vienna and Munich. This fact, combined with the tradition in Prussia from Frederick the Great to Wilhelm II, that the ruler be his own architect, makes the outlook depressing.

The second group and at present the strongest is that represented by the Kampfbund für Deutsche Kultur, an inner party organization for the purification of German culture. Their architectural hero is the newly appointed director of the Prussian state art schools, Paul Schmitthenner.

Though an outspoken enemy of *Die Neue Sachlichkeit* he claims modernity. His houses are sound, well proportioned but uninspired adaptations of the vernacular of the early 19th century, much in the same feeling as the best adaptations of the Cape Cod farmhouses in America. His larger buildings are in a half-modern tasteful style, better really than much work in Germany, more modern in intention. It is notorious that official architecture is conservative and Schmitthenner occupies the position formerly held under social democratic regimes by Hans Poelzig and Bruno Paul. He is as competent an architect as either of them.

The third group is composed of the young men in the party, the students and revolutionaries who are ready to fight for modern art. The most powerful of these is the new director of the National Gallery, Alois Schardt. So far the battle has been fought in the field of painting and mainly around the names of those venerable German artists, Nolde and Barlach, who are especially hated by Schulze-Naumburg. In architecture there is only one man whom even the young men can defend and this is Mies van der Rohe. Mies has always kept out of politics and has always taken his stand against functionalism. No one can accuse Mies' houses of looking like factories. Two factors especially make Mies' acceptance as the new architect possible. First Mies is respected by the conservatives. Even the Kampfbund für Deutsche Kultur has nothing against him. Secondly Mies has just won (with four others) a competition for the new building of the Reichsbank. The Jury were older architects and representatives of the bank. If (and it may be a long if) Mies should build this building it would clinch his position.

A good modern Reichsbank would satisfy the new craving for monumentality, but above all it would prove to the German intellectuals and to foreign countries that the new Germany is not bent on destroying all the splendid modern arts which have been built up in recent years. All revolutions, seemingly against everything of the past, really build on the positive achievements of the preceding decades. Germany cannot deny her progress. If in the arts she sets the clock back now, it will run all the faster in the future.

Architecture in 1941

Written 1942; previously unpublished.

This hitherto unpublished essay, prepared for an encyclopedia, remains an accurate and comprehensive view of architecture at a critical moment, just before the American entry into World War II and contemporaneous with the immigration of a number of key European modernists including Marcel Breuer, Walter Gropius, and Mies van der Rohe. Johnson reveals himself as not only a sound critic and historian but also a lively journalist, writing in a tone worthy of The March of Time. *It is interesting to note that his enthusiasm for Robert Moses and the motor car would change in the course of the next ten years or so, and that Johnson would become one of the earliest and most convincing critics of the American love affair with the automobile (see "The Town and the Automobile," pp. 81–83). The section of the essay devoted to "Design" isolates at an early stage the major regional schools which would figure importantly throughout the decade of the 1940's and well into the 1950's. The call for a "semi-political struggle" sounds more characteristic of 1930's radicalism and in a sense anticipates his later criticism of Modern Movement establishmentarianism in the 1950's and 1960's (see "The Seven Shibboleths of Our Profession," pp. 143–49).*

In the year of war 1941 the art of architecture took on, as was inevitable, a more public character. By the end of the year indeed it was obvious that private building for private purposes was nearly at an end. The period of skyscrapers, suburban residences, country clubs, and even churches, museums, and schools was—temporarily at least—over. The energy of architects all over the country was absorbed more and more by public commissions.

Official Architecture

Among the public works of the year some peacetime buildings were still being built. The most anachronistic were the Mellon Gallery in Washington and the Jefferson Memorial in the same city. The minds of the country were on less monumental problems and on less classical and eclectic design. Both buildings looked old-fashioned even before they were open to the public. Also in Washington stands the new National Airport which, with its out-of-scale reminiscences of Mount Vernon, and with much less justification, also belongs in the category of old-fashioned new buildings.

New York, our second capital city, fared better. Brilliant Commissioner Robert Moses continued his road building, making art out of traffic lanes. Most of his parkways and bridges are good architecture; the East River Drive winding in and out and up and down, crossed by light concrete footways, is very good architecture. Even the New York Asphalt Plant which Mr. Moses had to move away from the river front for his Drive is now a work of art. Its startling parabola is a welcome relief among New York's endless rows of walk-ups.

Except for New York, however, municipal architecture during the year was meager. The federal agencies did better. Most memorable will be the work of the Tennessee Valley Authority under the general architectural supervision of Roland Wank. Massive in scale and straightforward in detail, the dams, dynamo rooms, and control houses of the Tennessee Valley are much more nearly symbolic of our times than the correct dullness of official Washington.

Socially, perhaps even more important is the work of the San Francisco office of the Farm Security Administration. Besides making a dent in the migrant labor problem of the Far West, young architect Vernon De Mars has made a dent in the central problem of architecture-town planning. The F.S.A. camps at Chandler, Arizona; Woodville, California; and Granger, Washington, though they owe something in design to the great Swiss pioneer of contemporary architecture, Le Corbusier, are very clean, very neat, and very American.

Housing

The big new step in architecture for 1941 was public housing. Never before in our country have we seen governmental planning and architectural creativeness combined in the building of whole communities. Heretofore, our housing developments have been built speculatively, crowdedly, hit-or-miss, and, more often than not, entirely without benefit of architect. In 1941 the combination of necessity and leadership put the United States far in advance of the whole housing world. The necessity was the dislocation caused by defense requirements. Workers were suddenly needed where none had been needed before. The leadership came from the Federal Works Agency, especially from Defense Housing Chief Clark Foreman. The result is a whole series of planned communities. They are discouragingly inadequate to the problem, but they are a beginning.

Architecturally the most important is the New Kensington, Pennsylvania, project designed by two Harvard professors, Walter Gropius and Marcel Breuer. Here a new pattern of city planning takes the place both of the dull gridiron system of the nineteenth century, and of the romantic scattered house type of the "suburban" period. The houses are connected in rows of four to eight units, and these rows are grouped, carefully following a steeply sloping site, in a free, asymmetrical arrangement. The project will undoubtedly have a great influence on future housing. The largest project of the year was architect William Wurster's 1,600 units at Vallejo, California. Here site prefabrication cut costs and proved the desirability of large-scale undertaking in the field of housing.

Among the projects having freestanding single houses, the most interesting work was that done by Hugh Stubbins of Cambridge. The best-organized office for handling big work was probably George Howe's in Philadelphia. The most distinguished name among housing architects of the year was that of America's foremost architect, Frank Lloyd Wright, whose project at Pittsfield, Massachutsetts, had not been completed at the end of the year.

1941 may be known in our architectural history as the year when community planning started in the United States—the year when the field of activity of the architect widened from single buildings to congeries of buildings.

Prefabrication

With defense housing rose the demand for prefabricated houses: that is, the adaptation to housing of the mass-production methods of such industries as the automotive. It was only partially answered in 1941. Engineer-architect Buckminster Fuller produced a house made by a corn-crib manufacturer. For the Glenn Martin Plant near Baltimore, the Pierce Foundation built many houses using an insulating sandwich. The Pierce house is, however, not fully prefabricated. Others proposed plywood panel construction, and one man built an experimental house near Washington of "gunite" concrete sprayed onto a balloon-held framework of reinforcing rods. The only attempt at erecting a test community of prefabricated houses was a government project at Indian Head, Maryland. It was not a success.

Design

The trend in design during the year continued the direction of the past decade toward what used to be called "modern." Holabird & Root of Chicago in their work for universities and railroads continued to be the most successful adapters of contemporary design to conservative uses and for conservative clients. The Saarinens, father and son, continued their graceful style. William Lescaze finished his Longfellow Building in Washington, where it marks a clean contrast to the official stuffiness.

The major design problem of the last years, however, has been the private, freestanding house, and it is in this field that the various trends are clearest.

In the East, the influence of the Harvard Architectural School has continued to grow. The best houses in this strongly European tradition are the ones by Gropius and Breuer; especially good is the Chamberlain House in Wayland, Massachusetts.

In the Middle West, the tradition of Frank Lloyd Wright once more assumed the proportions it had a generation ago. Mr. Wright, after a long and undeserved eclipse, is once more a leader. His manner and that of his followers is somewhat influenced by European work of the last generation. The roofs are flatter and the windows more often reach the floor, but their houses keep the "Prairie" look which they had in 1910.

It is on the West Coast, however, that domestic architecture has had its real boom. It is only here that a "School" may be said to exist. The "California School" work shows the influence of Wright; of the Austrian Neutra, who works in Los Angeles; of European pioneers; and even of the Orient; but it is nonetheless original. The houses are simpler than Wright's, more fitted to wood construction than any European models, more straightforward than any eclecticism. The careers of some of these young architects should be followed: John Funk, John E. Dinwiddie, Gardner Dailey, Gregory Ain, and John Yeon.

Publications

The most important work on general architecture to appear during 1941 was *Space, Time and Architecture* by the eminent Swiss critic, Sigfried Giedion. It is an ambitious history of the background of modern architecture written as a morphology of history. Especially noteworthy: the story of the effect of engineering on aesthetics; the story of the effect of social patterns on architecture. In the field of American architecture, Henry-Russell Hitchcock's monumental illustrated volume on Frank Lloyd Wright will long be the standard work on our greatest architect.

The prize for the magazine of the year goes without question to *California Arts and Architecture,* a lively and discriminating review. The larger architectural magazines were beset during the year both with falling advertising revenue and with increasing pressure from advertisers to feature the expedient rather than the fine. The *Architectural Forum* carried the best reports on new developments.

Education

In recent years architects, like those in other professions, are faced with the problem of oversupply. As a result fewer young men went into the field, attendance at schools declined, and just at the same moment income from endowment diminished. The entrance of America into the war only hastened the trend. New York University had to suspend its architectural school entirely.

The quality of instruction, however, remained high both in the official academies and the one-man studios. It is in the field of education that the United States has most profited architecturally from the European war. Expatriates returned and émigrés came to teach. Walter Gropius and Marcel Breuer of the Bauhaus teach at Harvard. Moholy-Nagy has started a new Bauhaus in Chicago. Mies van der Rohe is the director of architecture at the Illinois Institute of Technology in Chicago. Alvar Aalto, Finland's most distinguished architect, taught in 1941 at Massachusetts Institute of Technology. Erich Mendelsohn of Palestine and Serge Chermayeff of London are now active here. Antonin Raymond, long an expatriate, has a studio at New Hope, Pennsylvania. Paul Nelson returned from years in Paris. All these men stimulated and influenced the art of architecture during the year 1941.

Politics

As 1941 closed, architects turned their attention perforce to the political scene. The great field of private construction seemed closed to them; on the other hand, government building was more and more kept in the hands of government architects and engineers employed in the offices of the Public Buildings Administration or in the Army and Navy bureaus. Architects in private practice did not seem very important in the rush of building cantonments, defense plants, and emergency housing.

If the architects were to be the leaders in the "space arranging" of the future and not merely allow the whole task to devolve upon engineers, military and civil, they would have to face, as a profession, a semi-political struggle new in their experience.

Architecture of Harvard Revival and Modern: The New Houghton Library

From the Harvard Advocate, *75th anniversary issue (April, 1942), 12–17.*

This is an important statement, which has remained obscure for too long by reason of its publication in a student journal and not in an architectural or general-interest periodical. Written while Johnson was a student at Harvard's graduate School of Design, it sees the issues of traditionalism and modernism in far less parochial terms than most of the university's community appears to have at that time. Johnson asks very tough questions in the guise of not asking questions at all; that is to say:

Without inquiring into Mr. Gropius' feelings when he sees from the windows of Robinson Hall the Georgian details of Houghton nor asking what Messrs. Perry, Shaw and Hepburn think of Harvard architectural education, we will look into this split in the architectural world to see how it came about, why, specifically, President Conant could build a Georgian Revival Library in the same year he writes in his Annual Report to the Board of Overseers, concerning Mr. Gropius' modern school: "The School of Design has in the last few years become the leading school of architecture on this continent, if not in the world."

Johnson's view of the situation is detached and historically informed; his invocation of Richardson as "America's greatest nineteenth-century architect" is rather more correct and less sarcastic than his subsequent use of the same term of praise in the case of Frank Lloyd Wright.[1] His discussion of what he calls the "uglification" of the 1860's and '70's is remarkably sympathetic to the High-Victorian Gothic style, then at the nadir of its reputation; his invocation of Memorial Hall's "strength of character and impression. . . . It is at least not a dull building" sure evidence, should we need it, that Johnson's intelligence and eye are exceptionally sensitive instruments, no matter what the fashionable ism or aesthetic of the moment might be. The discussion of Sever Hall is a sympathetic one. This is not surprising, given Hitchcock's 1936 monograph on Richardson; but Johnson goes beyond the conventional modernist search for ancestors, typical of the writings of the Swiss historian Sigfried Giedion and, to an extent, of the English historian Nikolaus Pevsner, to see in Richardson's building not only a remarkably inventive and skillful composition, but also one that incorporates strong references to the Colonial architecture that constituted the physical context of the Harvard Yard at the time of Richardson's commission.

Caught in the anti-Neo-classic polemic of the "Harvard Bauhaus," Johnson allows the super-scale of the Widener Library to blind him to the splendor of McKim, Mead & White's rather modest Robinson Hall, a building I believe he would find more praiseworthy today.

Over and over, as in the discussion of the Houghton Library, Johnson reveals himself a superb critic of architecture, no matter what the position of a given building in the battle of styles. This essay marks a new maturity and perhaps hints at the beginning of a wavering commitment to the canonical International Style. Modern and traditional buildings alike are discussed in a notably sympathetic manner; each is subjected to intelligent, critical examination, independent of Johnson's own biases, in a way that would have been unimaginable ten years earlier.

1. *"100 Years, Frank Lloyd Wright and Us" (see pp. 193–98).*

There are many who are shocked that Harvard University, which justly enough has a reputation for leadership in the cultural world, should build a Georgian Revival Library like Houghton at a time when modern architecture has gained such wide and general acceptance, an acceptance great enough for Harvard to establish and develop a school of *modern* architecture.

Others are shocked that a modern architectural school should be allowed in the hallowed Yard, and especially one led by the great exponent of uncompromising modernism, Walter Gropius, founder of the famous Bauhaus.

It is difficult to talk across the gulf separating the two camps, when the partisans of modern architecture consider Georgian and Gothic Revival buildings bad regardless of any intrinsic merits they may possess, while the older generation of architects defend the worst Revivalist buildings on the theory that they at least do not look like greenhouses or factories. Without inquiring into Mr. Gropius' feeling when he sees from the windows of Robinson Hall the Georgian details of Houghton, nor asking what Messrs. Perry, Shaw and Hepburn think of Harvard architectural education, we will look into this split in the architectural world to see how it came about, why, specifically, President Conant could build a Georgian Revival Library in the same year he writes in his Annual Report to the Board of Overseers, concerning Mr. Gropius' modern school: "The School of Design has in the last few years become the leading school of architecture on this continent, if not in the world."

The paradox of the present situation is, however, not merely a Harvard confusion; it is inherent in the history of the art of recent architecture. In fact, since 1888 (I pick that date because it marks the death of America's greatest nineteenth-century architect, Henry Hobson Richardson) we have had two histories of architecture: one, the history of Revivalism, the other, the history of what we shall have to call, for the want of a more specific term, modern architecture.

To make this dichotomy clear we will have to begin much before Richardson. Cambridge affords the best material for a study of this period, for Harvard University has always been in the vanguard of design, which in the confused welter of "styles" in the nineteenth century was no mean achievement; and not only did the University always do *the latest thing*, it did it extremely well. No other single locality in America so well illustrates the story of this century in architecture.

We need not start our history before University Hall, 1815. There is no disagreement on the excellence of the eighteenth-century buildings, especially the modest Hollis and Holworthy dormitories; and except for Jefferson's work for the University of Virginia, there is no finer college building in America of the period than Bulfinch's University Hall.

But after Bulfinch came the Age of Romanticism. Buildings were then built in Greek, Romanesque and Gothic *styles.* It is the fashion today to decry this "mixture" as in bad taste, to call the period jumbled, insincere, unoriginal or Victorian. Yet, just as *Victorian* is beginning to lose its pejorative connotations, so the fact that the Romantics used strange, copycat names for their architecture can no longer blind us to the excellence of their work, or to the inherent unity of design of the period. For the Romantics were no copyists. Dane Hall looks nothing whatsoever like the Parthenon. And Boylston Hall labeled "Romanesque" looks like no medieval building imaginable. In fact, if we look beyond the details to the massing and fenestration, the similarity of Dane and Boylston is more striking than their difference. The windows are extremely vertical, spaced far apart, emphasizing the massive character of the masonry. The detail in both is flat and simplified. Neither building could be mistaken either for eighteenth-century or for ancient structures. The "Greek" and the "Romanesque" must be kept strictly in quotation marks. Not so, however, the modern Revivals. Gore Hall on the river, built since the last war, is a correct copy of Sir Christopher Wren's Hampton Court in England. Gore can be called English Renaissance without quotation marks. The inspiration, the "style" in the deeper sense, is quite the Romantic spirit of the nineteenth century.

Dane Hall and Boylston unfortunately can no longer be admired; Dane burnt down in 1918 and Boylston had a Mansard roof added to it, now a monstrous hybrid. Gone too are the "Romanesque" Appleton Chapel, the original Gore Hall, and the old Library which was "Gothic." Two other Romantic buildings are left: Divinity Hall, which is excellent "Greek," and Lawrence Hall, in the "Italian villa style" and not too excellent. However, both have vertical and widely spaced windows and the fine masonry massiveness typical of the period.

By 1860 the inspiration of the Romantics had lagged, and there followed two decades of architectural horrors; Harvard kept well in lead. Except for such backward imitations as Thayer and Weld, Harvard remained progressive. Memorial Hall, for example, finished up the seventies, and has a strength of character and impression, though perhaps ugly ones. It is at least not a dull building.

In the middle of this period of *uglification,* the seventies, there came onto the scene that unique genius, Richardson. His Sever Hall, finished only four years after Memorial Hall, 1880, is the most important building the University has ever built. Older graduates have only to think upon old Hemenway Gymnasium, a contemporary of Sever, to realize the greatness of the latter.

Sever is today still a beautiful building, in spite of popular taste which condemns dark window trim, dark red brick, and heavy-handed, moulded brick decoration. The ugly qualities are few; every basic modern quality, Sever possesses. To be really appreciated it must be first viewed at night when lights are burning inside it; the *night view* is always the acid test of architecture. If the windows and doors of a building are well proportioned in relation to its solid wall surfaces, it is apt to be a good building. Too many an "attractive" piece of architecture pleases because of surface tricks, shadows from trees, ivy-clad walls, or questionable decorative motifs, which, at night, appear in full truth, without disguise. Three buildings in the Yard deserve night study: Hollis, Holworthy, and Sever, its neighbor, Robinson, a contrasting bad example. The eighteenth-century window pattern of Hollis is seen as regular rectangular holes cut in checkerboard fashion out of the wall surface, neither vertically or horizontally accented. The order is perfect, the proportion, good. Sever's window pattern is a series of horizontal bands, divided and subdivided by heavy mullions and thin muntins. The groupings differ from floor to floor in length and character. The order is not as obviously simple as in the eighteenth-century dormitories, but is just as strict. Robinson at night, on the other hand, reveals a window pattern that apes the eighteenth century, but has none of its simplicity and order. The windows are too tall and thin, too widely spaced to have the rectangular checkerboard quality of Hollis or the horizontality of Sever; yet they are not widely enough spaced to have the slit effect of Romantic architecture. The effect is one of lack of order and poor proportion.

Richardson was known in his time as a reviver of the Norman or Romanesque style; hence Sever is thought today to be vaguely Romanesque. Actually, the front arch is Syrian, the end bays and the towers on each side tinged with Romanesque, the massing wholly Colonial, though violently different from Colonial in proportion. In other words, Sever is a product of Richardson's fertile but disciplined imagination. The horizontal window treatment can only be called modern. And particularly modern is the startling horizontal dormer window on the rear, one continuous band of window panes such as was not used after that until the twenties of this century.

The twenty years between "Romanesque" Boylston and "Romanesque" Sever illustrates perfectly the difference between the Romantic Age and the beginning of the modern rational or functional approach to architecture. Boylston is careful, graceful, flat, even thin; Sever is tough, broad, thick in detail, a primitive of modern.

Up to and including Sever the historical outline is straight. It is after Sever that the bifurcation of architectural trends begins. Along one road, Richardson's influence toward functionalism broadened with time, though it was strongest in the Middle West and not in Boston. There Louis Sullivan and Frank Lloyd Wright were Richardson's especial heirs. Through Wright the inflence spread to Europe: to Le Corbusier, Mies van der Rohe and Walter Gropius; and through Gropius, of course, back to Boston and Harvard. This tradition, having grown so greatly, is now referred to as modern architecture.

The other section of the fork in the road, after 1888, is architectural Revivalism. It was a natural development. Richardson's contemporaries admired his work, but thought of him as a Romanesque revivalist. Instead of the Romantic connotations of "Romanesque," however, they gave the word historical connotations. Their work became, in fact, more and more Romanesque without quotation marks. By investigating actual Romanesque monuments they undoubtedly felt they were doing better than Richardson at his own trade. So as knowledge of past styles became more and more precise, as photography took the place of bad sketches as source of knowledge, architectural copies of Old World originals became more archaeological and less haphazard. Gradually it came to be held questionable taste not to know the "styles." Good taste demanded even more exact adaptations of the originals.

It was only natural that at first these copies should have been very bad. They had none of the freedom and strength of Richardson, and none of the real quality of the originals. A typical early Revival building is Robinson Hall, built just twenty years after Sever. It was designed by McKim, Mead, & White, the best-known architects of the day (Harvard doing the "latest thing"). Yet it has none of the modernity of Sever, none of the refinement of the later Revival buildings around the Yard; and not the smallest suspicion of the quality of the Renaissance. It is hard to say much of Harvard building of the period, 1900 to 1918. To list the buildings is sufficient commentary: The Harvard Union, Phillips Brooks House. The New Lecture Hall, Robinson, Emerson, Langdell, Pierce, etc., ending with that most brutal example of bull-market Classical, Widener Library.

No, nor did the period of the '00's improve the architectural harmony of the Yard as a whole. The Revivalists, essentially eager to make their individual buildings correct, did not worry about the ensemble. The Romantics had kept the college buildings in scale with each other. The Yard until 1888 was composed of two quadrangles of Colonial dimensions surrounded by Colonial-dimensioned buildings. The coming of Widener blasted the harmony forever.

Since the last war the Revivalist buildings became more correct and more correctly grouped. Gore Hall on the river is good Wren. Littauer taken from the Massachusetts General Hospital is only fairly good Bulfinch. The steeple of the new Appleton is in itself a fine and correct addition to Colonial Cambridge, though incongruous atop a Greek Revival portico. The new Houses are better. Particularly Lowell House which has two entirely enclosed courts, a sense of enclosed space superior to any other buildings at Harvard, far superior to the broken-up confusion of Dunster or the square dullness of Smith Halls. Certainly the Houses have never reached the nadir of McKim, Mead & White in their grouping of Robinson and Emerson with Sever.

Houghton Library is the newest addition to Harvard Revivalism, and by far the most elegant of recent buildings. The architects, Messrs. Perry, Shaw and Hepburn, who were in charge of the Colonial reconstruction of Williamsburg, Virginia, were at Harvard faced with a more difficult task. In the first place they were called upon to erect a building in a space where there was no room for a building. The site with its charming gnarled oaks was the last bit of informal grass slope left in the Yard, a rest to the building-weary eye. Any possible building was doomed to be entirely dominated by the weighty walls of Widener. Worse still, the steep slope of the site made a normal building out of the question. Lastly, to the confusion of the architects, it was obligatory to allow for an umbilical connection with the mother Library, which as executed reminds the observer of nothing so much as an "El" station.

Insignificant and modest buildings such as the Wigglesworth dormitories along Massachusetts Avenue might have fit in; but Houghton Library, housing as it does the treasures of Harvard, could not be insignificant. The architects chose, therefore, to create a façade to the east and treat the connection to Widener as best they could. It is unfortunate that this new building will most always be approached from the chasm between new and old libraries, and not from Quincy Street.

Yet if we accept the basic assumption of the Revivalists, that Harvard should be Georgian, tastefully and correctly done; and if, moreover, we take into account the all but impossible task of erecting a monumental building as adjunct to the Behemoth of Harvard we must grant the architects success.

The east façade, the essence of the design, is simple and dignified; the whole elevation is treated as a single story with very tall, narrow windows spaced extraordinarily far apart, which give the whole a massive monumentality. There are, on the one hand, no fussy pilaster strips, colonnades or engaged columns, and on the other hand there is no attempt at the domestic Colonial quaintness which detracts from the nobility of much of modern Georgian work.

There seems to be no one specific Georgian model for the design. Many Georgian country houses had "swell fronts" and long windows like Houghton. The best known to New England is the Garden façade of the Gore Place in Waltham. The Gore house is built of the same orange brick, and the windows are placed in the same relative position with each other. At Waltham, however, the balustrade, as in all Georgian houses was freestanding so that the low pitched roof was visible, whereas at Houghton, presumably for reasons of attic space the balustrade panels are, unfortunately, filled in. The Gore House being very late Georgian has very flat insignificant details, whereas the window embrasures of Houghton are large and protruding. The proportions of the two are very different. It can, however, be no adverse criticism of a Georgian Revivalist building that it is not copied from a single prototype. The Houghton façade can stand on its own merits.

The construction and materials of the building are, for the most part, of the best. Rarely, too rarely, these days, are buildings erected with such solidity of construction and such care for detail. All the stonework and brickwork is carefully cut, especially the bricks of the flat arches over the windows. Because of these excellencies it is all the more to be regretted that economy forced a few compromises: the seeming wrought iron grills are made of wood and the wall coping which looks like limestone is made of sheet metal.

The choice of salmon-colored, underfired brick in place of the ubiquitous red Harvard brick may shock the purists who believe that Harvard must always build with Harvard brick, but in this case the color is the much needed one. In their Longfellow Building at Radcliffe College, Messrs. Perry, Shaw and Hepburn have used this salmon brick.

Some details of the façade cause question. Why use white paint on the window trim, and putty-colored paint on the wooden balustrade panels above? Were these panels supposed to be of limestone, then changed to wood and painted to simulate the stone? Why does the front door not fill the limestone frame? In most Georgian Revival structures the inset doorway would be as high as the windows in order to fill out the enframement.

But these are minor matters. The large objections all concern the site relationships. A monumental axial façade, whether Georgian or any other kind, requires a setting and approach. Houghton has neither. The gardens of President Conant's house impinging upon the axis, force a diagonal, cramped approach, most disturbing to any sense of equilibrium. Since appreciation of architecture is, at least in part, kinetic, the effect of walking slantwise toward the façade of Houghton is architecturally unpleasant. We can absolve the architects, however; it is the fault of Harvard's traditional desire to have its cake and eat it too. We cannot have a good President's garden and a good Georgian approach to Houghton.

Less easy to understand is the slope of the site away from the façade toward the rear. A façade, unlike a stage setting, requires background and framing. A high retaining wall running south from the façade could have given the sense of level ground so necessary for a Georgian façade. The existing path could be carried down a full story height by a stairway.

The interior arrangement of the Library is difficult to criticize since it was designated expressly for the needs of a Treasure Library. The librarians are, themselves, pleased; a minor miracle, in itself, when architects please their clients. The functional problems of the building can then be said to have been solved. To those who are not librarians it seems illogical that the entry room, flanked on the exterior by great windows, need be lighted artificially. The artifical illumination, however, is necessary for the preservation of rare books, and the objection which functionalist critics raise, that windows of a building should serve to illuminate the rooms behind them may be met with the point, that the windows certainly do not detract in any way from the façade. The entry room, because of its lighting, shocks the observer by a claustrophobia.

The success of Houghton cannot answer the question which comes up and will continue to come up in the future: should Harvard not build modern buildings? There are favorable reasons, even precedents for it. Even the designated architects of the University, the favored architects of Georgian Revival, Coolidge, Shepley, Bulfinch and Abbott who designed the Houses, built the modern Biology Building for Harvard in 1931. This building was at that time the most advanced modern college building in the country. Whether it was that the University thought this building was far enough from the Yard so that "experimental architecture" could be condoned, or whether they felt that science being modern, a modern building might be allowed to house the scientist's work, we do not know. At any rate, it remains the *only* modern building at Harvard.

Other academic institutions have done much more in modern architecture. The Illinois Institute of Technology in Chicago has gone the farthest; they have given to the director of their architectural school, Professor Mies van der Rohe, the commission to design their whole new campus. Here in New England, Wheaton College held a notable competition in an attempt to acquire the most modern architects for their faculty. The Saarinens have been commissioned by Oberlin College in Ohio to design a new auditorium unit. Closest to home, fellow Cantabrigians, Massachusetts Institute of Technology have consistently commissioned architects for new buildings, logically feeling if an architect is worthy to teach students, he is good enough to be trusted with commissions.

In the case of Harvard, though Messrs. Gropius and Breuer have drawn up plans for Black Mountain College in North Carolina, they have designed nothing as yet for the University that employs them.

The most cogent reason for the Georgian Revival at Harvard is the plea for uniformity and consistency in Harvard architecture. Harvard was founded and grew great before the end of real Colonial architecture; is it, therefore, not logical to continue in the same tradition? Another point: persuasive, unanswerable: donors prefer Georgian. And Harvard is not going to refuse a new building on the grounds that some of the Board may not like the donor's architect, particularly an architect previously employed by the University.

To the plea for consistency and uniformity, however, there are rejoinders. Against the Harvardian tradition of Colonialism, we see the inevitable tradition of Progress. Up to McKim, Mead, & White the architecture of Harvard changed with the times, why should one think it will not continue to change with time? History is rich with such precedent: Oxford College changed from Gothic to Renaissance and then to Victorian Gothic

Revival without a change in the traditions of the University of Oxford. At Hampton Court, the home of kings, Sir Christopher Wren added his Renaissance Court to the earlier Tudor Gothic Palace. And since Wren kept to the scale of the original, the transition, then, or to-day does not shock the senses.

The east quadrangle of the Harvard Yard, in 1888, is a case similar to the above examples. Although Bulfinch Palladian pilasters face the Syrian portal of Sever, although "Romanesque" Appleton Chapel faced "Gothic" Gore Hall Library, the scale of all four buildings was similar. The same harmony, unfortunately, cannot be said to exist among the Georgian brick buildings around Houghton. The President's House, Wigglesworth Hall, and Houghton, itself, all are dwarfed by the colossal orders of Widener. Perhaps, like the Baroque Schoenborn Chapel tacked onto a Romanesque Church in Wuerzburg, a modern structure might have glowed by its very difference in scale and design against the Widener setting. Perhaps, a low modern building, needing no axial approach or monumentaility could have been built and might have remained comparatively harmoniously.

Style and the International Style

Speech, Barnard College, April 30, 1955; previously unpublished.

Johnson is witty, and often at his own expense. The self-mocking tone of many of his talks of the 1950's parallels the mocking pseudo-anti-Modern Movement tone of much of his work in design in the same period. Nonetheless, despite his tone, Johnson never gives up his belief in the forms, if not necessarily the theory, of the Modern Movement, which he tends to regard as synonymous with Modern architecture. In this sense, he contends that the inception of Modern architecture can be pinpointed in the year 1923, although elsewhere, as in "The International Style: Death or Metamorphosis" (see pp. 119–22), he cites 1922 as the "magic year," and that earlier date seems also to have made a tidier reference point for the "Modern Architecture" exhibition and publication of The International Style, *both in 1932. But Johnson, as much the scholar as the man of polemical invective, recognizes that while there are dominant styles in the history of architecture, these are neither uniform nor monolithic, and they are more the result of a generally accepted vocabulary of shapes than a set of commonly held ideological beliefs. Johnson sees the history of architecture visually: not as names and dates, and not as the record of events within and without the culture of architecture, but as the unfolding of shapes. Though he recognizes that Mendelsohn, Häring, Scharoun, and other figures of the 1920's shared many of the philosophical and social programs of the leaders of the Modern Movement, like those leaders he cannot fully accept them because their forms are not the canonical forms of the "International Style."*

In this talk, given when he shared the podium with Henry-Russell Hitchcock in the session devoted to "Modern American Architecture" in an American Arts Festival, Johnson retreats from the anti-revolutionary position of "The Seven Crutches of Modern Architecture" of the previous year (see pp. 137–40) toward a position that supports a continuing creative struggle against prevailing style, an endless creative journey from the "known to the unknown." In so characterizing the creative process and in suggesting that art simultaneously goes forward and backward to effect change, Johnson begins to articulate a position that runs against the stream of the abstract, anti-semantic, utilitarian, functional, and technological biases of the Modern Movement. In 1960 he would define his position as one of "functional eclecticism."[1]

1. See "Informal Talk, Architectural Association" (pp. 106–16).

The artist is traditionally inarticulate, his historical perspective blinded by prejudice. His reason for doing this, not that, is mere rationalization after the fact of blind artistic choice.

This is certainly true in my case. My learned friend Mr. Hitchcock, whom you have just heard, is articulate, so I shall try to be inarticulate, or rather to put things *subjectively,* as the artist must if he is not to lose the individuation which is art.

Now Mr. Hitchcock and I have a peculiar relation. He is not only a critic, he is "my" critic. I discovered him. So if some of the same phrases occur in my talk, it is no accident; they will be his, not mine. I collaborated as a junior partner with him in the exciting days of the thirties. I learned from him. I shall be delighted if I should sound like him, since to me the creative critic perhaps outranks the creative artist in responsibility for the total cultural picture. Even if this is not true in general, it is in any event true in this case. I am and will always be in debt to Russell Hitchcock.

Therefore, as a prejudiced practitioner of the art, I can be free to be as non-intellectual and uninhibited as I wish. I must explain the word "non-intellectual." I really mean anti-*word,* because the word kills art. The word is an abstraction, and art is concrete. The word is old, loaded with accreted meanings from usage. Art is new. The word is general—art is specific. Words are mind—art is eyes. Words are thought—art is feeling. It is easier for me to talk with a pencil and a few grunts; however, unaccustomed as I am to words, I shall eschew the grunts and do the best I can do with these awkward tools, to try to communicate to your perhaps awkward minds—accustomed as they are in the academic world to words, words, words, words.

History has always fascinated me—too bad it is written in words that kill the flavor of the story. I mean the story of architecture, which must be learned only with eyes, and our place in history in the middle of the century. Through my eyes it looks wonderful; through my eyes, it seems we are in the middle of a Golden Age—none more golden! Perhaps the other arts may be getting along; I wouldn't know.

The theater doesn't look as good as Shakespeare to me, however. Hindemith and Bartók may be great, but do even musicologists claim that they are Mozartian giants? Painting and sculpture may well be on a par with architecture. Maybe painting, to be great, has no need of a definite discipline and style, as does architecture. Individualism seems to be more rampant.

But with architecture, you have your feet on the ground. The field is not divided between realists and abstractionists like painting, nor even any more between modernists and traditionalists. No magazine publishes, no school teaches anything but modern, and modern architecture gets more and more beautiful every year. And without being chauvinistic, it

Philip Johnson and Henry-Russell Hitchcock

can be said that architecture in this country is the best in the world and is growing better and better.

The problem is how to describe a Golden Age when you are in the middle of it.

Maybe we should start at the beginning in the magic year of 1923. (To Mr. Hitchcock, that date is less explosive; he sees the continuance of history. I see barely anything before that date.) It was the year of the centripetal revolution; the revolution *toward* a style, *away from* individual styles. There were great architects before 1923: Sullivan and Wright in Chicago, Wagner and Olbrich in Austria and Germany, Mackintosh in Scotland, Gaudí in Spain. No, we cannot deny these men their genius, only their relevance. Except Wright, they existed in a vacuum. What came after? More centrifugal, splitting movements: romantic achievements, but a Golden Age needs more than geniuses. Each of us has learned something from these giants, naturally, as no painter today *cannot* not have looked at Cézanne. I have learned from Sullivan and Gaudí: Sullivan, who first knew how to handle the big office building (a new problem, don't forget, in the history of the world); Gaudí, who knew colors and curves—the sculptor predecessor of our great Le Corbusier.

But—and this is important—Mies van der Rohe, my associate (my biographee, to use a really horrifying neologism), finds only Berlage of Holland, a contemporary of both Gaudí and Sullivan, worthy of emulation. Berlage was the Master Builder of his time as Mies is today. His honor and respect for building as a technique of putting things together bricks, stone, steel, Mies learned from Berlage; yet the historian Mr. Hitchcock has not even mentioned Berlage in his story this morning. The men of the 1890's and 1900's were giants, but their work was mutually incompatible. I wonder if Gaudí ever heard of Berlage. There was no common style; no description of their common accomplishments could be written. Their achievement does not compose a corpus. Indeed, not since the breakup of the Baroque and its pallid Palladian manner in England and her colonies has there been a universal (and I mean universal in the Western sense) style. Yet every Golden Age (in architecture, at least) has a style. Witness the names you learned in school—the Gothic, the Greek, and the Byzantine. A style always has a number of understood (felt, in my language) concepts or presuppositions from which to start to design. At the flowering of each style, some very great monuments of smooth understanding have been erected. The Greek flowered slowly, the Renaissance with incredible rapidity, but a style was there each time. There was no style in our times until the year 1923.

I have excepted Frank Lloyd Wright from the list of early giants who had no issue. He is the exception that illustrates the rule. It is possible for genius to help create styles and yet be part of none. Michelangelo, for example, broke the bounds of the Renaissance style and to this day remains the enigma of architectural history. Frank Lloyd Wright is our Michelangelo. One day, more than fifty years ago, he founded modern architecture, and he has been founding styles ever since, but with ever-decreasing relevance. The Riverside Club of 1900 was the forerunner of the style of 1923, but Frank Lloyd Wright went on from manner to manner, until today, though deserving of his title as the greatest architect in the world, he is nevertheless less influential than he was five decades ago. The Baroque style analogously developed more from the Church of the Gesù by Vignola than from Michelangelo's grand distortions. Modern architecture owes much more to Mies and Le Corbusier than to Frank Lloyd Wright. Architecture today is a style, and Frank Lloyd Wright, though he has been much influenced by it, is not part of it.

Strange, just yesterday, I was thinking about taking a trip to recharge the batteries of the eye and considering where to go. It occurred to me that it is of greater interest for me to see Catalano's laminated wood, hyperbolic paraboloid house in Raleigh, North Carolina, than any of Frank Lloyd Wright's new houses. It seems more germane to the subject at hand.

But to get back to 1923. I could not, even if I would, tell you just what happened, but I am at home from that year on. The innovations of that year were innovations toward a common kind of design to which all architects today, including, I may confidently claim, the architectural students in this room, can turn back as to a common parent, so unlike the respect for a Chartres or a Parthenon. I can still, in my designing moments, learn the grammar of design, approaches to shapes from, let us say, the Brick Country House of Mies van der Rohe or the Ozenfant House of Le Corbusier, both of the year 1923. In much the same way, perhaps, did later Florentines look back to Brunelleschi, not copying but with a sense of continuing. There is more similarity between those works of 1923 and what is done in schools thirty years later than between these buildings and any work at all of the year 1913, only a decade before, so sturdy a hold on us has this new tradition.

I do not for a minute mean to say that all buildings now under construction conform to the new style. Far from it! But in an age of such fantastic building activity as today, it is only natural that cultural lag makes itself felt much more strongly than in earlier, less "civilized" times. The new crop of buildings on Madison Avenue has little to do with this discussion. Few buildings in any period carry the main story of art; perhaps today they are fewer than ever.

Rather than trying to define style, or even describe *our* style, an example from the cognate field of furniture design may illustrate the strength and vitality of our movement. You have seen the so-called Barcelona chair designed by Mies van der Rohe in 1928—perhaps in my house in New Canaan, or certainly elsewhere. It is current design at its best. It does not date. I have found none better in the twenty-seven years intervening. I know of no designer younger than I who would not agree. Yet in 1928, I remember, as we looked back twenty-seven years to 1901, to the quaint "objects" of Art Nouveau—the whiplash, curvy wooden chairs or the straight, stick-like Arts and Crafts chairs—we were shocked by a sense of change and revolution. There are new and good chair designers—Eames, Nelson, Saarinen, to name the Americans; but they are within our style, and do not render the 1928 Barcelona chair obsolete.

I leave to the historians the description of why it happened in 1923: the growth of rectilinear abstract painting; the final will to integrate steel and concrete into design; the worship of the machine; the end of World War I; the towering influence of Frank Lloyd Wright.

I only know that it happened, and that I am extremely grateful. I do not want to wander alone among the arbitrary wilds of "taste," as I would have had to in the last century. In that jungle, only a Richardson or a Sullivan could survive. Now I rejoice, I can lean on my elders, then hope to stand on their shoulders, reaching toward an architecture which will perfectly express my time.

A style is not a set of rules or shackles, as some of my colleagues seem to think. A style is a climate in which to operate, a springboard to leap further into the air. The onus of designing a new style any time one designs a new building is hardly freedom; it is too heavy a load except for the greatest of Michelangelos or Wrights. Strict style discipline hindered not in the slightest the creators of the Parthenon, nor did the pointed arch confine the designers of Amiens.

A style is not a set of rules to be applied by critics; it is a commonly held corpus of visual aesthetic canons, some of which can even be verbally expressed by laymen and critics. A few of these characteristics of the Modern style Mr. Hitchcock and I described in our book of twenty-three years ago called *The International Style.* It is interesting to recall what they were. I myself use these disciplines daily; not, of course, like a Bible, but more like the lenses of my eyes, or like what in German is called *Weltanschauung*—the how-you-look-at-things—rather than as a set of privatives. I paraphrase now, since I fear the exact phraseology of a quarter-century ago might date rather badly.

Naturally, we (I assisted Mr. Hitchcock in those days) tried to describe the differences between our style and older styles. We felt first, therefore, that out style had rejected the idea of mass as the aesthetic organizing principle for massing and fenestration, in favor of a weightlessness like that, for example, of a skeleton building. Even where we design with masonry walls, we build them straight and not pyramidally as in the styles of the past. Second, we felt that we design without using the axis as an ordering device, but rather using the march of columns themselves as modules of order. And third, we avoid the applied ornamentation of the past. These are not meant as a total description of a style—no words can be; but are they not as true today as a quarter-century ago? Are these criteria not used today by a growing body of informed laymen in looking at the buildings around us?

In studying the Lever House, perhaps the best building of any size in the Modern style in New York, certainly its effect is that of a weightless prism in which architectural order is expressed by the column spacing below, rather than by axiality; and it is uncluttered with applied ornament. The close observer might be bothered by the off-regular beat of the columns (a solecism in a strict *regular* style), or by the massive, weighty fire stairs appended at the rear of the weightless prism. These are minor points, not meant as a criticism of Mr. Bunshaft, the designer (I am too conscious of committing many more grievous errors myself); but the fact that these minor points are noticed reveals a common set of criteria that are used as the basis for judging.

I am reminded of an eighteenth-century British anecdote: a mason who forgot the closer brick at a window opening was laughed off the scaffold by the passersby. And yet in the entire city of New York, I do not know of any brick window embrasure where the closer is used correctly, and no one notices. The eighteenth century looked at brick bonding; we look at column spacing. Different styles, different focuses of attention, different conceptions, different standards.

Our style is not rigid, however. Rigid rules do help out bad architects but do not inhibit the imaginative. That is what is so wonderful! No single artist is conscious of the "rules" any more than of his *Weltanschauung,* his viewpoint through which he looks at the world. He just creates. Actually, he struggles the best he can *against* the style, *against* the known, *toward* the unknown, *toward* the original. It is this tension between style and change—known and unknown—that keeps a style alive. When Ralph Adams Cram was working on the Cathedral of St. John the Divine, he was not in tension with the Gothic, he was trying to comply with it. Every modern architect, on the other hand, being brought up with the modern style under his skin, can struggle against it with all his strength. If he is great he will bend it. I use the future tense because so far none has done so.

Style phases, however, there have been. In the twenties, stucco surfaces sprinkled asymmetrically with windows expressed the skin of our weightless volumes. In the thirties and forties, the cages, expressed and clear, took over, and even exposed masonry elements were no longer frowned on. In the thirties, also, there was much to-do about the free-form as a variant from the box of the twenties. A few Hollywood swimming pools and nightclub ceilings succumbed, but it was a passing fancy, like free-wheeling in automobiles. Today the cry, especially in the schools, is for thin-shell concrete roofs, which once more seem to offer a relief from a style that has been a trabeated, flat-roofed one. Very healthy—a new style phase, but hardly a new style. Ninety-nine percent of our buildings will still be multi-story—it is hard to walk on hyperbolic paraboloids. Wavy roofs do nothing to invalidate a style based on the undecorated cage, the expressed column. The most offbeat stylistically of any of our architects— and it is no accident that he is one of the greatest of all—is Le Corbusier. In striving for sculptural effects a few years ago, he designed a chapel at Ronchamp, to be built of gunited lathe—that is, of a net-like material on which concrete might be sprayed. But Le Corbusier is ahead of his time; gunite can't be used like that, so the building is built any old how— rubble masonry and concrete, mixed and all stuccoed over. The moral herein: Le Corbusier was thinking in terms of cages and volumes, not of masonry, even if our dull technicians are unable to keep up with his brilliant mind.

I want to close with a critique of the latest in the work of another of our really great architects, Mies van der Rohe. Mies has always been the purist, the Master Builder, as contrasted with Le Corbusier, the Baroque spirit, the painter, the sculptor of our style. The Seagram Building on Park Avenue is no exception; rather it is the distillation of the austere conception of the style, a concept which I share with him, as his partner on this building.

First, the site. As in the design of a cup, the emptiness is an essential element of this conception. The 100-foot-deep garden—larger than the court of The Museum of Modern Art—out of which rises the 500-foot precipice of the tower, is the main feature. Nowhere in the world can you see 500 feet straight into the air! The New York Central Building above the Grand Central Terminal at the foot of Park Avenue, for example, is not 500 feet high, and all other buildings in New York have setbacks, which conceal their true height. The proof: go to Long Island and look back—you will see towers you never saw from the streets of Manhattan.

The tower is a 5-by-3-bay rectangle—simple enough—but stiffened, as it were, by a spine at the back—a spine clothed in marble.

Like all great buildings—and I give you these points to help you examine buildings of past ages as well as our own—four important parts of the building are superbly blended: the corners, the crown, the base, the entrance. The shaft of the tower is all glass, the first floor-to-ceiling glass ever used in a tall building. (The U.N. and Lever House are only partially glass, in spite of the way they look.) But the corners go in and out, making a stiff bronze edging for the pattern of windows. The crown is an open filigree of their bronze mullions, three stories high, with a bronze housing for the elevators and such. The third item, the base, is a colonnade of noble piers behind which the glass of the entrance lobby runs. The *prisme pur* of Le Corbusier's first formulation, the building raised off the ground for appreciation of the weightlessness of its skeleton, is preserved. The entrance, and indeed the procession through to the great rooms at the back, is a symmetrical, majestic sequence of space experience, a clear march with none of the twisting and turning for elevators so familiar in our large buildings.

Compare the Seagram Building as you see it with other skyscrapers, bearing in mind these four points. There are no startling differences. You will miss the setbacks—those old-fashioned suggestions of mass and weight, wedding cakes—but study the crowns of New York skyscrapers. How many solutions you will find, all the way to useless dirigible masts, and how many successful ones! Mies has always said it is better to build good buildings than original ones. The Greeks of the fifth century must have said the same, and yet who on the Acropolis would complain of the lack of originality around him?

Seagram is possible because we have Mies, it is true; but it is also true that it is possible because we have an accepted style of architecture. It is possible because of enlightened patronage—as enlightened as the Medicis ever were—which again is possible because we have an accepted style.

Our Golden Age of architecture is only beginning. The founders are still alive, the style itself is barely a generation old. It is up to my generation, and it is even more up to the generation now in college and school, to take advantage of our future, to create the monuments which, like the buildings of other Golden Ages—Egypt, Rome, Byzantium— will act as beacons to the future, as physical reasons for remembering our times and our century.

The Town and the Automobile, or The Pride of Elm Street

Written 1955 (?); previously unpublished.

Johnson has been no more ambivalent about the relationship between cars and buildings than any other architect of his generation. In contrast to Wright and Le Corbusier, who embraced the automobile as a liberating force, Johnson sees it as a freedom fraught with peril: he states as fact that "the automobile is bad" and that "you must walk to appreciate architectural experience," yet he recognizes that "in America there is never going to be a town center without an automobile" and that "we cannot introduce the sidewalk café in this country" because Americans won't get out of their cars long enough to sit at it (New York being something of an exception to this generalization). In so saying, Johnson crystallizes a fundamental American dilemma: we long for European cultural experience, but we are not willing to, or at best cannot often bring ourselves to, make the adjustments in the tempo of our lives and the scale of our cities necessary to achieve it. Ironically, Johnson the architect has proved Johnson the theorist wrong. Though there is a "Main Street" running down the center of New York's Roosevelt Island, for which he and John Burgee provided the master plan in 1967, the absence of real traffic (as opposed to occasional, eerily silent, battery-powered minibuses) drains it of the vitality implicit in its name. Sadly, at Roosevelt Island we have streets without people, rather than plazas without cars.

The automobile is the greatest catastrophe in the entire history of city architecture. Is there any doubt of the fact? Just try to *walk* across the Place de la Concorde, a once beautiful area of Paris. Too dangerous; better take a taxi. Try to take a taxi across town in New York; better walk in rain, sleet, or snow. *Time* magazine has the best solution—put boards across the top and start over. Try another experiment, Wall Street on Sunday after seeing it during the week—exciting spaces: the Subtreasury corner is the best townscape in New York. Or try Easter on Fifth Avenue slightly before the crowds: the pedestrian is king; Fifth Avenue is an avenue—a space, not a crowded gutter. Better still, visit the two places in the Western world preserved for us: Venice and the Acropolis at Athens, the last places where town architecture can still be seen without automobile fumes.

And are not the towns the archetype of space experience, the summit of creative architectural endeavor? Surely architecture is the organization for pleasure of enclosed space. And what more magnificent enclosure than a town, a *place*, a place where the spirit is cuddled, made serene, made at home among his fellow spirits, made proud, happy, or excited depending on the ceremony, the day, the hour.

And, second, is not architecture the processional through exciting, ambient space? What greater experience than the path to the Parthenon front, through the Propylaea, past the Athena Promachos, past the Erechtheum, turning 180°, the eye sweeping the magnificent view toward Hymettos, and then back to face the east front of the greatest temple to a great civilization? How would you negotiate these experiences in an automobile? How the entrance to Venice? Imagine yourself met at the Piazzetta steps (you can approach Venice only from the sea, remember), being met by a taxi and whisked around the Campanile and through the length of the Piazza San Marco to your hotel! No, you *must* walk to appreciate architectural experience.

I would even go so far as to say you cannot get out of a car right in front of a monument of architecture. Please try, when you next visit Notre Dame in Paris, or Chartres, to get out of your car on the opposite side of the square and *walk* toward the west front. Kinesthetic experience has to do with aesthetic experience. You may have forgotten the statue of General Sherman at 59th and Fifth, but you probably remember the Prometheus Fountain in Rockefeller Plaza. One you drive by and the other you walk toward.

No, there is no doubt of the facts: the automobile is bad. But today we hate to face the facts: rather give up the art of townscape, the pleasures of gregariousness, the agora, the curia, the stoa, the piazza, the village square, than deny mechanical "progress" its due.

No one likes to admit the death of so great an art. Hence, there are experts, modern functional planners, who say the automobile can be "worked in," "taken care of." Can it be? Has it been? Is there a "town feeling" anywhere where the automobile is rampant? If not, what are we to do with our Frankenstein monster? We created it. We, the organizers of modern space, must decide what to do with it.

I ran into all the problems of the automobile working on a mining town which, alas, never was built. The problem of a small town of three thousand inhabitants was not like the New York situation, where nothing short of barring private cars would help any. (In Imperial Rome, they kept carts out of the city by day; maybe we could learn.) The problem of my town was how to keep the good architecture and yet keep the car. The advice which inundated me from amateurs and professional planners alike was to put the car in a parking lot and institute pedestrian malls—a tempting solution, one often used in shopping centers around the country.

But consider how shopping centers work: Framingham, Detroit, Cross County, and others. Your processional approach to the pedestrian area is through a forest of muddy mudguards and bumpers, and after this ordeal you enter the store by the back door and walk out again—through the back door. You never see the "architectural" part of the center. The pedestrian "mall" is a deserted back alley used for furtive shortcuts to other shops. The purpose of a square is to see people and be seen, to meet and to be met; and a back alley, no matter how big, can never fulfill this function.

To me, the essence of the American small town has always been the drugstore, with its high-school kids and their cokes. It is where anything happens that is going to happen. It is where everyone passes by sooner or later. In America there is never going to be a town center without an automobile. The machine has become part of our clothes, a symbol of pride—part of our identity before the world. We, at least in America, have become a race of four-wheeled centaurs, and what good would a pedestrian square do a centaur?

The clue to the problem of the automobile must exist somewhere in current practice. You cannot introduce foreign ways of living in America; we cannot introduce the sidewalk café in this country, for example. We don't live that way. The delicate operation of separating an American from the four-wheeled part of him has to be performed with tact.

In my town plan, I propose introducing the car right into the main street, a short and comparatively narrow street to give you a look-see. Maybe there will be no place to park, but at least you will see what's up, what is at the movies, who is standing in front of what coke parlor or, for that matter, beauty parlor; then like a good boy you will go around behind the row of stores and park and then come back to Main Street. At least your processional would be correct, not as good as Venice or the Acropolis, but pleasant. In addition, if you are lucky enough to find a parking place on the main street, in order to overcome the horror of walking behind a row of parked cars I propose raising the sidewalk two feet—a simple device which drowns the great steel hulks and joins the two sides of the street.

It is time to re-create the street as a centering device, instead of the splitting device it has become. In our talk of malls, piazzas, and shopping centers, we tend to forget the beauty and the togetherness of the street. Think back on the Main Street in Nantucket; Princes Street, Edinburgh; Beacon Street, Boston; Regent Street in London, before it was ruined. Streets of definite length, definite character, green on one side perhaps, or sloped or curved. The centaurs may be able to move in such places, if enough room is provided behind for them to shed their wheels.

There can be hope that the great art of townscape is not dead. Someday, people are again going to want processionals, are again going to want to dance in village squares. And when they want them, they will get them, and, like Easter on Fifth Avenue, let the automobile take care of itself.

Retreat from the International Style to the Present Scene

Lecture, Yale University, May 9, 1958; previously unpublished.

This is the transcript of a tape recording made of one of three lectures delivered at Yale in the spring of 1958 as part of Vincent Scully's survey course on "Modern Architecture." As with most of Johnson's talks, it is characterized by an informal, conversational style; a long chat with students on a Saturday in New Canaan in the late 1950's and early 1960's might have covered much the same ground in much the same way. Johnson is rare among practicing architects in his willingness to talk more or less publicly, in a frank and objective way, about his own work in relationship to the work of his contemporaries. Because this Yale talk and the two others of the series not included in this compilation were never intended for publication, they contain more of Johnson's opinions in an undiluted form than do many of his articles or more formal lectures. They also bring into sharp focus his extraordinary platform wit. He is at once a candid and irreverent analyst of the contemporary scene. The Yale talks also reveal him as a marvelously lucid and patient teacher, able to present complex situations in a remarkably clear manner.

Who will ever be able to think of Breuer or look at his work in the same way as before, once having heard him characterized as a "peasant mannerist"? Or Nowicki, Saarinen, and others as "the wavy-roof boys"? And what could be better—and more consoling—for a beginning architect to hear than that great architecture can be measured by the number of buckets one has to field to take care of the leaks?

Johnson's references to Kahn offer testimony to his sense of quality, but his admiration is not without irony, a little sense of déjà vu, *and even perhaps some jealousy.*

Now the question of the difference in situation between thirty years ago and today, and thirty years from now, is very interesting. We finished with the old boys now in their seventies, Corbusier, Mies; and Wright is almost ninety. And so today we have to consider the people who are coming up—whether they are coming up or not, I cannot say, since I am one of them. This is going to be a very embarrassing lecture, and I am not going to try to keep it objective in any way. I am just going to ramble among my contemporaries. An architect is, of course, not permitted by our idiotic code of ethics to discuss the merits and demerits of his fellow architects; so, of course, I will do so! I'll try not to, but no doubt you will gather through my tone of voice what I think. I hate them all. You can chalk that up to my smallness of mind, and it won't affect your judgment; you see, all I am going to do is to show the pictures to you, and you can pick for yourselves.

Now, there are eleven names, and with the eleven names, I am going to give you a little characterization of each. We start with Marcel Breuer, the oldest. (I am going to do it alphabetically, by the way, because any other way would be giving my hand away as to who I thought was good, and it also puts Johnson right in the middle, so it's all right.) First is Marcel Breuer, a mannerist, a peasant mannerist. He wouldn't like that, but somebody will no doubt repeat it to him, and I will have to go and explain. Next, *B* is Gordon Bunshaft, chief designer of Skidmore, Owings & Merrill, the biggest firm in the world. He is an academic Miesian, of course, pure and simple. Then comes Bruce Goff, a Wrightian romantic. Then *G, H, I, J,* Johnson, well we can't talk about *him.* I suppose he is a classicist—structural classicist, if you want; we have to have a name. Then there is Lou Kahn, who is a neo-functionalist; that is meant in terms of great respect, as you will see when we get there. Then we have Frederick Kiesler, who is a latter-day Leonardo. I mean, he does painting, sculpture, and architecture all in one building. Matthew Nowicki, who is dead, was the pioneer wavy-roof boy. Paul Rudolph is of course a decorative structuralist, and he takes his structures and makes beautiful decorations out of them. (I can explain that to him, so don't worry.) Then we have Eero Saarinen, who is the leading man; he is wavy-roof boy number two, whom you are very familiar with here in town. Then we end with Ed Stone, who is the screen decorator—the decorator with screens; well, anyhow, the man who hangs decorative screens on the outside of his buildings.

Now we go back and start our slides with Le Corbusier, the greatest of them all, now seventy-two years old. In the Philips Pavilion at the Brussels World's Fair, he is using the hyperbolic paraboloid on the edge, making what, I hope—since I haven't seen it—is a beautiful building. People don't seem to be as impressed by it as I think I shall be, but it doesn't weigh on you. He lifts you up as the Gothic people lift things up, and I hope it lifts you up with it. It is a curve made of straight lines.

A good deal of this new thing since the end of the International Style, a good deal of the revolt from it, was instigated by engineering, as was the case of Le Corbusier. We are fascinated—everyone, I think, in my generation—with Bucky Fuller's work, and with Nervi's, and with other engineers' works. Maillart was an early example. We got fascinated with the idea that you didn't have to use trabeated, that is, skeletal, up-and-down-and-straight-across forms. We got rather bored with the simplicity of the International Style, and the breakaway came through the influence of Bucky Fuller, who talks, as you know, eleven hours at a stretch in every university in the country. Now he makes these things, these geodetic domes, for the Air Force. (They lift them up and put them down in the Arctic.) But really he is an abstract mathematician, and you will see with what fascinating forms he has worked, his tetrahedral forms with triangular faces. But you notice one problem—how do you cover it? And if you cover it, how do you get in? As beautiful as these objects are, they are baubles in large scale—fascinating in their complexities of straight lines and curves, but they have not become architecture as yet. Another fascinating thing is his discontinuous compression column. (I think I show this example because I like the words "discontinuous compression.") These are the compression members; they are held together with turnbuckles and tension, but it does hold up anything you want, as long as you don't break one of these tension members. And the whole idea is such a mathematical fantasy: that you could hold enormous, endless columns with this very simple device of these discontinuous compression members.

Then to get more toward the architecture, we have a building by Nervi on the right, the Pirelli Building in Milan, and on the left the Seagram Building, to show what has happened to simple, normal planning, this being about the simplest tall building you could imagine, and it holds itself up of course. The system of triangulation on a high building is very complicated, with members that cross over between the uprights. Whereas Nervi's is a concrete building: lower, middle, top floors; the concrete getting less and less, and diagonal stress is taken up by actual diagonal parts of the building. Unfortunately, the building is ugly. It was finished by a not very good architect, but the plan is a fascination to all of us in its shapes. Now Nervi, of course, is our greatest inspiration right now, and this slide shows one of his early hangars before they put the roof on. These almost ogival curves at the corners and the lamella roof give you a wonderful feeling. You can see the size of a man down here. It's a marvelous feeling of a space frame and gives us all great excitement, the trouble of course being that you can't translate this kind of engineering into multiple-story buildings, because you can't walk on a hyperbolic paraboloid. But when you cover it up, look what happens. Here is another one, but it is the same kind of thing; and this is why, in a recent interview, which unfortunately was quoted, I called Nervi a ceiling decorator. But he is a lot more than that; he is quite a man to inspire us with his shapes.

Marcel Breuer designed Nervi's big conference room at UNESCO in Paris. This is a *toit plissé,* a folded roof, that carries into a folded wall; and this folded wall, of course, uses the minimum amount of concrete for the maximum amount of strength to hold up the roof, which, as you see, waves as it goes to express the actual stresses in the roof. And, of course, in this building the room looks exactly the same inside as out. It's all raw concrete, and it's the most beautiful assembly room (it is not finished yet) of our time. And it shows that fascination that all of us are getting for the more interesting shapes. Breuer was one of the Bauhaus products; he designed the spring chair and the things that have now become permanently established in our vocabulary, before he was even twenty years old. And, although much younger, he was of course one of the leaders of the whole International Style in Central Europe, and then in Switzerland, and then in England, and now in this country. This is his apartment in Doldertal in Zurich. I show this to show how he springs from a very strict Corbusier International Style in the thirties to what he is doing now with Nervi, and to what he is doing in his smaller works. I couldn't find a good slide of his own house, but if you come down to New Canaan, you will see two of his houses, and you will see what I mean by his peasantness and his mannerism. He likes the raw Connecticut stone, he likes to use just normal flooring for a ceiling. We usually use it on the floor; he uses it on the ceiling. There's nothing against it, I'm merely saying it shows his desire for more interest. For instance, he will take some stone and expose it, and the next plane will be painted bright blue and the next bright red. He likes to do twisted things, like this normal modern International Style chimney, and then just poke holes in it for the pure peasant hell of it. But that's part of his expressiveness. As someone said when Breuer got the job of doing the interiors of the new railroad trains on the New Haven, "How can you use a rubble wall in a railway train?" You know, it does sound as if I were criticizing these people; it's quite the opposite. Just because I stand on the other side and make all my things look classical and dull and cold doesn't mean that you should not—in fact, you *should*—do something about warming us all up, and that's what he does. For instance, in this large De Bijenkorf Department Store in Rotterdam, which was just finished recently, to gain decorative impact he has used rectangular stones on this façade and hexagonal ones on the adjoining façade.

Then we come to Bunshaft, our second academic Mies man, which is standard Skidmore, Owings & Merrill work. This is the Connecticut General Life Insurance Building, which you may have seen up here near Hartford, and you will see that the proportioning of the windows with the lower panes cut in half is an old Mies trick from the Illinois Institute of Technology buildings. Of course, Bunshaft has much more money and much more material to play with than Mies ever had, so all these things are very elegant stainless steel instead of being just painted iron. This other work, however, was done at about the same time as the Seagram Building in New York; it is the Inland Steel Company in Chicago. To differentiate it from the Academy this is, of course, purely the Seagram Building fins without the projecting **H** members, but to gain the freedom of interior spacing which rental architects frequently want, he takes the columns outside, so that you have all free space inside, and your partitions don't run into these enormous columns. The other problem in a tall building is the elevators: Bunshaft put them on the outside, which gives the impression of two buildings. These of course are very large, being the columns to hold up a very large building.

Then we have Mr. Goff, the Wrightian, who builds out of Quonset hut units; he is a Wrightian who likes to pile things up, but he also likes to use things that are lying around the house, like a quarter section of a Quonset hut. I think the section plan of this so-called Coal House in Aurora, Illinois, may show you a little better how he does this, and there is the balcony here; you can stand up here and look over these people. It's an extraordinary space feeling when you are in it. Mr. Goff builds extremely little, and I couldn't get any photographs of his later work. His office moved to the Price Tower (which I think is very fitting) in the little town of Bartlesville, from where he hopes to revolutionize architecture. Well, he might. (You know, I don't like this stuff.)

We come now to Wallace K. Harrison. I left him out the first time around, better put him in between *H, K,* and *J*—wherever he fits. Harrison is the symbolic expressionist of our day. He also, of course, comes from the International Style. He finished the U.N. Building when Le Corbusier went back to Europe, and this is his Alcoa Building in Pittsburgh, in which he developed a very interesting *bugnato,* reverse *bugnato* skin out of aluminum; that is, the square panels are punched inward to give them stiffness. It is an amazing building on the skyline and a perfectly logical approach to the skyscraper problem. Why not cover it all with a rhythm skin, and then have the windows a part of that rhythm? This is by far his best building. Now he has turned into a symbolic expressionist—this is a theater, for Oberlin College, Oberlin, Ohio, in which the trumpet, an open trumpet, was sort of an invitation into the theater held back by the wavy screen as a background for outdoor theatrical performances. But the most interesting of the buildings is the First Presbyterian Church in Stamford. This is the church you may have seen in *Time* magazine—it is shaped like a fish. It wasn't intentional, but as he worked on it, he rather liked the idea of the symbol of the fish as being one of the earliest Christian symbols, taken from the initials for the Greek words "Jesus Christ, Son of God, Savior" which make the word "fish." So he made the whole church like that. It is an extraordinary tour de force of pre-cast members, pre-cast and tilted up into place. Then to do away with any sense of roof or wall, the whole roof is shingled with slate tiles all the way to the ground. The difficulty is, of course, how do you get a door in a slanting wall? I always feel that the whale somehow got his back broken, and unfortunately he placed the entrance, the main entrance of the church, in the broken part of the tail fin. I would like to have you see this church if you are at all interested in architecture, because the glass is the most beautiful I have ever seen in my life. It was done in Chartres. In the shadow of Chartres Cathedral there is a workshop for this very thick, this one-inch thick, glass, which makes the most beautiful interior light in any modern church. It is some sixty feet high, but because the walls lean together like a tent, the apparent space is much reduced. You can hardly go further than this in a denial of the rigid structural simplicity that we have all been used to.

I put in a slide of Mies's here, because it is relative to my house which was built at the same time, but after I had seen Mies's designs. Naturally my work—my early work—is very Miesian; I am very proud of it. I have been called Mies van der Johnson—it doesn't bother me in the slightest, and it does seem to me that if our generation is going to stand on somebody's shoulders, we had better pick the best man to start with. Now this is Mies's famous Farnsworth House near Chicago. It floats on a plain which is sometimes flooded, but you see here his passion for articulated structure, his calmness of proportions; I think they show even in this slide. The house is entirely of glass, the only partitions are interior ones, which is also the case in my own house. His is white, and mine is black. The front steps are a very classical motif; you remember the podium is a feature of Mies's work. Now I will go to my own house—I won't say it's imitation Mies, because it is quite different, but it too is entirely of glass. The core there is the bathroom and the chimney, the kitchen is at your left, the bedroom on your right. This is pure International Style work except for the round chimney, which would of course be anathema to Mies, and the round chimney is made of the same material as the floor, which doesn't separate the planes; it is not very good style to have anything look as solid as that. Sculpture is of course very important to these houses to create space.

This is the Kneses Tifereth Israel Synagogue down in Port Chester— very different from Harrison's work, in that it is still pure International Style, with the decorated ceiling dripping around the slots giving you the light, which is never in your eyes because the reveal is too deep. Lou Kahn, especially, hates that ceiling; but then I dislike some things about his work, so that's all right. This is my latest work, the museum for the Munson-Williams-Proctor Institute, going up now in Utica, New York, with these great strap concrete members that hold the building up. The ground floor is glazed. It is again slightly International Style in the idea that the cube floats, but it's awfully heavy, and those enormous beams would never have been used in earlier times.

We come to our favorite man, Mr. Lou Kahn; he is one of the bright stars in our firmament, it seems to me. In the old days, when he started on the museum here (this was done how many years ago? since the war) it was purely International Style, without any articulation. The proportioning on the other street is much more careful and beautifully done. It has, of course, like all International Style buildings, a certain boredom, which was inflicted on him by the problem. He had to carry the floors from the old building over into this building, and I have often had that problem; it's insuperable. He also had the problem that they didn't put in the air-conditioning when they built the building, as they should have done, and that is now going in. The corner problem (which you remember is a problem we discussed) is that you have to watch out for the corners against the ground, the corners against the sides. If you walk around the corner of this building, there is a solid wall, where there are water tables to give you the scale of the floors behind. This water table then appears to be peeking around, like a little dot at the corner. In other words, the composition on one side was very hard to adjust to the composition on the other. No water table was needed or wanted on this façade, so it had to stop like the little dribble on the corner.

Lou Kahn, however, got hold of himself after this building and did what he had always wanted to do, and this is really one of the most exciting buildings that we have: it is the Richards Medical Research Building down in Philadelphia at the University of Pennsylvania, where he is now, and it shows him at his neo-functional best; that is, he feels he should pull the building apart and make every part express itself. These are the three laboratory towers, and the center is whatever is left over. These are ventilators (you will see them later in the model), and the stairs. He had to make these squares, because of the law in Philadelphia, but he wanted them round, as you can see. Every part expresses something different—out, away, even to the return here, to express that this is not *this* and is not doing the same thing as *that*. Lou even goes so far as this: When he had some air-conditioning ducts that he wanted to get from one side of the building to another, and the engineer said, "Well, we will run it diagonally across that way," Lou said, "No, if a man has to walk that way to get there, then the under-floor ducts should go that way, even though you never see them." That is the kind of aesthetic logic which is expensive, but rather wonderful, because it shows his absolute will, which is revealed in his exterior architecture by the articulation of every single part. Here are eight columns that make a two-way gridiron ceiling out of every room, forty-five feet across; the independent rooms each express themselves, but look what happens on the outside. This is an early drawing in which those towers that stuck out are expressive. They are expressing something very different from what we used to think of as architecture. See this tower, for instance: it is one of the ventilator towers, and of course it gets wider as you have more and more laboratories venting into it. The result is enormous congeries of San Gimignanesque towers with dark, very dark, corners between those great blocks where they went together, and very jagged sky projections. If you take the usual things we look at in a building, you'll see that the silhouette against the sky is unique in his work, and unique in modern architecture, and is most expressive. Where are the corners? All of these are corners—the whole thing. This corner is held by the things that project on either side—there are myriad corners. I'm sorry to say I haven't yet seen how the base is handled, but when this building is up, I imagine you will get a shock about a new way to relate the building to the ground. Kahn is one of the few really original revolutionaries against the classic type of modern architecture.

We now go to our Leonardesque man, Mr. Frederick Kiesler. He is an elderly Viennese. Well, is he an artist? It is hard to say. Is he an architect? He started life as a member of the group known as de Stijl, way back in 1925 in Berlin, and he knew Mies back at that time. Then he came to this country. He has never been successful as an architect, simply because he feels that architecture these days has become too separated from art, from painting, and that painting has gone its own way to easel painting hung on a wall, which destroys the wall, and the wall destroys the painting. He also feels that sculpture is something you go into a museum to look at, or you do what I do and set it up in an abstract space without connecting it. He believes that the total impression should be the one that surrounds you. Perhaps you have been to New York to see his art gallery, World House, in the Carlyle Hotel, in which he melded the walls and floors and ceiling all together; all of them surround you, and you can't say whether it is architecture or sculpture or painting. In fact, when he does a painting, he usually projects a piece of it out toward you, because he doesn't feel that anything flat or square could represent today. He takes the analogy from science, which more and more breaks down the divisions between biochemistry, let's say, and physics. He feels that art is a totality and only in that way can it be expressed. This is the piece he did for me, next to my house. It is a gazebo, a piece of architecture, a piece of sculpture. It's about twenty-five feet across and about twelve feet high with enormous primitive-like chipped wood that he has carved himself— a triangular piece with other pieces sticking up like a giraffe's head. It's a very impressive and again unidentifiable thing. Is it sculpture? Is it architecture? His only piece of architecture is the Endless House, which we have shown at The Museum of Modern Art. This is just a model of it, made of concrete. The working drawings are now being made (some foundation gave us the money to do that). It will rest like an egg on a stone base. The windows are particularly important. They are slits, that is, they do not break the continuity 'of the exterior shell; and inside, all the rooms are curved and rounded, and the beds are all built in as part of the architecture. There are all kinds of light organs that come down from the top, and they whirl around and change the color inside. Of course, about fifteen years ago, I remember seeing the early drawings for the house, and I merely laughed at them, but it is not so laughable anymore as Kiesler joins the main lines of architecture. He is by far the oldest man that I am talking about today, but he has been so seminal that he deserves listing with the rest.

This is Nowicki's Livestock Judging Pavilion for the State Fair Grounds at Raleigh, North Carolina. He was a man in his thirties when he designed it, a great friend to all of us, probably the most brilliant young architect that any of us ever knew, and he was about to build Chandigarh before Le Corbusier was hired to do that city, and on a flight returning from India the plane crashed, and he was killed. This pavilion was completed after his death, and he worked, I remember, all one summer making sketches and casually, because he lived that way, on this conception which has been, I am sorry to say, almost ruined in execution. His idea was those two enormous beams that crossed each other, by their laying themselves down, would form the pressure to counteract the enormous plastic roof that swung the whole way. The problem, of course, in all these wavy-roof buildings, the one we find here again at the Saarinen skating rink, is: how do you close it in at the ends and at the bottom? Now Nowicki's theory here was perfectly simple, but when he had this problem of closing an end, then he ran into the problems of wind, and he had much prettier tension cables that came down at a pitch like this, to prove that they were merely holding this thing from flopping in the breeze—a pure tension wave. Whereas when the engineers got down to figuring it out, they found that these elements were necessary as wind braces, and unfortunately they looked like columns, at least to me and to people who have been there; and they do look as if this was what was supporting that ring, therefore losing the whole point of the sway itself doing the work of holding up the roof. But it was a very, very daring thing for a man in this thirties to accomplish and extraordinary that the state of North Carolina should have commissioned it; and it has been extremely helpful to all of us ever since, and to Saarinen in particular, to have this model in front of us. Now that is the wavy-roof beginning.

This is John Johansen, who as you all know teaches here. This is his new house that he is building in New Caanan, and I merely wanted to explain how far the wavy roof has come. They have come to toothpaste-tube architecture at last: you squeeze it out! This is built by spraying on concrete over mesh with a gun. As you know, there are many swimming pools made that way now; you just shoot the concrete onto the ground, and there is your swimming pool. This is one of those pools. The beds in this house again, as in Kiesler's, are organized into the mass itself. These projections here are the structural beams. You see, if you hold up something like this it tends to collapse on you if you don't have a beam on the curve; so this, this, and that are all the beams that hold up this very intricate house. Again, the courage is terrific! No one has done this, and I am not sure that they should, but that's an old man's reactionary talk. Let's build it! The problems, of course, are obvious: how do you scribe the glass, or Plexiglas, to those curves? What do you do about insulation?—and a few minor details like that. But if everybody had stopped, when they had an original idea, to figure out how you were going to keep the water out of it, you wouldn't ever get the architecture of the next generation. So the wavy-roof boys really are the leading revolutionaries today.

Now we will go on with the one of our heroes called Rudolph. I can hardly say how much I admire his work. I am very jealous of him—I hate him, and it's respectfully reciprocated, but that, of course, is all part of the natural development in the history of architecture. But when this house came out, I really was green with jealousy. This is a delicious little Guest House for the Walker family on Sanibel Island near Sarasota, out in the terrible sandy country that Florida has too much of, and the idea is terribly ingenious. It's a glass house, back in there, but on each of the four sides making a Greek cross are these outriggers which are held up by double 2-by-4's here. Out on that rides a line with a weight on the bottom of it. As this weight comes down, the plywood cover on the house (you need that in Florida) comes up and makes a sun shade for the house. It is all so ingenious, it hurts. But apart from that, if you will, notice how extraordinarily strict it is from an International Style point of view (and this is only 1952), but how extraordinarily light every single feature is, how strictly classical the composition. Rudolph called himself at this time the poor man's Mies. (He doesn't like to remember that he ever called himself that, so don't remind him.) But it's interesting here how he uses wood, which Mies has never used. He uses wood to gain the same degree of lightness and clarity that is obviously in the very best of the International Style of work. A little different is this house that he built on the edge of the water, again with nothing but glass shutters as walls, but with an extraordinary floating roof of plastic, which makes the whole thing float like a pavilion out across the water, these being the diagonal members that keep the thing solid and in tension—structural troubles, but all this is characteristic with pioneer work. We used to rate our houses by counting the number of buckets we had to collect the water from leaks. Frank Lloyd Wright built the Fallingwater house and that was a seventeen-bucket house; I counted them. My house is a four-bucket—no, pardon me, a six-bucket house. In a storm we had once, we had to have six buckets. The only answer is the one that Mr. Wright gave Mr. Johnson, the Johnson Wax man, when he was in his great new $300,000 or $400,000 house. He was sitting at the head of his table at a dinner party, and he called over to Mr. Wright. He said, "Really, Mr. Wright, this is too much; the rain is coming right down on my chair. What are you going to do?" Mr. Wright said, very simply, "Move your chair." Now, this is very serious advice if any of you are thinking of becoming architects. Architecture is only one thing, trouble, and especially about rain falling on people's heads. The best thing to do is to become inured to it first, get a thick skin, such as Mr. Wright has developed over eighty years. Just develop it younger, so you won't suffer from ulcers and the other things we architects get.

This is one of Paul Rudolph's new buildings. It's the headquarters for the Blue Cross–Blue Shield in Boston. It is going to go up soon, and this illustrates the phrase I gave you in the first place: structure as decoration. Here his structure is entirely free to do with what he pleases—it is no longer the International Style. Thin columns gracefully placed; these are deliberate decorations. Obviously, you only need half that many columns to hold up the building in the first place; obviously, you don't have to project them out here and bring them in there, at arbitrary angles. In other words, he feels the necessity, as we all do now, of tying the building together organically, whether you use just the minimum structure and the broadest spans you can; but we must grab the thing as we grab any piece of composition, as a stone is held by its setting claws, for example, as this building is. The structure is the ribs that hold the neutral area behind it. Even Rudolph's spandrels—and these change from time to time as he works out the building—become a function of the column. See, they are like little branches on these trees that go up. There is no longer any normal spandrel as such, the spandrel being, as you remember, the part between the windows in an office building. The only really peculiar part, and this won't show, of course, from below, is that this angle goes straight into this, but what's that angle? It's a very hard thing, a corner (remember our problems on corners). He has a new way of turning a corner, which is to chop it off, to chamfer it, which to an International Style man like myself is anathema. Because, what is the size of the building? You see as you get around it; does the building stop there, or a little bit further? You see his unclarity of the corner is, however, part of his intention here to make the façade go around. He doesn't want to look at this side and then at this side. He wants to emphasize the fact that this cage is something holding. He would, I suppose, like to have made it octagonal, had he been able. But Paul Rudolph is one of the pioneers of this post-Miesian age, and it is interesting that going up right now in Florida is a purely Miesian school, at the same time that this building with its lacework structure is going up in Boston. We live in a transitional age!

We get now to the man who has done the most work in our generation; as *Holiday* says, perhaps America's leading architect, Eero Saarinen. He is the man of course we are all most jealous of, because he builds more than we do. So it is very simple, he is much more successful than any of us; so if you find a slight note of hysteria, why don't mind. This is Saarinen back in his International Style days. It is the Milwaukee War Memorial, which projects out over Lake something-or-other—Lake Michigan. (No, I have been there, that's all right. Just because I come from Lake Erie, I never can remember Lake Michigan.) Here you see all the characteristics of the International Style: tension, cantilevering in the extreme—it's the biggest cantilever in the world. This cantilever is held by the wall behind this one, way back through to here. It is an extraordinary feat of engineering, and it is held on a Miesian podium, and then a gap as Le Corbusier would do it, and then a simple projecting block of boxes with the window set in back. The museum is here, and that's the American Legion. I would like to reverse it, but you can't always have your own way with these city-planning people. This was done five years ago, before he got the wavy roof. This was designed one night, or rather described. We had a conference of middle-aged architects at my house about four years ago, when Paul Rudolph was just a child, then Saarinen, Pei, myself, Johansen, and one or two others, and he drew that. Well, now look what he is doing now. We have here the new T.W.A. Terminal at Idlewild. This is, of course, again toward the expressionism of Harrison, toward the thin shells of Utzon—not that you remember that, but he is the man who won the competition in Sydney, Australia, for an Opera House with great wavy sails. You feel the Opera House (it's on the ocean) is about to sail off across the sea. In the Terminal these, of course, are enormous wings that represent flight perhaps, or perhaps it is merely his desire for large spans of shells. This slide shows the flight theme better. You drive in in the middle, and all things are held up with four enormous piers that bifurcate and hold up these four separated shells. This, of course, will be glass, and it will be interesting to see whether the same thing happens here as happened in Nowicki's pavilion in Raleigh, North Carolina: whether the mullions that hold the glass won't look as if they were holding up the shell itself. Actually the shell, of course, is held from way back here and is one enormous, huge cantilever. We'll go up closer to one of those columns. This is something new since Mendelsohn's day, when he did the Einstein Tower in 1923—the attempt to make large architecture sculptural, or vice versa, to make large sculpture into architecture, just by using your thumb. This is a model designed without drawings; that is, you just take your clay and your wires and your thumb and create these shapes which are structural enough. I mean, it is not the work of an engineer, it is the work of an architect. We want to make shapes that please and arouse awe out of the shapes that the engineers are giving us on their drawing boards. The question now before the house is, can you build this? They are now figuring it out.

A building which, however, is built, is perhaps more interesting to discuss, in that the problems here are much the same, although this is an infinitely simpler and easier building to build. This is the Saarinen skating rink, which I think is one of the most wonderful places to sit in that I have ever been in. I think when it is active that you feel a central feeling there that you won't feel in any other skating rink or rather arena of that kind in this country. The conception is so simple. There is an arch that goes the long way, which is extraordinary to begin with, and ends down here, and then there is the ring, the same ring of course that Nowicki had. This ring here (this is just wood) holds this in compression and keeps it stable. It didn't, but that was the theory. Well, you cannot judge a building by whether it works or not. You see, I would never have the courage to do this, old classicist that I am; I'd figure out how I would hold it up first and then hope to build it. But this approach is a more romantic one and a more popular one today. "We will build the building and then see how we can hold it up." And it is actually held in place, to avoid what the engineers call flutter, by cables stretching from the arch down to here. But the conception of the tent-like form over a great longitudinal arch at once gives a feeling of central space, of quiet, of calm, almost of classicism. The only trouble Saarinen ran into was how to get in—which is another one of our points we had to consider when looking at buildings. His arch, the way an engineer would do it, would normally reach the ground way across the street. Well, he didn't want that, so he curls the end of the arch back inside where you can't see it. It is an architect talking. This is where he really departs from any interest in structure that we were all brought up to have. He takes the structural member and tips it up into a Napoleon hat for an entrance, just deliberately flouting the idea that this member is your main structure. Never has anyone thumbed his nose so directly at the tradition of structural integrity. Most of the rest of us are still stuck thinking of structure as something you handle as a theme in design. He doesn't. This ring comes around; this is the compression ring that holds these great cables. Now when you get here, you still have to have cables; so if you go in, you will find a steel truss along the roof there, jammed in to do the work. So here we have an arbitrary entrance made in direct opposition, and intentionally so, to the structure itself.

Now we will go on to the last man, who is just the opposite from Saarinen, and that is Ed Stone. He is certainly the most popular modern architect today. As you know from the papers, he did the United States Pavilion for the Brussels Fair, which as you know is turning out to be very good. This is The Museum of Modern Art building, done twenty years ago, before you were born. This is rather a fascinating story. Ed Stone did that part of the façade, and this, and this. John McAndrew did that ceiling (he was Curator of the Department of Architecture at that time) with the holes in it; and Alfred Barr, the Director of the Museum, designed this strange-shaped canopy that sticks out toward Fifth Avenue. I just found that out the other day in talking with these gentlemen; but this is a very pedestrian piece of International Style work. Nineteen thirty-seven was too early in this country for it and, as Le Corbusier said, "My God, they can't even copy me!" Then we jump to Stone's most famous work (don't laugh, because we have only three minutes), to his most famous job, the United States Embassy at New Delhi, which is certainly a beautiful thing. If they do succeed in gilding the columns, it will be even more gracious. It is on a Miesian podium with a Miesian stair, but it is a more classical arrangement. You come right through the center door in the long axis and the screens then are hung over two floors. It is not a great hall, as you might think from looking at it from the outside, but a more graceful combination of screens in classicism could hardly be imagined. This is Stone being still more graceful in the Stuart Company Factory, a pill factory in Pasadena, with wonderful troffers letting the light down through the center (these are the structure), but the light is so high that it never blinds you, it just filters down through those troffers. Of course, a great deal of this room is the planting, which I regret to say next year will look like hell. Then we end with a rather sorry slide, his own house on 64th Street, but he put it in his own work. A little lacking in scale perhaps. I had to put that in because it illustrated my own remark in *Time* magazine, in which I said I thought there was more to architecture than hanging screens all over structure.

So that is the end of the course, and please remember that these boys are going to be good, if they are not now; and it is your duty, it's your bounden duty, to see that some of them become great architects.

Where Are We At?

From Architectural Review, CXXVII (September, 1960), 173–75.

This piece finds Johnson in a particularly expansive mood, filled with confidence in his opinions, a sense of his own importance as an established architect and principal intellect of the second generation of American modernists.[1] *Tackling what was the most provocative book about the history of the Modern Movement to be published since Sigfried Giedion's* Space, Time and Architecture *of 1941, Reyner Banham's* Theory and Design in the First Machine Age, *Johnson again, as in the innovative presentation of his Glass House in 1950 (see pp. 213–25), chose the English magazine* Architectural Review *in which to bring his ideas before an international audience. That the essay is provocative goes without saying; but that it is more significant for what it reveals about Johnson's biases at a critical turning point in his own career than for what it tells us about the history of the Modern Movement now seems of even greater interest. A year earlier, in the same magazine, William Jordy had characterized this critical shift in Johnson's work in an article appropriately titled "The Mies-less Johnson."*[2]

Johnson's essay lays bare the fundamental "art for art's sake" narcissism of the Modern Movement or at least of its International Style:

Architecture . . . has its own validity. It needs no reference to any other discipline to make it 'viable' or to 'justify' its value. . . .
  For the sake of the argument let us admit that we do live in a machine age. We can hardly call to question an architectural style that evolved in that age for not expressing it. The International Style 'expressed its age' merely by the fact of being prevalent at that time.

Though Johnson talks a bold l'art pour l'art *line, I would submit that at the core he is still very much concerned with utilitarian functionalism; more importantly, even his attitude toward the use of history is pragmatic, as can be seen in his concept of "functional eclecticism." For Johnson, the history of architecture is the history of forms rather than of architectural ideas. Prevailing culture, programmatic and technological considerations, are little more than glittering footnotes to the real issue, which is form.*

Johnson is quick to admit that the ideas which Banham examines carefully, if irreverently, were once his as well: "I blush at the absoluteness of our beliefs." And, oddly enough, he singles out as revelatory Banham's "keen analysis of Guadet and Choisy as ancestors of our planning and structural functionalism" when he himself had cited the latter in a similar context only a few years earlier in his presentation of the Glass House.

Johnson's concluding paragraphs reveal the complexity of his position, the breadth of his understanding, and his own self-doubts while in the midst of that most perilous Mies-less stage of his career as an architect, which seems to most critics at the present writing to be his least understood and least lovable period.[3] *Johnson applauds Banham's explosion of the myth of a monolithic modernism; he acknowledges the death of the International Style, but he goes no further toward making an attempt to reintegrate such non-International Style modernists as Häring, Scharoun, and Mendelsohn into the canon of the Modern Movement. Two years later, he will see the death of the International Style as the "end development of the Modern Movement . . . the end of Puritanism and false morality in architecture."*[4] *But for now, at least, though he perceives the death of the avant-garde, and despite efforts to keep a stiff upper lip, he seems apprehensive about just wandering around aimlessly; he loves the freedom of the "foggy chaos . . . the multiplicity of it all," yet he feels the loss of "the lovely helpful beliefs of the last generation."*

1. For a discussion of generations in the Modern Movement, see Robert A. M. Stern's New Directions in American Architecture. *Revised edition (New York: Braziller, 1977), pp. 7–8.*

2. Architectural Forum, *CXI (September, 1959), pp. 115–23.*

3. See, for example, Robin Middleton, "Book Review: Philip Johnson: Architecture 1949–65," Architectural Review, *XXXVII (March, 1967), p. 107.*

4. Article for the Kentiku *(see pp. 247–48).*

For an American addendum to the soul-searching about "Whither Away" which the *Architectural Review* goes in for every month, I may not be the best one for the *Review* to hire. There are Scully and Hitchcock and Drexler, McQuade and Jordy to pick from, but I do have one disadvantage-advantage, and this is that unlike the others I do practice—with much difficulty—architecture. I am outside the writing-historical club and I can be as arbitrary as I want; be willing to be labelled—and mislabelled—any way they, the club, want. Although it is never pleasant for a practical person to be pejoratively pigeon-holed (one feels caged into a small sub-category that robs one of the self-glorificatory freedom that artists like to boast of), it will nevertheless be fun to be a sub-species for such astute and intellectual categorizers as the English intellectuals.

One of the major keys to any discussion "Where Are We At?" is Banham's important book *Theory and Design in the First Machine Age.* It is a wonderful and perverse book. I can't follow his *parti pris:* "What distinguishes modern architecture is surely a new sense of space and the machine aesthetic." As one minor architect (maybe not even "modern") I have no new sense of space nor am I encumbered with a machine aesthetic.

Nor can I go along with his title, and I quickly propose another one: "Architectural Theories of the First Half Century." It is not that I would have historiographers without a point of view (I like Scully's introduction of Greek topography in his book on Wright), but I find it hard to follow the author when he takes one of the more peculiar beliefs of the twenties, the faith that we live in a Machine Age (note the capitals), and makes it into his criterion for the validity of an architectural style.

Architecture, one would think, has its own validity. It needs no reference to any other discipline to make it "viable" or to "justify" its value. We might even question whether words like value or morals are applicable to an architectural style. The International Style, for example, needs no one to say it was good or it was bad. Greek and Gothic styles were loved and reviled throughout subsequent ages and neither opinion affected the architecture itself, but were comments rather on the state of mind of the lover or the reviler. The International Style is its own justification. We can dislike it, which most of us may today, but we are obviously much too close to have any interesting views on its future influence or its position in the history books.

For the sake of the argument let us admit that we do live in a machine age. We can hardly call to question an architectural style that evolved in that age for not expressing it. The International Style "expressed its age" merely by the fact of being prevalent at that time.

As for the discussion in the book of the fine distinction between the first machine age, which is apparently on the way out, and the second, which is coming in, it is not an interesting dichotomy architecturally, and has only marginal interest as part of an otherwise fine history book.

Once the reader has passed through the machine-drenched prose of the introduction, however, he will find a treat awaiting him. I know of no author but Dashiell Hammett who can keep me more fascinated page by page. Reading as a student who had arrived in 1930 on the European scene, I keep having the feeling "Oh, yes, I did believe that then," or "Now I understand where I derived that idea from." For example, the preposterous idea that Gothic ribbing carried inert panelling and that therefore it was morally "good" to separate structure from infill, took up my whole horizon as a young designer. Or when I remember our worship at the shrine of Plato's *Philebus* because he wrote there of the beauty of the pure mathematical shapes and their solids. I blush at the absoluteness of our beliefs, which Banham makes such intelligent fun of. Again, the keen analysis of Guadet and Choisy as ancestors of our planning and our structural functionalism is a revelation. I did not know before how much that I take for granted came from the prejudices and whims of men so far before our day.

The author's chief interest, however, it becomes clear, is Futurism, and the lyricism about Marinetti is far different from his wry humor about, for instance, Le Corbusier's theories. From Marinetti to Buckminster Fuller represents a line of development outside of what the *Architectural Review* would call (in capitals) the Main Stream, a line of technology, a sole god, an autophagous design animal, the story of which in Banham's prose has the exhilaration of a Coney Island roller-coaster. The ride, however, leaves me cold because, as Banham admits, Futurism was more important as ideology than as form.

The Main Stream is more interesting to me: the English influence on the Werkbund has never been better brought out, Muthesius better evaluated. (As is often the case in this book, the non-architect talkers: Muthesius, Marinetti and so forth, are more stimulating than the plodding practitioners.) Parenthetically, it is amusing to read an historian of the ideas *about* architecture (Banham) at the same time as an historian of the *forms of* architecture (Hitchcock). They both stimulate; history is after all the story of what goes into the mentality of all of us designers today. Both the Banham book and the Hitchcock Pelican volume [*Architecture: Nineteenth and Twentieth Centuries*] deal with the architecture of the immediate past; both are brilliant, but since they seem almost not to overlap one should perhaps read one in alternate chapters with the other. If one misses in Hitchcock the broad wit and generalities that Banham serves up, one is grateful nevertheless for the specific story of forms, since forms in design beget more forms, whereas ideas barely have influence on them.

New *aperçus* appear throughout Banham's book: Berlage appears fresh to me, for example. It has always been clear that he was influential (especially to Mies's development) but his work when visited seemed relatively modest, even uninteresting. But with Banham's outline placing him in his Zurich lecture as the bridge between Wright and the European modern movement, all becomes clear.

But even Banham cannot tell us what happened at the Bauhaus. All Bauhaus members deny de Stijl influence in the 1923 revolution against Itten, and yet our eyes tell us otherwise. There is no doubt of the personal battle between van Doesburg and the Bauhaus in Dessau which would cloud the eyes of both sides involved. And there is also no doubt of the Lissitzky influence (which all since admit); but Lissitzky was not de Stijl. Also in Berlin in 1922 there was such a confluence of interweaving streams that perhaps it really was a spontaneous combustion. But can one imagine the interlocking cubes of the Meisterhaus at Dessau or the Bauhaus itself without a direct line from de Stijl?

Thanks to Banham we get a sixties view of the whole German twenties. Mies and Hilberseimer turn out to have been the most perspicacious of the practicing architects, Hilberseimer for his books and Mies for his choice of leaders at Weissenhof. Who, with 20/20 hindsight today, would pick differently the four leading architects of that year, 1927, to give prominent space to in an international exhibition: Le Corbusier, Mies, Gropius, and Oud? It is a pleasure to record that a practicing architect, not a critic, was the chooser.

It is especially welcome today, to read a book that can be written about the twenties without being propaganda for the International Style. At the time we could not appreciate a de Klerk or a Sant'Elia (I still cannot) or a Mendelsohn or even Domenicus Böhm (whom Hitchcock, but not Banham, cites). Even Scharoun and Häring were suspect, so strait was our gate. (Look up who was included in Hitchcock and Johnson's *International Style,* written in 1930–31.) But time makes perspective, and both Hitchcock and Banham can find new ways to look at those dear, dead days.

When the story of Banham's book changes to the emerging critics of the end of the twenties, the names of Giedion and Hilberseimer come up, but what of that American Barr-Johnson-Hitchcock circle that Banham refers to in articles, but not in his book. He makes fun of the propagandist historian Giedion for falling for the functionalist doctrine of the times, but does not mention that Hitchcock did not. Read his *Modern Architecture* which appeared in 1929. It was clear to the author then that the 'New Pioneers,'' as he called them in his first book, were doing something radically different and confluent and it had nothing to do with functionalism or for that matter a Machine Age aesthetic. Perhaps I am being U.S. nationalist about this point, but Hitchcock's physical distance seems to have given him an eye for the form as being more important than the palaver. And, incidentally, the sobriquet "International Style," which Banham uses throughout the book, first appears itself in a title of a book by Hitchcock.

Which brings us to the end of the book: the chapter I wish Banham had left out. In it he seems to take the position that the International Style should (morally, that is) have symbolized a machine age. Why? After demolishing functionalism through the book as a false propaganda term that was really never practiced by the very leaders who used the word, a restricting, negative, unrealistic idea, he now attacks the leaders for not designing buildings according to another belief, that was also mere propaganda and illusion. He does not blame Mies that the Barcelona Pavilion is not functionalist, but he blames him because it is not symbolic of a machine age, or, in Banham's language, a Machine Age. Here is a stray quote from page 325: "But because of this undoubted success [of the International Style] we are entitled to enquire, at the very highest level, whether the aims of the International Style were worth entertaining, and whether its estimate of a Machine Age was a viable one." Who cares? The main question is, were the products of the International Style beautiful, and not even eternally beautiful, but relatively beautiful to those of us who enjoy looking at well-designed buildings.

Banham's insistence on the moral demands of the Second Machine Age ends the book. He seems to be a "beyond architecture" believer. Pure technology will carry us onward and onward. Buckminster Fuller is quoted *in extenso* with a perfectly valid criticism of the architecture of the International Style as being concerned with design, and not with plumbing, chemistry, and scientific technology. He was, and is, quite right. *All* architecture is more interested in design than in plumbing. I feel like crying (but not for quotation): Let Bucky Fuller put together the dymaxion dwellings of the people so long as we architects can design their tombs and their monuments.

But once more, whither away? The International Style is dying and the *Architectural Review* is looking for "a new compelling, unifying slogan." But if we live in an age when we do not like "compelling slogans" or styles or disciplines or even capital letters, can't we just wander around aimlessly? "The world is so full of a number of things": and so forth. I am free to admit that I love in my work to comment on history! The Italians like funny shapes; I don't like them, but who am I? The English like the Jaoul Houses. Paul Rudolph likes Ronchamp. More power to them. We are going through a foggy chaos. Let us enjoy the multiplicity of it all. Let the students have a different hero every year. Maybe it is good for them.

Certainly Banham's book will further the chaos by analyzing away the last of the beliefs (the lovely, helpful beliefs) of the last generation.

Informal Talk, Architectural Association

Lecture, Architectural Association, School of Architecture, London, November 28, 1960; previously unpublished.

Johnson at peak form: exquisitely agile on his feet as he fields the jibes of a characteristically critical audience of English architects and architectural students, letting his audience know from the outset that while he is very interested in what they are doing (and especially in the then-emerging proto-Archigram work which was to be found on the drawing boards of the Architectural Association school), he is also ready to tell them that he doesn't think much of their work.

Johnson's visit to the American Museum at Bath opens him up to new lines of speculation about relationships between history and current practice. His concern focuses on two issues: 1) the insufficiency of International Style theory and form to deal with the problem of new buildings set within historical contexts, and 2) the awful agony of doing late International Style/Modern Movement work after having visited and enjoyed the great monuments of the past.

Jumping into the lion's den, Johnson opens to serious reconsideration the great bugaboo of stylistic imitation, though he does not develop this theme or return to it in later talks and articles. Despite the seeming irreverence of his tone, he still places a higher value on the coherence implicit in the idea of an International Style than on the "terribly scattered" direction of his own work. In defense of the recent work he articulates a concept of "functional eclecticism." Though this is very much a parallel to Eero Saarinen's idea of the "style for the job," Johnson fails to make the connection between it and his own concept; in fact, he comments rather negatively on Saarinen's work.

Johnson's discussion of his own entry in the competition for the Franklin D. Roosevelt Memorial is interesting in light of the scenario which unfolded as the dynamically composed stelae selected by the jury were unfavorably received in virtually all quarters of the public and the profession. The nature of Johnson's explanation of his own scheme for the Memorial—the comparison of Roman domical architecture with the thin-shell domical segment employed by Saarinen at the Massachusetts Institute of Technology—suggests that, despite claims to the contrary, Johnson believes in rules; not the easy rules of the International Style, as he had laid them out with Hitchcock in 1932, but the rules of history.

Johnson's remarks about the likelihood of a "Brutalist" building appearing "some day" in an international competition takes on a special significance in light of his later participation as juror for the international competition for the design of the Centre National d'Art et de Culture Georges Pompidou (or, as it has come to be called, Centre Beaubourg). The jury for that competition, which included Johnson as well as the Brazilian architect Oscar Niemeyer, chose an obsessively "Brutalist" mechanistic design which draws on the late, Archigram-dominated phase of Brutalism. Johnson's remarks about the potential importance of Brutalism and its offshoot "Archigram-ism" take on a double irony, as Richard Rogers, one of C.N.A.C.'s designers, was then a student at the A.A.

Johnson's discussion of his participation in the Roosevelt Memorial Competition takes on another interesting dimension in light of the references he makes to contemporary politics and to the radical politics of the 1930's. However casual these references may appear now—uninformed, even, as his comments on the Nixon-Kennedy rivalry now seem—their very inclusion in the talk testifies to its "informal" nature and to Johnson's new self-confidence; at last he regards himself as an Establishment figure, secure enough to look back on the political dalliances of his own past.

The end of this "talk" may at first reading seem wordy, argumentative, and overly specific; but for me it represents much more. Faced by a critical audience, Johnson works out his ideas as he talks. Though he may deny it, he is in the best sense a functionalist, committed to a recognition that buildings must "work," though not necessarily in a strictly utilitarian sense. This is nowhere clearer than in the discussion about theater design, fresh on his mind after just having delivered a speech on the subject in Berlin. Here the somewhat unresolved conflict between Johnson's recognition of the programmatic aspects of current practice (which can be described as the modern situation) and his commitment to history, image, and a sense of place is addressed with candor and passion.

I am glad that I arrived a little ahead of time. It has given me a chance to go up and see whether the Architectural Association was still here! We have a very strange impression of your school in the United States. I do not know whether you send us your best or your worst, and I hope to be here long enough to learn from you which it is. Our impression is that if one goes to the A.A. one designs so as to put the boiler rooms on the roof, and on top of that, again, towers in all the strangest possible shapes— arriving somehow at the ground in little columns. And you also have this strange way of rendering. If I am on any international jury I can tell straightway when the work of an A.A. man comes up.

This is the first time I have been in London for ten years, so I have been very interested in what has been happening. I am probably starting at the wrong end in referring to these strange designs. What is going to happen to Britain with all these boiler rooms floating in the sky? It is going to be an interesting period; it is not now. We managed to pass three Lever Houses along the way from Paddington, each worse than the one before. I did not have to make that comment; as a foreigner, of course, I am not allowed to. Britain is splendid! I had a most articulate taxi driver, very much like the ones we have in New York. I felt very much at home. Usually English taxi drivers take you where you are going and that is all. He asked me to take a look, through that strange glass you have in your taxi cabs, at Castrol House. I said, "What do you think about it?" He said, "I think it is terribly boring." I thought that was a wonderful comment. I had not realized that higher architectural criticism had reached that level. It was an extraordinarily good comment and indicated that he felt that all these tall buildings lacked character. He asked me what I thought of the American Embassy and volunteered the information that it was an architectural monstrosity. We passed over that. The only one he liked was the Thorne Industries building. Is it just as bad?

It is better.

You see—he is a great critic. Since I made my formal lecture in Berlin last week on another subject [see Bibliography, p. 279], I did not prepare anything for you: I felt that as I was just drifting through town, I had just as much right to expect information from you.

It is becoming increasingly difficult to talk about architecture. Twenty or thirty years ago, before you were born, it was relatively simple. We had a battle to fight. We knew who the great men were and the direction in which we were going. It was easy to get into the great fight. In politics in the thirties there was the Spanish Civil War. It was quite easy, and if you went into an intellectual meeting you knew which side you were on.

It was just the same in architecture. Either you liked Le Corbusier or you were a "square." (I am glad to know that the beat slang is much more prominent in England than it is in America. I hope I manage to learn some of it. I acquired a new phrase or two from an English architect in Copenhagen yesterday.) Modern architecture is going to pot, and this makes it difficult to talk about. I was in Bath yesterday and today, visiting the new American museum down there. It does seem an oddity. Have you ever been there? Mr. Gibberd has a very ugly building right in the very middle of town. But, after all, I am not so sure that it is ugly. How can you do modern work when you see the old Bath around you? How can you do a housing project after you have seen the Crescent? We do not have that problem in America. There history is so unimportant—as Henry Ford said. But you have it here, and, as I have said in a rather contradictory fashion in one of my lectures, you cannot not know history. It should be easy to do a building in downtown Bath. It is easy to do reconditioning jobs in architecture. When you build a new college at Oxford, we are told, you must not copy the Gothic or the Renaissance but strike anew. I am not so sure anymore. Boiler houses flying in the air over the Oxford colleges! It is something that one has to think about.

An extraordinary thing happened in Germany after the 1914—18 war. We saw the growth of what we still call in the book "Modern Architecture." 1923 was a magic year for all of us. It was the year of Mies's great designs. It seemed certain to me when I was your age that we were entering an era comparable only to the Georgian: that the main themes would be worked out by Mies, and that the rest of us would do the ancillary buildings. We were certain that by 1960 there would be a universal peace of great modern architecture. Just the opposite happened. The next war came, and the International Style has disappeared except in such places as Castrol House. In looking through the designs, I found only two done in this style. One was a filling station, and you can do very little with that. There was also a market that looked vaguely modern. I am using the word "modern" in its more exact sense—architecture between the wars. It is called in England and America the International Style—an expression perhaps more prevalent in my own country than in yours; and there is only one exponent left, Mies, and he will not change. I think it is wonderful that forty years afterward he will not do so. It is a rather stabilizing influence, and we might all pay regard to it.

Today I am ashamed of the terribly scattered work that I do, and its lack of direction. I am perfectly willing to admit that your work lacks it also. After all, you cannot always build boiler plants quite so high in the air! What can we do about it? It is all very well to say that we admire Mies, and that some discipline is a good thing for young minds, but what if one is bored, if one cannot look at Castrol House? If you go to Germany you will see the local versions of Lever House; they are worse. Or go to Denmark and look at the S.A.S. building—by far the worst of all. It has no scale and is rather like a piece of blotting paper with a drawing on it. It has no shape, height, width, or atmosphere. The discouragement, as one wanders around, becomes deeper and deeper, and the only outcome is that one gallops off in all directions.

The nineteenth century was complicated too—so much so that a book about it, written by my friend Russell Hitchcock [*Architecture: Nineteenth and Twentieth Centuries*], seems very heavy going indeed. If you have not read it, I am sure that your teacher has. The author tells me that the best place to start is at the chapter on the house.

I studied philosophy as an undergraduate, instead of architecture. Perhaps that is why I have none now. I do not believe that there is a consistent rationale or reason why one does things. Whatever the philosophy, the buildings always come out looking quite different from one another. It is nice to see Jim Stirling's shapes, but I don't know that he gets them where he says he does. He likes strange-looking props, just as you like putting boiler plants on the tops of buildings! He is a very sensible Englishman. They all are, by the way. We always come to England for the words that we need. We are a pioneer land and rather inarticulate. You may have heard the Yamasaki lecture at the R.I.B.A. the other night. "Aw shucks." That is the American attitude. "I'm just a little boy at heart." He is just as arrogant as the rest of us! You should hear Charles Eames. There is a real American high-school boy talking, but underneath he is a first-rate designer. He should have an Englishman to write the scenario. That is why I come to England—because I like to talk to the *Review* and the boys who know something. If Hitchcock had been born in England, think what that volume would be. Pevsner was not; but what lucidity, what industry! *An Outline of European Architecture,* and one is on the way—and knows where he is going!

Coming down in the train, while trying to think up a philosophy, I was admiring your scenery. Englishmen do not appreciate it enough in the way that Wordsworth did. The trip to the west of England would be like going to a suburb, if one were in New York, but as soon as one is out of London the scene begins to change as you go from brick to stone, from one landscape to another. We are not used to this telescoping. The scenery was so good that my philosophy was not well developed, but it is sometimes useful to have labels to hang on to or disagree with. The English are wonderfully good at it. They invented something called the New Empiricism, which came from Sweden. It did not last long, even in the *Review.* Then came Brutalism, and so on.

In short, my philosophy is *functional eclecticism.* It is not at all simple, but then the new Brutalism did not mean what it said either. It is quite all right for labels not to mean what they say. Humpty Dumpty put it rather well when he told Alice that words mean what you want them to mean. What I mean is that nowadays, since there is no formal discipline that one can catch on to—apart from boilers—one might as well use this approach. I am a historian first and an architect only by accident, and it seems to me that there are no forms to cling to, but there is history. There is nothing today like the wonderful faith of Cézanne and Picasso in primary colors, instead of the dirty browns, reds, and grays we seem to prefer. No one that I know of, except the neo-Neo-Plasticists, who love to appear more so, would use a red door, a blue frame, and a white wall. In Rotterdam in 1925 I saw my first Neo-Plasticist building, and for the first time I found everything serene, simple, and uncluttered. Primary little colors were things that one could defend. One could defend the straight line. One could, and did, feel passionately about things, as about politics in the thirties. All my friends were members of the Communist Party then, or close to it. They do not mention those things now! It is a great help in life if one can feel passionately about things. I am too far gone in my relativistic approach to the world really to care very much about labels. I have no faith whatever in anything. It neither hurts nor helps my architecture, though it may produce some rather funny results at times.

In Berlin there is a theater that is the best in the world, and to it come rich people and also those who have not enough to eat—just to watch. The fact that the latter are devoted to whatever they are devoted to shows in every gesture, in every movement. They have only to step up to the edge of a platform and what they say communicates. You have seen it in the people with passion in this country, perhaps. (I am afraid that we have Kennedy and Nixon, who are organization men.) Where there are political passions, it is easier to have architectural passions. Since passion is absent, let us do what we please. It may be the end of the world, now that the Chinese have the atom bomb. But we may have five or ten years, and they may be good ones. We may have twenty, and die from decent causes. In the meantime I think we should splinter up in any way we please.

Briefly, functional eclecticism amounts to being able to choose from history whatever forms, shapes, or directions you want to, and using them as you please. I entered a competition for the Roosevelt Memorial for Washington, and, because it had to fit in with the Capitol Building, I sent in a Roman dome. It was thrown out first thing, I should imagine, by the modern-minded jury—perhaps rightly, but it seemed most proper to me. I have no really expressible attitude on architecture, and if we are going to have chaos I feel that we might as well have nice, juicy chaos. Let us, instead of merely talking about tolerance, practice it. I have a terrible time practicing it because, for instance, I do not like Saarinen's work at all.

It is natural for me to adopt an historical approach, but if you prefer boilers, there is no reason why you should not cultivate that attitude. Perhaps some day we shall see more of them in the international competition entries from this school. My philosophy does have some regard for functional justification, if only in a vague way. If I like a dome in a certain application, I use it and prefer it to Saarinen's crown. To me it should go on top of a building, not on the ground, looking as if it had been unable to rise up out of the ooze. You should see the new ones at M.I.T. or Idlewild: there you have the bird that really could not get off the ground! Is there anything terribly wrong with the Pantheon? Acoustically the dome may be impossible, but it has some dignity and centrality about it.

My new theater in New York will look very much like the Altes Museum in Berlin. It seemed to fit in with the other buildings at Lincoln Center. They will probably tell me that I am a Fascist. At least my philosophy allows one to play around with a little more freedom than usual. In the eighteenth century, if they wanted a tall building, they were just as likely to put up a Chinese pagoda, because that was the tallest they had seen. If one wanted a ruin on a hill, one built a fake tower of some kind. I do not see what is wrong with that attitude today.

The question is, "What should you be doing?" Certainly, I do not think that you ought to be in a school of architecture. You are all learning the wrong things. The sooner you leave, the better. If you really want to be architects you had better go and work in an architect's office. That is impossible advice to follow in the States, and I suspect that it is here also. One has to work for fifteen years in the States before getting a license in that way. All one can learn in school is the functional part—how to arrange it so that one can get in the door, are the stairs too narrow, and so on. The real object of architecture must be to make you excited. All real architecture is interior architecture—the city square, the church, even the house—though none of us likes to do houses; we would rather do palaces. One should be able to make squares and create Baths, and feel marvelous inside as a result. Bath had nothing to do with economics or planning. It could not have. It would have been built over long ago. You should forget about economics, about the costs of building, about toilets and elevators, and just think of shape. Those wonderful boiler plants waving in the breeze—that is architecture. I recommend you to leave the school as soon as possible and begin playing with boiler plants.

There seems to be a similarity between the work of five or six men—Saarinen, Rudolph, Stone, Bunshaft, etc. What accounts for this uniformity of direction, which seems to have been developing in America over the last fifty years or so?

You amaze me! I would have considered them to be following very different paths. Russell Hitchcock has referred to this sort of thing before—for example, the similarity between the houses of Wright and Corbusier, who loathed each other. The history books will trace a connection between them. No doubt you are referring to the fact that one of these men hangs a particular kind of lace on a building and Mr. Stone or someone else hangs another kind. I hang things on buildings and so does Bunshaft, but he can't even speak to me on the street anymore.

There seemed to be a united movement towards what Gropius called "functionalism," but this broke up suddenly a few years ago. Why did it break up so suddenly, and into so many parts?

It was a great disappointment to people of my period, who all felt that that kind of modern, International Style was thoroughly well established. My taxi driver would not have found Castrol House boring five years ago. Lever House was the main thing then—I heard it even from England. It is not now. If you had to do an office building, the Seagram Building would be the *end.* I cannot imagine what happened. I thought you might know, because the English seem to be ahead of us on all this. I remember discussing it with Smithson some years ago. I thought it was crazy, but who is crazy now? Saarinen does a different building every time he puts pen to paper. Do you feel there is a connection between what Saarinen does and what I do?

To a degree, yes. One can more easily compare Yamasaki and Saarinen. Both are going off in a new direction each time and then apologizing for what they are doing. I had in mind the American Embassy structure.

It is still modern, though very much dependent on texture. I do not like it. Obviously, I did not get the job! It is Mies-modern, but instead of using a steel H he has taken a single shape. It is multi-repeating on pins. There is no top, bottom, or corner. All my corners, tops, and bottoms are becoming stronger and stronger. Architectural design changes so rapidly that today's prototypes are out of date tomorrow; but the similarity you mention is very interesting. It would surprise you how much of your work looks similar by the time it gets to the States.

So much of your building seems to be done on a large budget. Suppose you had to build with some attention to cost, how would you approach it?

My new Yale laboratories are built to a budget. Unfortunately, they look a little like Stirling's.

Do you not think some of your problems would be solved if, instead of having the one-off job, you had to ally your architecture to a social program? It would force it all into a clearer pattern. It would not be so centrifugal?

I do not have to do it that way. The Russians do it, of course, but just because the Russians do it badly, it does not mean that we should not be able to do it. We do not seem to have the social controls in the States even to start it. I expected to see signs of control over here, with the London County Council and the various planning commissions in existence, but it looks very capitalistic to me. Germany is even worse than America. They build any old way in any old place. My theory is, "Let us relax." I see no prospect of having social discipline of that kind in our time. Social democracy has been around for a very long time and nothing has been done.

Has your relaxation come about as a result of disillusionment with the political situation?

I am not interested in politics. It perhaps comes from the fire that one had originally dying out somewhat, but there is no cause for discouragement. One should use the very chaos, the very nihilism, the relativism of our architectural world, to create whimsies. Stirling and I do not agree on that.

To many of us that seems almost irresponsible?

More than almost—yes, I have been accused of irresponsibility, but how could one put up a Seagram Building if one thought only of social responsibility? What was needed was a lovely building.

Are there any architectural problems in America slightly more difficult than covering a statue or doing a luxury museum? Maybe in America you have no problems to be answered?

We have all the ones you have, but no one pays much attention to them. I am doing a whole series of science buildings for Yale, and they have to be built for thirty-five dollars a square foot, which is just half the cost of a museum. I have been able to do them in concrete and build cheaply. We gave up housing some time ago. Architects build only about ten percent of our housing anyway. Some of the housing that is put up is rather horrifying. The problem has largely been ignored, except by Mies, who had a rich developer who thought he was God's gift to tall buildings. I am sure he would much rather do monuments. I see nothing wrong with the trend toward monuments. It is one of the better things that have emerged from the collapse of the International Style. No one could be ashamed of doing a monument to Roosevelt.

You have shown us those monuments as being important?

I have that kind of practice.

I imagine it is by choice?

I suppose everyone in the end gets the type of work that he wants. If I suddenly am made to feel irresponsible, should I rush off to the nearest housing developer—they do frighteningly bad work here too—and ask for work? One does not apply in that way. Smithson did a very nice one, and it almost killed him. One has to be a very rich man to be a responsible architect in the sense of taking up housing as a main interest.

Do you think of art as something free, which does not involve itself in a dialectical situation at all—something that is practiced when one is not going to be responsible to people? Is one responsible to art?

Art is a very emotion-arousing word, and it means something more than responsibility.

Do you feel that your art changes from one building to another?

English people know so very much more about how to use all these words than we do . . .

Many Englishmen still believe that form and content grapple together and that what comes out is art. It is not an easy matter.

I wish it were. Art is the greatest mystery of all. One cannot hide behind imperfections in form and content. In housing there are many loopholes. One can always say, "We could not afford this or that," but if you let yourself go and put boilers on the roof, you will be judged by that alone. I welcome this school's absence of responsibility in that it is prepared to put them up there. I have tried out the housing-estate side. One day I got my sense of responsibility out of the back drawer where I always keep it. We are all the product of our age and not without this gnawing sense of guilt. I hope you are not bothered with it.

Do you think that the human race has become panicky?

I think we are all taking it much too seriously. It is either going to be over in a couple of years or it is not. I am very glad to be alive. I could not imagine a more exciting time. Art is a complicated matter. Just think of Michelangelo and his work—was it a good or bad thing from the point of view of social responsibility? Whiskey does not raise a smile in this country, but in America, where we are prohibitionists, building the biggest whiskey building in the country is hardly a recommendation for the next job. Wright could always bring down the house by saying, "That whiskey building," as if it was a house of ill repute. What kind of people were the Medici anyway? They probably stole as much as our own robber barons ever did. What is wrong with the Frick Museum? It was left behind by someone who was probably very rich. If I started building housing I should be poor in no time.

Apart from the moral side, is there not the aspect of enjoying the work of art? Some of us may feel that some of your buildings are facile?

That is because I am a bad architect, but it is not given to all of us to talk about how good or bad we are. Neutra says that he is the greatest architect in the world. That is easy. He is not. It is harder to say about some of the others. One must obviously have some sense of responsibility, because one is trusted by the client to produce the kind of building that he wants. He does not know what it should look like. He will probably say, "We want a good-looking museum for so much." That is responsibility if you like. Some eight thousand people a day go into the Seagram Building, so I must have been thinking of the great masses after all.

If one likes smooth, easy forms one will do that kind of building. Others may like much tougher forms?

You mean "facile" in the sense that there is too much perfectly plain granite? I am glad you are not bringing morals into it. You do not mind my being irresponsible?

Stay as you are!

I have been making a number of nonsensical remarks about boilers on the roof. I do not mean it really. You have a direction that we find very interesting. The best students in America are ex-A.A. people. They come to us from a very interesting background, more interesting than any other school I know. Four or five years ago I did not enjoy it, but we all change.

You have acquired something of a reputation for producing these gnarled, strong-looking forms which seem a little outré, or peculiar, to some of us. I should like to know what revolutionary impetus led to this and would be glad to have something in writing if you cannot answer it now.

Your use of the word "functional" in your philosophy implies a certain discipline?

I am glad that you brought that up. I did not work out my philosophy properly. It does not mean "functional" in the usual sense, but the very opposite, in that a memorial should look like a dome, for instance. The great example of non-functional eclecticism is Mies's chapel. His philosophy is that all buildings look alike because the technology of our day requires us to use a steel structure (it does not, but he says it does), and that when one is to do a chapel the same feeling begins inside one as when one is about to do a school or a factory. If you mention structure to anyone else in America they are likely to say, "No one here ever bothers about structure." I don't see why you cannot draw upon the best that there is, as long as it fits. You can use Adam's columns, Soane's breakfast room. You can begin with the Syon House. I remember that I was building a "pink room" which was three times too long—3 to 1. You know, that is not a room—it is just there. When Adam was faced with the Syon House library he did incredible things to pull it together here with the aid of pilasters, and let it go there. He produced a beautiful corridor. Why not learn from such things and apply the knowledge elsewhere?

I have a problem with my New York State Theater. One can make a theater out of this room, but for that building at Lincoln Center I am to do an opera house. An audience of twenty-five hundred is too large for an opera house, because one gets the sense of being in a barn. Would I be wrong to adopt the old-fashioned conventional standpoint and just put in seating? You would have a room, not architecture, and it would be somewhat like Utzon's long parquet floor in Sydney. But forty-five rows back you cannot see, and you cannot get any feeling of atmosphere. However, vision is of no importance; in amphitheaters you cannot see anything. At the other end is the cinematographic approach. The architecture is done by the director, who wants to set the mood of his piece. All one sees is the scene created by his imagination. I am at the opposite pole in this matter. I believe in the importance of the "experience" of going to the opera. The mere fact that one dresses specially to go there helps to create the special feeling of "occasion." You will know the atmosphere I mean from having been into an Italian opera house, or Covent Garden, and many others. I am not in favor of the architectureless, featureless, acoustic box of the kind one can find at the Salle Pleyel in Paris, or here at the Festival Hall. Peter Moro was saying in Berlin the other day that he was responsible for a trend toward boxed drawers in the German opera houses because he had begun it in the Festival Hall. I must say that

I do not feel like putting on a dinner jacket to go to the Festival Hall, which is a modern opera house.

Is it not a concert hall?

Would you build an opera house like it? I think you will agree that we ought not to take it as an example. Which direction should we go in? The modern requirement is for acoustics, sight lines, and structural clarity— the idea of flowing space, with the foyers and the entrance hall all part of one great room, together with the stage. One does away with the proscenium arch: it is not modern! I say that that is nonsense. In Covent Garden one did not know what was inside, and this was true of any normal opera house. I claim that the bell-shaped form is essential for a good room. One cannot see the stage at La Scala or the Metropolitan—from one-third of the seats anyway—and I am sure that if I made certain that everyone could see, it would be such a big barn that no one would come.

Surely people come to listen to the music, not merely to attend in their dinner jackets?

You see, there are some modern people! I do not believe that what you say is true.

It is a highly functional use. Are you not putting a very low interpretation on functionalism? One surely has to try to bring everyone as close as possible and tier them in some way. I agree that one has to balance considerations of how well one need see with other considerations. It is a matter of give and take.

It is certainly an endless matter of give and take. Generally speaking, the art of creating a room that one is glad to be in is more important than getting the largest possible number of people close to the stage. I am very glad to say that my client thinks so too. One might very well have a client saying that as many as possible should be able to get close to the stage. It would be a moral imperative, of a kind. Why not switch it and say, as a moral imperative, that one should rejoice in the opera house and see as best one could? I may add that I have never compromised so much in my life as I have since I began that design. I am in trouble because I am a hundred feet from the stage when I should be eighty. Surely you would not advocate giving up everything to sight lines, etc.?

Was not the Festival Hall specifically designed for music? The design comes out internally. The sight lines and acoustics are surely most important.

It is in a slightly different position. I am sorry that I keep bringing it up, but so many things in it remind me of the German opera houses. There are twenty of them, and they build them like mad. They are also a little smug about them. They all have these drawers and are as cold as ice water. One can see from every seat!

The German people go to the opera more than any other race in the world. They spend more money on theaters than anyone else.

I wish the English did to the same extent, and certainly our own people. I do not mean to be reactionary, but I am wondering whether it is possible to take up the traditional approach in some new way. The Italian horseshoe, with its tiered style, has lasted for three hundred years, right through the nineteenth century and into this. Should that carry any weight with us, or should we give in to the new demand for acoustics and sight lines? Some of the opera houses in Italy had to be burnt down because people could *neither* see nor hear. They gave up seeing years ago, but they did enjoy the music. Perhaps we should face the whole problem of watching a spectacle anew.

I must leave now for Paris, where I shall go to the theater!

The International Style— Death or Metamorphosis

Speech, Architectural League Forum, Metropolitan Museum of Art, March 30, 1961; excerpted in Architectural Forum, *CXIV (June, 1961), 87.*

This talk before a large audience in the auditorium at The Metropolitan Museum of Art provided me with my first glimpse of Johnson as a platform personality; from the moment I saw him take the microphone in his hand, I have been convinced that there is no one in architecture today who is a more skilled performer-showman than he. The talk, sponsored by the Architectural League, was delivered as the opening statement in a debate with Reyner Banham, the English historian and critic. Banham, then on his first visit to the United States, was well known to the cognoscenti of the New York scene for his editorial work at the Architectural Review *and for his recently published book,* Theory and Design in the First Machine Age, *which Johnson had reviewed (see pp. 100–03). The audience had anticipated a stimulating evening of debate, in which the principal spokesman for what the English were presumed to view disdainfully as American pragmatism and art-for-art's sake frivolity would be attacked by the leading polemicist for what Americans viewed almost enviously as the kitchen-sink school of Brutalist earnestness. The expected, however, did not occur. Though Johnson's bold and provocative opening statement gave ample opportunity for the witty rebuttal which everyone had surely expected, Banham failed to rise to the occasion. Despite Johnson's brilliance, the encounter was little more than a memorable non-event. Johnson fired the audience up, but Banham proved unable or unwilling to rise to any of the master showman's bait.*

Johnson's concluding remarks now seem the most important in the talk. Articulating the distinctions between two streams of late modernism, the commercialized Miesian and the brutalized Corbusian, Johnson reintroduces the issue of the differences between our native pragmatism and European idealism. This issue had for a long time gone undiscussed in relation to the distinctly different patterns of development in the Modern Movement in architecture which had emerged in Europe and American during the post–World War II period. Though Johnson emphatically endorses historicism, he does not see it so much as a positive direction, a "third stream," to use his own phrase, but more idiosyncratically (and some would say, frivolously) as a manifestation of his restlessness within the limitations of the current scene. It is also expressive of his desire to épater the masters of the Modern Movement, in particular Walter Gropius. The anti-historical biases of Gropius, his naive belief in program-as-form-generator, and his philosophy of materialistic as well as social progress were not only crippling to his students at Harvard but also grossly contradicted in his own highly commercialized practice, as typified by his rhetorical and expedient use of "onion domes" at the Baghdad University complex and his elaborate circumlocutions in defense of his very mediocre Pan Am Building.

The phrase "International Style" has had a varied career: accepted by some historians, reviled by Giedion and most architects—perhaps a majority of you here tonight. The latest history of American architecture by John Burchard and Albert Bush-Brown says, for example: "The International Style was a new and unfortunate tag to the movement from which it has not quite been able to escape."

It might be well, therefore, to preface my remarks with a word of explanation of what the phrase meant to its inventors. Alfred Barr and Russell Hitchcock used the phrase first in 1931, when we were all searching for a name for the obviously clear line of work being done in the twenties by men like Le Corbusier, Mies, and Gropius. It was obvious it was a style. It was obviously different from the individualist work of before the war. That the practitioners of it at the time did not consider it a style was only natural. None of us architects want to feel we are working in straitjackets. But it is nevertheless the duty of the historian to point out styles when they occur in history.

As Hitchcock pointed out in our book *The International Style,* it was the first style since the Gothic to be developed on the basis of a new interpretation of structure, the Renaissance being only a surface change. Steel and concrete skeletons at last became the essence of a new style. Axial symmetry, pyramidal composition were replaced by an aesthetic brew derived from extra-architectural sources such as Constructivism, Cubism, and de Stijl. Ornament was completely rejected, roofs were flat, columns exposed; everything was trabeated, skeletal, and the word "piloti" came into the English language. Le Corbusier's *prisme pur* was the shape of the day. The machine became an object of worship—grain elevators the rage. This movement started with a bang in the magic year 1922 with Le Corbusier's Citrohan project, Mies's office-building project, and Gropius and Meyer's Chicago Tribune Tower project. It was a centripetal movement of such power that it has lasted almost forty years. Quite a style; the High Renaissance in contrast lasted barely thirty years, till Mannerism laid it low. The International Style lasted even longer than Barr or Hitchcock could have foreseen thirty years ago.

What caused this great style to emerge so suddenly, the historians will be telling us for the next few decades. It is clear that some such implosion was bound to occur, when we think of steel and concrete lying unrecognized out in the backyard of architecture, so to speak. Also, when we think of the vagaries of ornament of the nineteenth century and early twentieth, we can only welcome their abolishment.

In addition, long before World War I, a wave of sociological puritanism had formed against the decorative, repetitive, revivalist styles. All of a sudden, a building had to be suited to its function first, and then, only afterward, well designed. We can quote Nikolaus Pevsner on this—Pevsner, who is a self-proclaimed "modern" of thirty years ago, and who has remained holding his thirty-year-old convictions: "This new sense of social responsibility expressed itself in the principle of functionalism, that is, the principle that form follows function, in the sense that a building must function first of all, and nothing on its exterior—or inside either—must reduce its well-functioning; or, the other way round, that the beauties of the exterior must be developed after the assurance of the fullest functional fulfilment, and never at the expense of it."

And piled on this puritanism was the puritanism of structural expression descended from Viollet-le-Duc. The structure should show, the outside should express the inside. Even economy of structure was important: the least possible column size, the greatest economical spans. Mies has strictly said, "I hope you will understand that architecture has nothing to do with the invention of forms. It is not a playground for children, young or old."

The International Style spread and spread, far beyond the limits Hitchcock observed in 1932. Almost a generation has passed and here we are in The Metropolitan Museum (not, I regret to note, in The Museum of Modern Art, where the name was born) discussing whether or not it is dead, and if so, what if anything is springing from the ashes.

The Style spread and spread and, as will happen, began to decay and decay. By that I do not mean it got bad, but extraneous, interesting growths stretched out from it, until today at its most widespread (look at the magazines) it is almost ignored by the adventurous of all ages.

It is fun to see what the four great founders listed by Hitchcock thirty years ago did in subsequent years.

Le Corbusier now looks down with disgust on the twenties; and, actually, he was the first to turn against lightness, clarity, logic, rationalism, to arbitrary sculptural shapes, until at Ronchamp we have a building which some say is not architecture at all. It assuredly is not International Style. J. J. P. Oud, the brilliant Dutch de Stijl designer, turned against the theory in the thirties and finally in 1939 built the Shell Building in The Hague in a style more fussy and decorated than Berlage's fifty years previously. Walter Gropius kept to International Style architecture with his team until recently, when we have onion domes. Mies, of course, is the purest of the pure. The newest buildings on his drafting board are piloti'd steel cages with glass infill. The strongest man we have.

What happened? Le Corbusier is obviously too much of a sculptor to want to go on doing straightforward building; besides, how could you solve individualistic buildings in the simple trabeations of the *prismes purs?* Mies's chapel at the Illinois Institute of Technology rather jolted all of us, I think. J. J. P. Oud had never liked modern architecture and its functionalist straitjackets. He left when he could. Gropius's team designs in the Moslem mode are part of a much larger Neo-Historicism which is all over the country. The English have invented this capital-letter word

Neo-Historicism (cap *N,* cap *H*) to mark what is happening, and though they don't like what is happening, they are as always good at naming.

These various directions that the great men, now all in their seventies, took are symptomatic of what has happened with the rest of us in the following generation. We have spread off into ways that seem to Pevsner, for example, anti-rationalist, neo-formal, and heaven knows how sinful from the thirties point of view. Ernesto Rogers, a C.I.A.M. devotee, bewails that after the great generation there is nothing. What are we to do?

Obviously, go on. How to go on is our subject tonight, and an area in which Reyner Banham and I shall profoundly disagree. I am going to pay him the compliment of setting out a few thoughts that he can then take potshots at. I would much prefer it the other way around, but my lot is to come first. I shall do him the further compliment of using his terminology, the easier for him to demolish my points. (I must admit parenthetically, however, that I use his nomenclature because I have none of my own. Somehow, we in this country do not know how to indulge in the heady theorizing of British intellectuals.)

Anyhow, to the point! My picture of the recent past from which we inescapably extrapolate to foretell the future is a simple one. I recognize three quite interesting ways of doing architectural design right now, intertwined, none of them a style, but all exhilarating, all forward-looking, all fecund, I would say, for future form. The one-line direction still the strongest is the International Style. Mies is by no means through creating. The fine designs of S.O.M. (one does not dare mention names in this association) are doing better and better: the Air Academy, for example, could hardly have been better. The new Yale Library is a new twist in the *prisme pur.* I. M. Pei's New York apartments are clarity and sophistication itself. In the West, Killingsworth and Craig Ellwood are exploring worlds of small houses that we in the East know nothing of. Let us not write off this grand, modern, forty-year tradition. After all, who wants the job of doing New York's next all-out skyscraper? Eero Saarinen has the job; God give him the strength. Ever since the Philadelphia Savings Fund Society by Bill Lescaze of 1930, the International Style has provided the most viable grammar for skyscrapers. What now will Saarinen do?

The second great stream that I recognize is what the British sometimes call Brutalism—not a good name, but a name. It is an attitude, not a style, not even a way of forming. It stems from the attempt to fulfill as clearly and simply as possible the environmental purposes of the building. For form the Brutalists are apt to bring us great concrete beams—muscle-flexing, one English critic calls it—and tiny windows, funny shaped, scattered in great brick walls. Much inside and outside movement, and a great many pieces of concrete exposed. This is functional variety. Formalistically, since, in my opinion, forms always follow forms and not function, their designs are apt to be taken from the Jaoul Houses by Le Corbusier. The regular skeletal rhythms of the International Style are gone. The intent is strength, originality, and a certain crudeness. In this country we have brilliant examples in the work of Rudolph of Yale, Katselas of Pittsburgh; much not built, as indeed is the case in England, but coming.

The Brutalist attitude melts, however strangely, into the other popular direction, which, to use the British word, is Neo-Historicism. To many, this idea of a return to an interest in history is a slap at the whole Modern Movement, capital *M,* capital *M.* I claim that it is not. In the time of the Bauhaus and the time of the early days at Harvard, history was not considered a proper study. And today, how different! We find ourselves now all wrapped up in reminiscence. We cannot today *not* know history. It's a stimulating and new feeling of freedom. The English and Italians are apt to look back over a shorter period than are we; to de Stijl, or, for example, late Corbu; but in essence the new view of history is a new and stimulating impulse. We no longer have to judge buildings by how little or how much history they have in them. It is not neo-Baroque, it is not anti-international, it is not anti-Modern, it is only faintly anti-function-alist. It is also slightly anti-rational—but in being anti-rational, aren't we merely following in the philosophical trend of our day? We have no wish to revolt against the past; we can acknowledge the leadership of our great elders. But we can be freer.

Letter to Dr. Jürgen Joedicke

Letter of December 6, 1961; published in John M. Jacobus, Jr., Philip Johnson (New York: Braziller, 1962), 120–22.

Johnson wrote this letter spontaneously in response to his reading of Jürgen Joedicke's recent survey of current international architecture. It can be seen as a footnote to the earlier "Where Are We At?" (pp. 100–03), carrying forward his ideas about the ever-widening split between the "theory" of the pioneers of the Modern Movement and the "practice" of the second, American generation. Johnson sees himself as making a clean break with the Modern Movement, yet almost despite himself it seems he finds it not so easy as he might like to cut loose from its moral imperatives. The discussion of eclecticism reveals his wavering commitment to it as a philosophically justifiable design strategy. There is also more than a suggestion that he regards the very term as a pejorative one. Maybe the New Harmony dome is pure form—one rather doubts it; and maybe it isn't based on Borromini; but what about Hadrian?

Johnson's preoccupation with originality is almost obsessive and certainly not very compatible with an anti-Modern Movement polemic. In fact, allowing for the passage of time, his Spenglerian evocation of the Zeitgeist—"Old values are swept away by new with dazzling but thrilling speed. Long live Change!"— sounds not very different from many of the hortatory incantations of the polemicists for a new architecture in Germany in the teens and early twenties.

I am very much impressed by your summation of modern international architecture in 1961. Your sense of organization and characterization in a field as fluid as ours is clear and consistent . . .

Two points I should like to bring out. First, I wish you had the time to study American architecture more at first hand. The architects best known to European colleagues and journalists are the ones you especially discuss. To us Schindler might be singled out instead of Neutra—Kahn instead of Breuer and so forth. Also in talks perhaps we could make clear the differences between Stone, Yamasaki and myself.

May I say parenthetically, you are very fair with me. Borromini should not be mentioned in connection with my work. The New Harmony shrine is pure form—ugly or beautiful—but pure form.

There is, as you realize, however, a basic cleavage in our points of view. You criticize from a standpoint (*Standpunkt*). You take a stand (*Stellung nehmen*), on a moral basis of the Modern Movement. You understand the modern movement as deriving "Form" from the proper program (*Aufgabe*) and from structural simplicity and honesty. You take especial stand against using structure shapes as mere applied decoration. You would agree with Goethe: *"Der Pilaster ist eine Lüge."*

In line with this, you naturally would see the danger of a new Eclecticism in our new approach to history.

Is there not, however, another position we could take? Namely, that the entire modern movement—looked at as an intellectual movement dating from Ruskin and Viollet-le-Duc, going through the Werkbund, Bauhaus, Le Corbusier to World War II—may be winding up its days.

There is only one absolute today and that is change. There are no rules, surely no certainties in any of the arts. There is only the feeling of a wonderful freedom, of endless possibilities to investigate, of endless past years of historically great buildings to enjoy.

I cannot worry about a new eclecticism. Even Richardson who considered himself an eclectic was not one. A good architect will always do original work. A bad one would do bad "modern" work as well as bad work (that is, imitative) with historical forms.

Structural honesty seems to me one of the bugaboos that we should free ourselves from very quickly. The Greeks with their marble columns imitating wood, and covering up the wood roofs inside! The Gothic designers with their wooden roofs above to protect their delicate vaulting! And Michelangelo, the greatest architect in history, with his Mannerist column!

No, our day no longer has need of moral crutches of late 19th-century vintage. If Viollet-le-Duc was what the young Frank Lloyd Wright was nurtured on, Geoffrey Scott and Russell Hitchcock were my Bibles.

I am old enough to have enjoyed the International Style immensely and worked in it with the greatest pleasure. I still believe Le Corbusier and Mies to be the greatest living architects. But now the age is changing so fast. Old values are swept away by new with dizzying but thrilling speed. Long live Change!

The danger you see of a sterile academic eclecticism is no danger. The danger is the opposite, the sterility of your Academy of the Modern Movement.

Review of Robin Boyd:
The Puzzle of Architecture

From Architectural Forum, *CXXIV* (*June, 1966*), 72–73, 93.

Johnson was fascinated by this book, which for a long time he felt offered a kind of Rosetta stone to the new directions in architecture and which now, rather contrary to Boyd's intentions, seems little more than an account of modernism in disarray. All three of the "phases" that Boyd discusses and Johnson makes so much of merely document parallel tendencies in the Modern Movement as it was playing out its hand in the mid-1960's and do not touch on the really new directions, which were then already quite clearly articulated in the work of Venturi, Moore, and Giurgola—work that Johnson was aware of but felt unsure about.

In reading Robin Boyd I cannot help thinking of the time, a generation ago now, when Henry-Russell Hitchcock was similarly engaged in writing contemporary architectural history in his monumental *Modern Architecture* of 1929 and the picture book, *The International Style: Architecture 1922– 1932.*

Like Robin Boyd, Hitchcock was writing history about buildings barely off the drawing board and, like Boyd, trying to find good and great architecture in the maze of contemporary work. I cannot help but think Hitchcock's task was a simpler one. In the early 30's we could see the triumph of the International Style. The dominance of Le Corbusier was already complete. The Barcelona Pavilion had already established Mies, and the Bauhaus building, Gropius. The continuation of that triumph seemed assured. And indeed it was.

But today, and I wonder if the fact that I am sixty has anything to do with it, the picture does not look as clear, the lines so well drawn. Indeed, my own sense of lack of direction is quoted against me by Boyd. Apparently I said somewhere, "Why can we not wander aimlessly?" I was all for a principle of lack of principles, as it were. Boyd will have none of this, and his description of the situation today in the world of architectural design is completely convincing. At least to me.

Since I must recommend that every architect read every word, it may seem unnecessary for me to paraphrase the main thesis; but since Boyd does dress up his main points with discursions and, especially at the end, with a moral appeal for Realism, Functionalism, and even Truth (values I find too elusive to be satisfactorily invoked), it might not be out of place to give my impressions of his history.

A word of warning: The following resumé may differ from Boyd's in many ways. He himself is quite accommodatingly liberal, not to say loose, in his terminology. For example, he labels the Kurashiki Town Hall by Tange as Third Phase, when quite obviously it is Second Phase. We can afford in these murky waters to be slightly indistinct.

It seems then there are three phases of modern architecture of the last generation. By using the word "phase," the author reduces the dangers of the brickbats that Hitchcock received for the nasty words International Style. (It is amusing to note that no matter how much vilification we received for using the words International Style, the term is still used, even by the present author, and still means exactly what we meant it to mean 35 years ago when Alfred Barr first coined it.)

The First Phase then includes the International Style, all the work from the 1920's revolution to the present. This phase is based on the now old ideas: structural honesty; repetitive, modular rhythms; clarity, expressed by oceans of glass; the flat roof; the box as the perfect container; no ornament. Today Mies is the lone giant still sensitively producing works of art of the First Phase. Many fine S.O.M. skyscrapers and much lesser work by lesser architects continue the tradition. Fortunately or unfortunately, the First Phase principles were easily adaptable by commercial and industrial builders, and the rallying cry of the intellectuals of the twenties and thirties became the slogans of the speculative builders of the fifties and sixties.

Came the reaction and the Second Phase. All over the world we were bored. The fifties were groping. On the one hand, decoration came back; on the other, historical reminiscence. We have only to think of Paul Rudolph's Wellesley Gothic, Edward Stone's Venetian Huntington Hartford, my own Classical Lincoln Center, or Yamasaki's Gothic tracery. Although Louis Kahn belongs to a later story, his love of castles and San Gimignano. One of Boyd's words for the main tenets of the Second Phase is the jaw-breaking word "monolithicism." That is, we stuffed our functions in those days into preconceived geometric volumes. The cube, the cylinder, the rectangular solid. Or even into warped shapes or bunch of grape clusters, my Dumbarton Oaks being one example. The shape was primary. We even went in for vaults, hyperbolic paraboloids, gables, even for symbolic shapes (consciously or unconsciously) like the winged bird of Saarinen's T.W.A.

The special story of Kenzo Tange is illustrative. Starting with pure International Style (First Phase) at Hiroshima, Tange quickly went Second Phase with his famous town halls. Two features stand out: his love of Japanese architecture and the fitting of function into shapes, shapes, shapes. The best of those is Kurashiki. The plain rectangular block is made of pre-cast concrete "logs" that lap at the corners like a log cabin. The building is lifted off the ground, clearly recalling the Shosoin at Nara. The windows are cut in at arbitrary but effective spots.

The Third Phase, what is happening out front in architecture in the sixties, is naturally hard to explain. In art, labels are better attached after a long wait. I think of "Gothic" and "Baroque," both pejorative terms when they were invented. So Boyd is in a spot and I am, too, since it is obvious from the book that I am essentially Second Phase.

My description, therefore, of the Third Phase may be (1) prejudiced (age envies youth); (2) sympathetic but inaccurate (papa never understands junior); (3) absurd (old goat pretending to swing); (4) fair (I have seen everything). (A footnote to this talk of "age." It is meant only as between Second and Third Phase architecture. Both Louis Kahn and José Luis Sert are, in years, older than I.)

Anyhow, easier than talking principles, let us quote buildings included in the canon of the Third Phase today and deduce a few basic threads of consistency. Boyd lists specifically Kahn's Richards Laboratories, Rudolph's Arts and Architecture Building, Sert's Married Student Housing, Tange's Yamanashi Press Building, and Johansen's Taylor House.

Why he omits the key English building, Leicester University Engineering Building by Stirling & Gowan, I can't imagine. It beautifully illustrates the Third Phase and is perhaps the strongest of the lot. Consider it included.

What have these buildings in common that makes them a group? What identifies the Third Phase? Since what something is *not* is easier to make precise than what that something *is,* these buildings are *not* rectangular skin-interesting boxes like the First Phase, they are *not* arbitrary shapes like the Second. They are *not* all glass with even-bay systems poised on pilotis above the ground like the First Phase, or carefully smooth-materialed monolithic "significant" forms like the Second.

On the contrary, within the general modern movement with its emphasis on functionalism, structuralism, anti-axiality and anti-ornamentation (all these modernisms are scrupulously present), the Third Phase has found a new way toward the synthesis of unity and diversity, clarity and complexity.

In many cases a functional element has been picked out and exaggerated to make breaks and strength of intent, viz., the exhaust pylons of Kahn's Richards Laboratories, the vertical communications of Tange's Yamanashi Press Building, or the toilets in Paul Rudolph's Government Center. Sometimes a single element is repeated but at various scales, like the sun boxes of Rudolph's Milam House or Johansen's Taylor House. Sometimes great gashes are introduced in tall rectangular masses to emphasize depth and make an impression of strength, viz., Sert's Boston University and Stirling & Gowan's Leicester University. In some buildings like Kahn's and Tange's, even Johansen's and Stirling's, the Second Phase enclosed volumes seem turned inside out. The great spaces are *outside* the buildings, not in. The change from Kurashiki to the Yamanashi Press Building is a case in point. The Second Phase clothed great rooms with a single significant shape. The Third is a play of external space semi-enclosed by functional elements strongly expressed.

Often the Third Phase, unlike the First, but like the Second, reaches back into history but is more apt to pick more recent models. Stirling's Leicester reminds me of Hannes Meyer's drawings for his entry in the League of Nations competition of 1927. Häring's Garkau and Tatlin's utopian schemes are especial favorites. Wright's "looseness" as in the Robie and Kaufmann House designs is analogous to the play of space in the Third Phase.

The Third Phase is contemptuous of careful finishes. Coming from Le Corbusier and his English Brutalist followers, the "toughness" of raw concrete, unpointed brickwork is favored. It seems to the sixties more honest (handicraft is gone forever, anyhow), more of our era.

Functionalism has taken a new turn. Every architect realizes that function is not the sole maker of form, but the functional parts are made the *basis* of form much more than in the Second Phase. "What the building wants to be," in Kahn's phrase. Johansen's proposed library for Clark University expresses separately almost every varying function in the building. Big rooms hang out big, small rooms small.

Perhaps the most "far out" building actually to be realized yet in the Third Phase is Tange's Yamanashi Press Building in Kofu City, Japan, now nearing completion. At first it strikes the observer like an A.A. student's design made into a big instead of a small model, since so much of the "plug in" quality seems already to be there. It seems that seven round towers were casually spaced around the site. Suspended among the towers are the various floors. At one major point three whole floors seem to be left out making a vast, impressive void. The effect is staggering in conception. I hope it will be great in reality.

This caveat is necessary because like much early work of a phase, the ideas are apt to outrun execution. I am reminded of the beauty, clarity and slight unbuildability of early Le Corbusier and Mies sketches. There are many problems ahead for the Third Phase. It can disintegrate or it can become, as Boyd profoundly hopes, *the* architecture of the 20th century after the "failures" of the First and Second Phases. To a devout Second Phase man like myself, the danger ahead for it seems alarming!

But there can be no doubt the phase exists. There are too many elements in common. There is too much polemic, moralization and mystique simply to say it does not actually have validity. As a clincher to a doubter like me, too many good architects whom I have admired for more than a decade are leaders of the Third Phase today.

Boyd does not speculate too specifically on the why of this Third Phase; whence it arose. Matthew Nowicki once wrote "Form does not follow function; it follows form." The Third Phase forms must have come from somewhere. The answer seems to be Le Corbusier. Although Ronchamp is certainly shaggy and additive in its elements, Boyd seems to consider it Second Phase. More of a clean ancestor is the design of the Jaoul Houses. The British Brutalists derived an entire manner from these two houses. Their powerful vaulting, their crude in-and-out random fenestration seem to have liberated a whole generation.

The key building, however, is Le Corbusier's Dominican Monastery, La Tourette, of 1957–60. Although it is a rectangle, the functional or pseudo-functional divergencies, the casual treatments of the "façades," the top-heavy treatment of the cells, the total lack of conventional base (one might think the building was designed upside down) are presages of the agglomerative style of the sixties. This group impressed every designer in the world. Most of us could not if we would follow Ronchamp, but La Tourette could speak to all, not translatably, but conceptually. The Third Phase was born.

To repeat, every architect must have this book. To narrow my recommendation, read pages 142 to 155 where the characteristics of the Third

Phase are outlined. From page 155 to the end of the book, Boyd moralizes. Perhaps this is most important but not to this reviewer. I believe architecture, even present architecture, just happens. Rationalizations are interesting; Mies (less is more), Kahn (servant spaces) have interesting minds and their theories illuminate their work. But architecture will have immortality for different reasons that are hard for contemporaries to fathom. First, Second, Third Phase, all can be good (or bad). History will tell.

There are a few annoying things about Boyd's book. Being a collection of essays, the point of view shifts uncomfortably from section to section. Sometimes Boyd is writing for the general public, sometimes for the initiated critics, historians, and fellow architects. Sometimes he is analytical, sometimes hortatory. Small price, however, to pay for the insights, the appreciative vignettes, the basic rightness of his story.

The drawings accompanying the text are by the author and are intended only to recall the buildings to the educated reader. Unfortunately, in drawing my Glass House he omitted the axially symmetrical entrance door, which changes the character of the design. Accidents will happen. In all sketches of this kind, the sketcher sees what he wants to see. The axiality of the Glass House was *not* what he wanted. Postage-stamp-size photographs would surely have done as well.

On the Art of Architecture

The Seven Crutches of
Modern Architecture

*Informal talk to students, School of
Architectural Design, Harvard University,
December 7, 1954; published in* Perspecta 3
(1955), 40–44.

*This is still the best and wittiest discussion of the plight of architectural theory
in a pluralist and existentialist society. But how the worm does turn! Now the
dreaded crutch for many architects of the younger generation is not the
utilitarianism that Johnson fought in his architectural youth, but rather an
emerging historicism. And, despite all his disclaimers, and however abstract and
seemingly uncompromising the images of his buildings may seem, in day-to-day
professional practice Johnson remains a functionalist to the core.*

*One can only begin to imagine the impact Johnson's "Seven Crutches" must
have had in 1954, when they were first enumerated in a talk at the School of
Architectural Design. The afterglow of Gropius's ideas was still very bright at
Harvard in those days, and much of what Johnson said was surely regarded as
pure heresy by the faculty, if not by the students. Not surprisingly, the talk was
published by the students at Yale, where Johnson's point of view was far more
sympathetically embraced than at Harvard. And my own reading of it in
Perspecta when I began to study architecture made me an instant convert: as if
in answer to what then seemed (and continue to seem to me) the pseudo-rules of a
banal first-year studio, here was a document that appeared to say it all. With a
couple of classmates, I hopped in a car on a Saturday afternoon, drove to New
Canaan, and signed up for that continuing Glass House seminar on architecture
which Yale did not list in its catalog for the late 1950's and early 1960's, but
which existed nonetheless, contributing a primary influence on a whole younger
generation of architects trained in New Haven.* [1]

*Then as now, Johnson stands for intelligence; for a commitment to action
within a framework of ideas; a love for architecture as a manifestation of culture
and not merely as a by-product of mathematics, utility, and technology.*

1. *For a further discussion of this, see Robert A. M. Stern, "Yale 1950–1965,"*
Oppositions 4 *(October 1974). Published for the Institute for Architecture and Urban Studies
by Wittenborn Art Books, Inc., New York.*

Art has nothing to do with intellectural pursuit—it shouldn't be in a university at all. Art should be practiced in gutters—pardon me, in attics.

You can't learn architecture any more than you can learn a sense of music or of painting. You shouldn't talk about art, you should do it.

If I seem to go into words it's because there's no other way to communicate. We have to descend to the world around us if we are to battle it. We have to use words to put the "word" people back where they belong.

So I'm going to attack the seven crutches of architecture. Some of us rejoice in the crutches and pretend that we're walking and that poor other people with two feet are slightly handicapped. But we all use them at times, and especially in the schools where you have to use language. It's only natural to use language when you're teaching, because how are teachers to mark you? "Bad entrance" or "Bathrooms not backed up" or "Stairway too narrow" or "Where's head room?," "Chimney won't draw," "Kitchen too far from dining room." It is so much easier for the faculty to set up a set of rules that you can be marked against. They can't say "That's ugly." For you can answer that for you it is good-looking, and *de gustibus non est disputandum*. Schools therefore are especially prone to using these crutches. I would certainly use them if I were teaching, because I couldn't criticize extra-aesthetic props any better than any other teacher.

The most important crutch in recent times is not valid now: the Crutch of History. In the old days you could always rely on books. You could say, "What do you mean you don't like my tower? There it is in Wren." Or, "They did that on the Subtreasury Building—why can't I do it?" History doesn't bother us very much now.

But the next one is still with us today although, here again, the Crutch of Pretty Drawing is pretty well gone. There are those of us—I am one—who have made a sort of cult of the pretty plan. It's a wonderful crutch because you can give yourself the illusion that you are creating architecture while you're making pretty drawings. Fundamentally, architecture is something you build and put together, and people walk in and they like it. But that's too hard. Pretty pictures are easier.

The next one, the third one, is the Crutch of Utility, of Usefulness. This is where I was brought up, and I've used it myself; it was an old Harvard habit.

They say a building is good architecture if it works. Of course, this is poppycock. All buildings work. This building [referring to Hunt Hall] works perfectly—if I talk loud enough. The Parthenon probably worked perfectly well for the ceremonies that they used it for. In other words, merely that a building works is not sufficient. You expect that it works. You expect a kitchen hot-water faucet to run hot water these days. You expect any architect, a graduate of Harvard or not, to be able to put the kitchen in the right place. But when it's used as a crutch it impedes. It lulls you into thinking that that is architecture. The rules that we've all been brought up on—"The coat closet should be near the front door in a house," "Cross-ventilation is a necessity,"—these rules are not very important for architecture. That we should have a front door to come in and a back door to carry the garbage out—pretty good, but in my house I noticed to my horror the other day that I carried the garbage out the front door. If the business of getting the house to run well takes precedence over your artistic invention the result won't be architecture at all; merely an assemblage of useful parts. You will recognize it next time you're doing a building: you'll be so satisfied when you get the banks of elevators to come out at the right floor you'll think your skyscraper is finished. I know. I'm just working on one.

That's not as bad, though, as the next one: The Crutch of Comfort. That's a habit that we come by, the same as utility. We are all descended from John Stuart Mill in our thinking. After all, what is architecture for but the comforts of the people that live there? But when that is made into a crutch for doing architecture, environmental control starts to replace architecture. Pretty soon you'll be doing controlled environmental houses which aren't hard to do except that you may have a window on the west and you can't control the sun. There isn't an overhang in the world, there isn't a sun chart in Harvard University that will help. Because, of course, the sun is absolutely everywhere. You know what they mean by controlled environment—it is the study of "microclimatology," which is the science that tells you how to recreate a climate so that you will be comfortable. But are you? The fireplace, for example, is out of place in the controlled environment of a house. It heats up and throws off thermostats. But I like the beauty of a fireplace so I keep my thermostat way down to 60, and then I light a big roaring fire so I can move back and forth. Now that's not controlled environment. I control the environment. It's a lot more fun.

Some people say that chairs are good-looking that are comfortable. Are they? I think that comfort is a function of whether you think the chair is good-looking or not. Just test it yourself. (Except I know you won't be honest with me.) I have had Mies van der Rohe chairs now for twenty-five years in my home wherever I go. They're not very comfortable chairs, but, if people like the looks of them they say "Aren't these beautiful chairs," which indeed they are. Then they'll sit in them and say, "My, aren't they comfortable." If, however, they're the kind of people who think curving steel legs are an ugly way to hold up a chair they'll say "My, what uncomfortable chairs."

The Crutch of Cheapness. That is one that you haven't run into as students because no one's told you to cut $10,000 off the budget, because you haven't built anything. But that'll be your first lesson. The cheapness boys will say "Anybody can build an expensive house. Ah, but see, my house only cost $25,000." Anybody that can build a $25,000 house has indeed reason to be proud, but is he talking about architecture or his economic ability? Is it the crutch you're talking about, or is it architecture? That economic motive, for instance, goes in New York so far that the real-estate-minded people consider it un-American to build a Lever House with no rentals on the ground floor. They find that it's an architectural sin not to fill the envelope.

Then there's another very bad crutch that you will get much later in your career. Please, please watch out for this one: the Crutch of Serving the Client. You can escape all criticism if you can say, "Well, the client wanted it that way." Mr. Hood, one of our really great architects, talked exactly that way. He would put a Gothic door on a skyscraper and say "Why shouldn't I? The client wanted a Gothic door on the modern skyscraper, and I put it on. Because what is my business? Am I not here to please my client?" As one of the boys asked me during the dinner before the lecture, where do you draw the line? When do the client's demands permit you to shoot him and when do you give in gracefully? It's got to be clear, back in your own mind, that serving the client is one thing and the art of architecture another.

Perhaps the most trouble of all is the Crutch of Structure. That gets awfully near home because, of course, I use it all the time myself. I'm going to go on using it. You have to use something. Like Bucky Fuller, who's going around from school to school—it's like a hurricane, you can't miss it if it's coming: he talks, you know, for five or six hours, and he ends up that all architecture is nonsense, and you have to build something like discontinuous domes. The arguments are beautiful. I have nothing against discontinuous domes, but for goodness sake, let's not call it architecture. Have you ever seen Bucky trying to put a door into one of his domed buildings? He's never succeeded, and wisely, when he does them, he doesn't put any covering on them, so they are magnificent pieces of pure sculpture. Sculpture alone cannot result in architecture because architecture has problems that Bucky Fuller has not faced, like how do you get in and out. Structure is a very dangerous thing to cling to. You can be led to believe that clear structure clearly expressed will end up being architecture by itself. You say "I don't have to design any more. All I have to do is make a clean structural order." I have believed this off and on myself. It's a very nice crutch, you see, because, after all, you can't mess up a building too badly if the bays are all equal and all the windows the same size.

Now why should we at this stage be that crutch-conscious? Why should we not step right up to it and face it: the act of creation. The act of creation, like birth and death, you have to face by yourself. There aren't any rules; there is no one to tell you whether your one choice out of, say, six billion for the proportion of a window is going to be right. No one can go with you into that room where you make the final decision. You can't escape it anyhow; why fight it? Why not realize that architecture is the sum of inescapable artistic decisions that you have to make. If you're strong you can make them.

I like the thought that what we are to do on this earth is to embellish it for its greater beauty, so that oncoming generations can look back to the shapes we leave here and get the same thrill that I get in looking back at theirs—at the Parthenon, at Chartres Cathedral. That is the duty—I doubt if I get around to it in my generation—the difficulties are too many, but you can. You can if you're strong enough not to bother with the crutches, and face the fact that to create something is a direct experience.

I like Corbusier's definition of architecture. He expressed it the way I wish I could have: *"L'architecture, c'est le jeu, savant, correct et magnifique, des formes sous la lumière"*—"Architecture is the play of forms under the light, the play of forms correct, wise, and magnificent." The play of forms under the light. And, my friends, that's all it is. You can embellish architecture by putting toilets in. But there was great architecture long before the toilet was invented. I like Nietzsche's definition—that much-misunderstood European—he said, "In architectural works, man's pride, man's triumph over gravitation, man's will to power assume visible form. Architecture is a veritable oratory of power made by form."

Now my position in all this is obviously not as solipsistic, not as directly intuitional as all that sounds. To get back to earth, what do we do next? if we don't hang on to any of these crutches. I'm a traditionalist. I believe in history. I mean by tradition the carrying out, in freedom, the development of a certain basic approach to architecture which we find upon beginning our work here. I do not believe in perpetual revolution in architecture. I do not strive for originality. As Mies once told me, "Philip, it is much better to be good than to be original." I believe that. We have very fortunately the work of our spiritual fathers to build on. We hate them, of course, as all spiritual sons hate all spiritual fathers, but we can't ignore them, nor can we deny their greatness. The men, of course, that I refer to: Walter Gropius, Le Corbusier and Mies van der Rohe. Frank Lloyd Wright I should include—the greatest architect of the nineteenth century. Isn't it wonderful to have behind us the tradition, the work that those men have done? Can you imagine being alive at a more wonderful time? Never in history was the tradition so clearly demarked, never were the great men so great, never could we learn so much from them and go our own way, without feeling constricted by any style, and knowing that what we do is going to be the architecture of the future, and not be afraid that we wander into some little bypath, like today's romanticists where nothing can possibly evolve. In that sense I am a traditionalist.

The Seven Shibboleths
of Our Profession

*Speech, 11th Annual Northeast
Regional A.I.A. Conference, Oceanlake,
Oregon, October 12, 1962;
previously unpublished.*

*This essay is a corollary to "The Seven Crutches of Modern Architecture."
Not so much a comment on the art of architecture as an indictment of the conduct
of the profession, it reflects Johnson's concern for the future of the Modern
Movement as he observes a late manifestation of the International Style becoming
the dominant formal expression of the corporate commercial programs of the
1950's, and once-radicalized architects participating in "mid-century American
affluence." This indictment of the "business' orientation of mainstream modern
architecture not only testifies to the success of American architectural practice in
the 1950's and 1960's, but also reflects Johnson's view of his own career as
somehow purer than that of many of his colleagues. Of course, he fails to mention
that personal circumstances permit him better than most to support his ideological
commitment and remain independent of the marketplace. Johnson's anti-
commercialism should also be considered in light of his current practice, which
has become increasingly involved in the kinds of programs and issues he was so
exercised about in the late 1950's and early 1960's.*

What is wrong with our Art of Building today? I think we all feel slightly ill at ease about it. In the midst of the most affluent society the world has ever seen, is our Art the greatest the world has ever seen?

To ask is to answer—NO.

Compare, if you will, the state of our art with the art of painting and sculpture in our day and country. In past ages, we read in history, architecture was the mother, the patron of the other arts. Though Michelangelo and Bernini were both sculptors and architects, there is no doubt which art was considered primary in their day.

Today—and I refer you to the Seattle Fair—the painters and sculptors have the advantage. I do not say that the *architects* of the Fair are poor architects—exactly the opposite; I maintain they are the finest—but the total impression—at least to us foreigners from the East Coast—is that the painters and sculptors are free spirits, accomplishing really new formulations on canvas and stone for our culture. They make valiant and magnificent forms for us.

I feel the architects were hampered. They could build no Crystal Palace as in 1851, no Eiffel Tower as in 1889. They could build no White City as in 1893. They could build no Palace of Fine Arts as in 1915.

And safely I can prophesy that the picture will be gloomier in New York in 1964. There the thirty-year-old sewer lines impose the new plan. Paul Manship's crude steel ball replaces Seattle's soaring Space Needle; and there is to be no fine-arts section at all. So much for World's Fair culture!

No, the painters have every advantage over us today. Besides being able to tear up their failures—we never can seem to grow ivy fast enough—their materials cost them nothing. They have no committees of laymen telling them what to do. They have no deadlines, no budgets. True, an architect leads a hard life—for an artist.

True, but is there perhaps a way we can help ourselves more than we do? If the artists are free, can we architects make ourselves more free? If we have drudgery and practical headaches, is a revolt possible? Is there no way out?

I think so. To me there are seven reasons for our condition in the midst of this mid-century American affluence. There are seven (probably more, but I am fond of the number seven) values of life, seven shibboleths, which we can perhaps change. A shibboleth, you remember, is a criterion, a catchword, a touchstone. Well, I shall pick seven virtues or values of our culture which in turn by their very nature have become *obstacles* to the practice of architecture as an art. All seven are good, clean virtues, but when turned into shibboleths they can hurt.

The obvious number one is *Utility*. Surely no one can say that a building should not be useful. But the danger is in stopping there, saying to ourselves, "Well, at least I designed a useful building." Alas, ninety percent of what we design are *merely* useful buildings—naturally not architecture; but do we even try hard enough on the other ten percent?

We have every right to blame the times we live in. It is a materialistic age. The arts and crafts of the Middle Ages went into church buildings, not office buildings. We live in a world of business and school committees who want useful buildings. In fact, *Utilitarianism* is a one-word definition of our scale of values. We check every other value pragmatically. "What use is it?" "Does he really mean business?," etc. These are *the* important questions in our culture. Small wonder that we architects, a small cog indeed in this vast machine, are influenced by it—and away from art.

Actually we architects in America are a smaller cog than anywhere else in the world. I wonder if it is true, as I have heard, that ninety percent of the cubic feet built in this country are built without any architect? And I do not wonder, I know, how little of the ten percent that is left which has an architect's name on it is really "designed" (in quotes), since most of the cubage has the stamp of an architect to comply with the law, but otherwise is manufactured (if that is the word) by a package company that employs architects as necessary evils in its back rooms.

We are almost helpless; our business clients on the one side, our non-paying artistic inclinations on the other. But let us not get sucked in too far. Maybe if we can be conscious of false values, we can resist better.

Erich Mendelsohn once said, "An architect is remembered by his one-room buildings." A corollary might be, an architect does his best work in non-useful or downright anti-useful buildings. The two prizes that I have received from our profession were both for anti-useful buildings, the Roofless Church in Indiana and the monumental Nuclear Reactor in Israel. I do not feel posterity is going to get excited about my college dormitories and office buildings. Incidentally, my most famous house, the Glass House, if not anti-useful, is at least non-useful, or at least it is often attacked as such.

The second shibboleth to question is a corollary of the first; the value called *Economy*. It is surely a virtue, one must say, to be able to build cheaply. But is it art? Are not all the memorable buildings of the world expensive? I once figured out, erroneously no doubt, that the equivalent cost of the Parthenon, if we were to apply most of the workmen and talent of America over thirty years to build a monument, would be some twenty billion or so. True, it is not much when we think of forty billion for a single trip to the moon, but from our worm's eye point of view in the profession, it would be heaven. Think of all that marble, all that bronze!

And why should we not spend the money? Our economy needs a lift, our cities need redoing. What a WPA project! And what a cultural lift! First, the critics of America might be more impressed with us. We might even be compared with the great Mayan culture. After all, cultures are remembered by their expensive buildings.

Maybe, again, there is little we architects can do. We are all sickeningly familiar with the final cuts to our plans at the last moment: why not take out the landscaping, the retaining walls, the colonnades? The building would be just as useful and much cheaper.

The word *cheap* brings me to my third shibboleth: *Material Progress.* The so-called virtue of cheapness can make us use brick instead of marble, cement block instead of brick, aluminum instead of bronze, two-inch partitions instead of six. This "virtue" (in quotes) leads to another, the lure of a new material. The cult of progress has brought some good things—steel and glass, for example; but it is not necessarily better to be novel. Plastics are not always good and beautiful. Granite is better and more beautiful. Mies van der Rohe judges material by how beautifully it ages: parchment, marble, bronze, grow old beautifully.

Same for technology: A hyperbolic paraboloid roof is a new technique, but will it be art? Sometimes; and so will a fieldstone lintel. (Stonehenge!) Pre-cast concrete, the panacea for our decade, *is* really a miserable material and strangely enough often more expensive, in New York at least, than limestone.

But again, we live in an age of progress, which again rubs off on our psyches. I wish I could fight it, but let me add parenthetically, I fall for all these virtues myself. I chortle with joy when I build a cheaper, newer building for a smiling client. I have even built one pre-cast building. I am always delighted when a smart salesman comes to the office with a *new* something or other that will catch my progressive fancy. We can't abstract ourselves from society. Only the really great, like perhaps Frank Lloyd Wright or Le Corbusier, can do that.

As we believe in Progress, with a capital *P,* in technology, so do we in Progress for Human Betterment. We believe in it so thoroughly that one of our most distinguished architectural schools has now become a School of Environmental Studies. I have heard no protests from artists at the switch. It seems perfectly natural in our melioristic, materialistic world that it be more important scientifically to analyze and physically to improve our surroundings than to go in for "prima donna" architecture and useless monuments. This shibboleth of *Social Progress* (my fourth, by the way, if you are keeping count) is eminently unimpeachable. I would rather be known to be against motherhood! Only a little voice way inside keeps saying (and perhaps today out loud, too, since this meeting has been called on "The Art of Building") "where is art?" Can't we have Art with a capital *A,* as well as Progress with a capital *P?* Are we to have no buildings for vicarious pride any more? We used to have. The plan and the old buildings of Washington, D.C., we still visit. The New England church, the Southern mansion, our California missions, and more lately that most glorious monument to uselessness, Maybeck's Fair buildings in San Francisco.

Now that it occurs to me, the Palace of Fine Arts is my private touch-stone for this meeting. It represents *my* criterion. It is *my* password of the day. It was built for glory alone; it was expensive; it will again be expensive to fix up. It represents the will of the community, a sort of monumental symbol for San Franciscans. A great public symbol, almost a temple. There are no overtones of progress, of technology (quite the opposite!). It helps no poor person to a better kitchen. It is useless. It is just plain glory. And San Franciscans (unlike New Yorkers, who won't even stir a finger to save their doomed glory—Pennsylvania Station) are going to preserve it. Why save it? I answer: Why should the question arise? There is no reason but art.

I suppose housing and roads and factories are terribly important, but the Art of Building is not going to be furthered by such a study. We do not know how the Greeks lived—like pigs, some tell us—but their temples we remember, their art we remember, their poetry we remember. Let us not get so carried away with material progress that we forget the Art of Building.

Another result of our cultural pattern is our fifth shibboleth: *The idea that our buildings be democratically acceptable* to at least a majority. At its worst this virtue leads to a vanity about magazine and book popularity which can be disgusting. But it is a legitimate virtue. No one wants to be a non-building architect. All of us believe in our own non-hermit, non-monastic society. We legitimately want to belong. We like praise. But, do we not like it more sometimes than integrity itself? Do we not sometimes design for the pages of the *Architectural Forum,* do we not design too deliberately for an Ezra Stoller color shot? Is it not merely fashion we aim for? And I speak for a great number of us. It is clear from a few names what integrity and non-fashionableness really mean. Lou Kahn and Mies van der Rohe are way outside the world of fashion. And do we not admire tham all the more because of it? Is it perhaps not our duty as architects to stand sometimes against the mass?

Another danger of our mass identification today, our immersion in what Wright called the mobocracy, is an identification with what we might call our Establishment—namely the world of business. It is surely a virtue of sorts to belong, but the shibboleth of *Democratic Capitalism* can be a danger. "We have to make money, don't we?" "We had to take that job to pay our overhead." These are indeed problems, but they have precious little to do with the Art of Building. You remember perhaps Whistler's answer to a young painter who showed him some rather inferior work he had done. "Well," the young man said in self-defense, "one must live." Whereupon Whistler answered, "Not necessarily." Eating is not as important as art. *Ars longa vita brevis,* said the Romans.

Soon, under the influence of the marketplace, we architects begin to count our success in dollars of income. One architect—who shall remain nameless—once told me of his $600,000 "take" one year. He had the grace to be almost ashamed, but he was pleased at this sign of success, and I must admit, I was envious. Imagine envy of a few thousand dollars. I *ought* to be envious only of Lou Kahn, Le Corbusier, the immortals, whom no money can touch.

But architects are much like other people. We are tempted when we are shown the cities of the plain. So much so that we organize teams and even stock companies in those states that allow it. We have organization charts, all the paraphernalia of big business. The American pride of bigness overtakes us. The head of the firm can no longer design or practice architecture in any sense. Instead he flies around the country "selling" jobs. Then, for a very important job, he sets a *team* of designers (boys in the back room) to work and picks what he and the client can find out of the chaos. Architecture has *become* business—Madison Avenue business.

Architecture has even been defended as the outcome of teamwork, by some of our leading masters of the art. It is said architecture is too complex for the artist alone. It is necessary and wise to have a team. A strange concept, born of a business world! Can you imagine Michelangelo, who had in his day far more work than he could do, making up a team for finishing St. Peter's? Perhaps Matisse needed some help finishing his chapel at Vence? Can you imagine what these artists would have answered you? Have you ever heard of a Frank Lloyd Wright team or a Le Corbusier team? No, the attack on prima donna architecture is made by those who do not love architecture. And the answer to them is easy; to quote J. J. P. Oud, the great Dutch architect, "What would they have instead of prima donna architecture, chorus architecture?"

Maybe that is the best we can do in America. It is, alas, only too true that the individual, artistically gifted youngster is woefully inadequate in the game of finance, estimating, cost cutting, speedup, deadline meeting, that the business clients of our day have become used to. The non-building artists of our day are often impractical dreamers whom practical people are right, perhaps, not wholly to trust. We can only accomplish as artists what our patrons will stand still for. We cannot expect them to change to Medicis and Pope Juliuses overnight. We cannot step out of our times.

But could we not fight just a little bit harder for art—for *our* art—than we do? Instead of fighting for our art, what do we do? And not just as individual artists, but even under the banner of our professional organization, the A.I.A. We offer ourselves as a "service" profession, a humiliating, salesmanlike verbiage. A shibboleth indeed! *Service* is certainly a virtue, and terrible architects we would be, if we did not serve. By all means service. But how far does service go? Are we, hat in hand, to go to the back door of our clients' homes? Do we rate higher than the Fuller Brush man? How much higher? Madam will have a Rococo boudoir? Certainly, madam. Mr. Developer, will you have a little split-level-Colonial-ranch-home touch to your development? Certainly, sir. Mr. Bank President, you need another million a year income and therefore want to cover over the entire block so no one can see your building at all? Certainly, Mr. Bank President.

Raymond Hood, in the twenties, told me he was perfectly willing to put a Gothic doorway on one of his modern skyscrapers if he was asked to. "Is that not our business," he said, "to serve the client?" And this year we are asked by our leaders to expand our services. I have not heard them issue a call to expand an artist's work! Maybe we should appoint ourselves a committee of the five or six of you who would join me, a "Committee for Taking Ten Minutes out of the Office Day to Think about the Art of Architecture." On second thought, the name of the committee would be too long, and our national headquarters would never permit it.

Perhaps we do not have to go so far as Frank Lloyd Wright in individual crankiness. He said, you remember, that he was indeed arrogant, but he preferred an honest arrogance to a false humility. He lost many clients, but it is possible he may be remembered more than most of his contemporaries. And he may be remembered for just those virtues that seem contrary to the virtues most of us practice.

Which brings us to the point of this discourse: Are the virtues we live by really good for us as artists? I have named seven this morning, seven good values, seven touchstones, that we use daily in defending our work to ourselves and to the world—seven shibboleths.

We have talked about the virtue of *Utility,* but we find that the useless are the most beautiful. Who can use the Parthenon or Maybeck's Palace? We have talked about *Economics*—yet great buildings are always very, very expensive. We have talked of *Material Progress,* that we ought to use the newest techniques, the newest materials; but are not granite and bronze still the most beautiful of materials? We talked of *Social Progress,* which heaven knows we need; but is not art longer than life, is not art outside social values? We mentioned *Art to Please the Majority;* but does this not become a mere popularity contest for magazine approval? We mentioned the necessity and virtue of *Earning Money* for our families, the need to organize as a business; but when we do, do we not find less and less leisure for thinking, sketching, designing—in short for art? And lastly we have mentioned the virtue of *Service,* which is apt to put us on a level part way between a salesman and an exterior decorator.

No! Painters and sculptors in this culture are luckier than we. None of these terrible dilemmas confine their thinking. No wonder their status has been rewarded even on the marketplace. The value of paintings in the last twenty years has gone up 1,300 percent, as against automobiles, 400 percent. Quite a tribute to the art of painting on the part of our business public! Has your net grown similarly? I don't have to ask; even that barometer fails us.

No! We, as artists, are in trouble, not to mention our difficulties as businessmen. And surely it is not our fault but that of the times, the clients, the climate of opinion which is so definitely against us. Our status is low. Why, in New York State, members of the medical profession, that great profession of Dr. Kildares, have special license plates on their cars. The profession of journalism can carry a PRESS sign in their windshields and park with impunity; we get tagged when we so much as park at our job sites. I mention automobiles and parking advisedly, since they are the status symbols dearest to the American heart. I can't wait personally till I can afford a long, black Cadillac with chauffeur, a low license number with some sort—any sort—of badge that will let me in places.

But these are vain dreams today! Michelangelo in his day was called the Divine, while he was still alive. Frank Lloyd Wright was considered a crank. Louis Sullivan died an unappreciated pauper.

And yet, could we not be the artists of our environment? It seems to me, prejudiced though I know I am, that we *could* rebuild our country closer to our hearts' desire, so that our culture could outstrip all others in history in building, as we do in science and technology. Are we less in any way than the Italians of the quattrocento?

I can't believe it is a matter of inborn talent, that we are not as great as in the Renaissance. It is a matter of values—of what we in America think is important. We spend money on military hardware, liquor, hairdressers, automobiles. We could—if we were so inclined—spend money on making America beautiful. If we thought it important to build magnificently, I maintain we could build magnificently.

We may not make it in our lifetime. But hope we must. *Ars longa, vita brevis.* Life is short, but art is long.

Whence and Whither:
The Processional Element
in Architecture

From Perspecta 9/10 (1965), 167–78.

Johnson's fundamental premise—that architecture can be qualified as any one thing, whether Wrightian-Rudolphian-Zevian "space," or Corbusian sculptural shapes (either mass or void), or his own "organization of procession"—seems uncharacteristically simplistic. Yet if one goes beyond this, the essay is a serious contribution to the as yet rather stunted body of modern architectural theory. Written especially for Perspecta, *it offers a clear analysis of the role of procession (i.e., spatial sequence in time) in archetypal situations, from the Parthenon through the Seagram Building and the Carpenter Center. Johnson reminds us that architecture is related to time, not in the pseudo-scientific way Giedion proposed, but in an experiential sense, dependent on the multiple perceptions of a man in motion and not frozen in place as in a photograph. In this regard, Johnson's essay can be seen as complementary to Christian Norberg-Schultz's writings and to the work of Kevin Lynch, especially his book* The Image of the City.*

The false lure of photography is a theme Johnson returns to from time to time. Much as he admires the very cool, super-real photography of Ezra Stoller (he used to say that no building of his was "official" until it had been "Stollerized"), he, like his colleague, Henry-Russell Hitchcock, is critical of those who judge buildings from photographs, and, like Hitchcock, he almost never comments on a building he has not seen at firsthand, that is, experienced "processionally."

Architecture is surely *not* the design of space, certainly not the massing or organizing of volumes. These are auxiliary to the main point, which is the organization of procession. Architecture exists only in *time*. (That is the modern perversion of photography. It freezes architecture to three dimensions, or some buildings to two.)

It is known to the veriest tourist how much more he enjoys the Parthenon because he has to walk up the Acropolis, how much less he enjoys Chartres Cathedral because he is unceremoniously dumped in front of it. How much better St. Peter's Square used to be before Mussolini ruined (opened up) the approaches. Vincent Scully's temples in *The Earth, The Temples and the Gods* are sited for approach as well as all the other considerations he has outlined for us.

But approach is only one aspect of processional, one moment of feeling. The next is the experience of entering, the shock of big space, or dark space, as it encloses (in time always) the visitor.

The Parthenon itself has no entering experience. Its entire feeling of procession is taken care of by the Propylaeum. The entire feeling of St. Peter's is taken care of, or was, by the filtering in through the barricade of Bernini's columns.

For modern examples take Mies's Seagram Plaza: the visitor crosses usually diagonally (an old Choisy-Beaux-Arts principle). Then he penetrates only glass, slowing slightly, to be faced with the three elevator corridors. But what elevator corridors! It seems simple enough, now that they are there, but compare these with any other. Where else in a modern skyscraper entry is the ceiling twenty-four feet high, or where else are the elevator lobbies in a direct line from the street? The visitor can look back to Park Avenue as he waits for the ride. In every other building there is a corner to be negotiated. The visitor has to wait in the first, second, or third box, has to take the first, second, or third turning to the left or right. In Seagram's it is a straight line.

Unfortunately, the entire experience of Seagram's leads but to the elevator, which, next to the automobile, ranks with the destroyers of architectural glory. That claustrophobic box brings visual, processional beauty to a complete dead stop. The visitor can only be restored, if at all, by looking out a high window. Elevators are here to stay, but one is not forced to love them.

Much better in that regard is the Guggenheim. (Never use the elevator! It murders Wright's great space.) The processional entrance experience is different from Mies's. It is again diagonal, but the jump into the hundred-foot-high hall is exactly the opposite kind of feeling from the typical grand axial entry to Seagram's. The visitor comes through a tiny door (too tiny, some feel) and is sprayed into the room. Breathtaking it is.

In both cases, the experiences are not static but temporal. The beauty consists in how you move into the space. There are as many ways of introducing space as there are architects, but it strikes me that clarity is one of the prerequisites. At least in the Guggenheim and in Seagram's the processional is as clean as the Acropolis or St. Peter's. The walker-through-the-space is never lost, ever in the slightest doubt as to his orientation, whence he has come or whither he aims. *Whence* and *whither* are positive, not negative, architectural virtues which are basic to the entire discipline of the art.

Take an extreme example, Le Corbusier's building for Harvard. Heaven knows it is easy to get lost in the basement. (What a surprise it is to come upon the "front" door with its label "Carpenter Hall.") Yet the building is, as a whole, a beautiful study in processional excitement—even a study in "clarity." It is impossible to miss the effects that Le Corbusier has prepared. The shifting, rising, declining, turning path that he forces on us gives varied, solemn, laughable Coney Island experiences that please the stomach. The feeling of "entrance" is certainly lacking, since one enters only to be thrown out into the street in the next block, but what fun! (There is a report that the main entrances in the early studies used to be off the ramps. It would seem more logical than the present arrangement.)

In contrast, take Paul Rudolph's Art and Architecture Building at Yale (interestingly enough built to house similar functions to Le Corbusier's Harvard building). The approach is, to say the least, off axis. Like Frank Lloyd Wright's Buffalo Larkin Building, the main door does not exist. At Yale, bicycles are kept there. A postern entry only—a side gate. The explosion into space is again like Larkin and, like Larkin, very impressive indeed. There are, however, no further attempts at clarity, but rather a mannerist (do we dare use the word Mannerist?) play of spaces off the main space (Imperial Hotel Lobby?), which baffles and intrigues. I shall probably have to take back what I wrote in the previous page about clarity being of the essence. The House of Architecture has many mansions. There are, I guess, no rules.

But for me there are. So let us take an example from work in progress, my design for the temenos in which is to sit the Kline Science Tower at Yale. Again the design may or may not succeed, but an artist's intention is at least of direct, though in the end only marginal, importance.

What I intend there is space seen in motion. A walk with change in direction with changing objectives. Also a slipping by of people, like a Giacometti "Place," like the diagonal walkings on the Seagram Plaza. Primary to this is clarity. One cannot, I hope, for a second be confused or, worse, annoyed in the turnings. One is forced to the entry of the Tower.

Walking up the hill at the upper end of Hillhouse, you enter through a propylaeum, a covered, columned portico. To the right the bastion of Gibbs; straight ahead—nothing. Perhaps in the future other buildings will rise above the cincture wall. Before you a paved square section with a colossal statue placed, I hope, inevitably; a point around which movement can circulate. Dominating your view is, however, immediately to your left, the Tower with its 100-foot-wide entrance steps. (It is too bad that the great increase in population has made great staircases obsolete. It was contrariwise lucky that the Mayans did not mind steep inclines. Our stair is modest.)

Before you enter the Tower, you note at the north, or right of it, a grove of young trees, shade, green in the summer, twigging in the winter.

An alien but relieving element. The temenos is not square but rectangular, and the Tower penetrates one corner far enough to call the remaining space an ell.

How it is enclosed is a major point. There can be no space without enclosure. West, a brick wall against Sterling (we are ten feet below grade here, which increases enclosedness), vines over the parapet, etc. The north, one brick wall, broken by an entrance from the Kline Chemistry on the left. The east corner, a vista—tightened by Gibbs and the wall— of East Rock, a visual proof that we are high ourselves. The east, Gibbs Laboratories; the south, the propylaeum and a retaining wall, a view down Hillhouse. A wall going down is as enclosing as one going up. Vézelay, Monte Pincio, Villa d'Este. And a going-down containment is a quiet eye relief from too much wall.

The processions through the plaza vary. There is a back stairs in the corner to the Tower. There is the entrance between Sterling and Osborn, one on the north corner, one at the north end of Gibbs, and Gibbs's front door itself. You should be able to get *from* any door *to* any door *clearly*. That is, at any rate, the intention. The means of clarification are porticos at all entrances; walks crossing the green are thin, uninterrupted visually one to the other.

Basically, the position of the Tower itself should clarify since it is strongly axial north and south. The Tower and the base of the Tower are *both* always visible. (It has always confused me that I still cannot find the bottom of that wholly admirable landmark, Harkness Tower. How many can remember what the ground floors of the Empire State Building look like from the street?)

Inside the building, whether you enter from the front or from the rear, you enter into the foyer facing the plaza, with the plaza on one side of the long hall, the elevators on the other. With the entering of the elevator, all processional is lost; it is the end of a chapter of architecture.

A few of the attempts and results of whither-whence: The New York State Theater, whatever stand one takes on its art works or decorative features, whatever one's views of Neo-classicism *vs.* concrete, is designed as a procession. The pop up the "baroque" stairs into the Mississippi-steamboat Promenade is of the essence. So are the side stairs up to and down from the upper balconies. So are the silhouetted moving people who form the living friezes to the space. This is all a question of procession.

Memory, by the way, plays a much larger part in architectural experience than is acknowledged. One feels better in a theater seat, I contend, if the spaces traversed getting there are uncrowded *straight*—in other words, clear.

Even a remodeling: the rearranged Museum of Modern Art is a case in point. The problem was to make possible bigger crowds than before. It was approached as a problem of procession. Confine the crowds as little as possible. The design result is almost Beaux-Arts axial. A clear main axial view into the garden from the street. A cross axis leading to galleries right and left. As usual, vertical flow stopped by elevators (only the elevators at the New York State Pavilion of the Fair are pleasant). In the garden we had more luck with the vertical. We took space enough for STAIRS in the old sense. We hope people will climb stairs, an experience lost in modern architecture, the ramps of the great Le Corbusier being the noble exception. In our garden about two domestic stories are climbed by many who would never go to the attic of a suburban house without complaining. It is the experience of the change of direction of what one sees as one rises. The speed of ascent (slow in the Museum stairs) is crucial. Time to look around, to feel the change that a rise gives. The curiosity of what is on top, the question: What will I see from up there? The comfort of a slow, obvious, and wide ascent. All of these considerations are more important than the "looks" of the stairway. Architecture is motion.

A final example, an old one. My own New Canaan house was started with the driveway. Such a disturbance is the automobile that its handling is the first consideration in the design of any home. In my house I had to buy the land next door to keep the monster from seeing my glass home. It now sits lurking behind a six-foot wall. The visitor gets out without seeing the house, rounds a corner (not 90°—about 45°—very important) and sees the house at another 45°. Again a Choisy-Greek principle: never approach a building head on: the diagonal gives you a perspective of the depth of the building. To help you round the corner, to enhance the importance of the glass unit, there stands on the right a solid box, urging the visitor to turn away toward the Glass House.

The Glass House is on a promontory, a peninsula, to make a "cup" of the experience of entering. A dead end so you know you have arrived; there is no further to go. Within the house there is more procession, however. The "entrance hall" (the pushing together of the chimney and kitchen cabinet) forces you (gently, to be sure) between them into the "living room," where you climb onto the "raft" of white rug which is the ultimate arrival point, the sitting group which floats in its separate sea of dark brick.

I purposely exaggerate the processional aspects, which in reality are not obvious to the casual visitor. But then what is obvious to a visitor about the quality of architecture? I am supposed to be an architect, but I cannot tell you, nor can any historian, why the Parthenon is the masterpiece it is. We can but grasp bits and pieces.

The whence and whither is primary. Now almost secondary is all our ordinary work, our work on forms, our plans, our elevations. What we should do is to proceed on foot again and again through our imagined buildings. Then after months of approaching and re-approaching, and looking and turning, then only draw them up for the builder.

Our Ugly Cities

Commencement speech, Mount Holyoke College, June 5, 1966; published in Mount Holyoke Alumnae Quarterly, 1 (Summer, 1966), 86–88.

This essay finds Johnson in an uncharacteristic role, that of a mildly pontificating commencement orator. In spite of what now seems an over-optimistic view of what had been accomplished in the way of social progress in our cities, his mood in respect to architecture is pessimistic. The roots of his mood of pessimism lie deeper than the exigencies of the occasion; a great and productive period in his career has drawn to a conclusion. He is under the sway of "postpartum blues": Richard Foster, his partner for eight years, had decided to strike out on his own; a clutch of remarkable work is behind him, including the New York State Pavilion, the New York State Theater, the Kline Science Center; and no new major commissions seem on the horizon.

Johnson senses that our escalating commitment to the war in Vietnam is bringing with it a new anti-monumental mood and a new anti-heroic generation to give it physical expression: Moore, Venturi, and Giurgola are emerging as important figures, and he is caught off guard. For the first time since the early 1950's, he no longer commands the attention of architecture students and younger practitioners. Moreover, with relatively little work in the office, in a rather too self-conscious fashion he attempts to keep up with the emergent preoccupation with issues of "urban design," devoting a good deal of his time to a project for a so-called "Third City" in New York's East Harlem Triangle area. This abstract, grand plan for the nation's most conspicuous urban ghetto makes only too obvious and painful the alienation of the practitioners of the Modern Movement from the issues and situations which were everywhere around them, and which were to become the predominant focus of energies and concerns in the 1970's.

In this period I observed Johnson very closely, working under his direction at the Architectural League in 1965–66, and in 1966–67 assisting him in establishing themes appropriate for a television series in which he discussed new urbanistic developments in New York. Johnson's concern with urban issues manifested itself in his active support of, and participation in, John V. Lindsay's first campaign for New York's mayoralty in 1965, and in his talk about founding an institute for architecture—an idea that reached its fulfillment in The Institute for Architecture and Urban Studies, begun under the auspices of The Museum of Modern Art in 1967. Johnson formed a new professional association with a much younger architect, John Burgee (they have been partners since 1967); his practice has taken on a new vigor; and his clientele among the big real-estate developers and speculators has increased in proportion to prestigious institutional clients.

I have spent the winter designing (for my own amusement, I hasten to add) an Ideal City. It seemed to me pointless when I started and even now strikes me as the height of foolishness. No one will look at it. It will never be published, or if it is, there are very few who will read. Reading a plan is so, so difficult. And with absolute certainty, no one will build it.

The reason for telling you about my lonely troubles is to point up for you the gap, in this cultural ambience of ours, between values I hold dear and the values that make our country run.

Here we live in the most affluent society the world has ever known. No one in the old days ever dreamt of universal literacy, to say nothing of universal toilets and (heaven forbid) universal automobiles. It is clear we can have anything on this earth we want.

Yet, can we? Well, we cannot, or, as I believe, *will* not, make our environment a place of beauty, our cities works of art.

There can surely be no discussion whether we have ugliness around us or not. I never heard anyone tell me that Bridgeport was anything but an ugly city, or Waterbury, or Pawtucket, or Holyoke. And New York where I am at home, is it so handsome? Exciting, even breathtaking, but beautiful only in spots, only for a few blocks. Otherwise, for miles and miles in all directions ugliness, ugliness, ugliness.

And can there be any difference of opinion that it has been getting worse and worse? I do not think I am being distressingly old to point out that New York was handsome a mere ten years ago, and argue further that it was handsomer even then than twenty, thirty, fifty years before that.

A few examples:

Item: The Brooklyn Bridge, one of the great bridges of the world, had not yet been ruined by a double deck.

Item: The Pennsylvania Station, which cost in today's dollars 600 million, still existed to give the commuter and newcomer a great gateway to a great city. That romantic, magnificent room is gone.

Item: Coenties Slip and other water inlets in lower Manhattan still gave us a romantic feeling of contact with our harbor. No more. The water is filled in; a superhighway cuts off the water view.

Item: Park Avenue used gracefully to flow around the wedding-cake delicacy of the Grand Central building. Pan Am settled that.

Item: Fifty-ninth Street, our other great axis, now terminates in that cheapest of all cheapies, the Coliseum.

Item: The pile of needle-like '20's skyscrapers that we loved to look at from the harbor is gone, ruined by the new scale of Chase Manhattan Bank, and soon to be settled entirely by the Trade Center.

Item: Our last plaza at 59th Street and Fifth Avenue on Central Park is going now to a supercheapy, built ironically enough by our richest corporation, General Motors.

Item: We used to be able to see the water. After all, Manhattan is an island. We have finer water nearer at hand than Paris or London, yet you can see the Seine, you can see the Thames. In New York, no more. Elevated highways!

It is amusing to note that when the much maligned robber barons were building railroads into New York, they built them well, they put them underground. Must our generation then do less with the successor to the iron horse, the automobile? Why are our motor roads not underground? Only Gracie Mansion, the residence of our Mayor, looks out over the water, the cars comfortably passing underground. It can be done, do we but will it. What Commodore Vanderbilt did for our city, we can do again—for ourselves.

Item: We used to have streets lined with brownstones, now we have areas dotted with cheap brick towers, all of which are built with lowest standards possible of ceiling heights, paper-thin walls, and execrable bricklaying. In other words, we used to have slums, today we have built but superslums.

Why? Why have we done this to our cities at the same time as we have done away with illness, illiteracy, hunger. At the same time as we have given every citizen a car, an education, elegant clothes, travel. Why does part of our culture advance and part decline so disastrously?

I must admit that at 60 I am getting a little bitter, so I dream up cities where I should like to live and, meanwhile, try to figure why, outside my dreams, the city decays.

It is clear our cities decay for the same reason that our air becomes polluted. We do not care enough. But that only pushes off the answer, why don't we care. Clearly our values are oriented toward other goals than beauty. Two values stand out, two cherished goals that we Americans think more important than beauty. Money and utility. Oh yes, we like at least at church on Sundays to think of commercial values as Mammon, with a capital *M,* as an evil, but then on Monday through Friday quite the opposite. Why else would a body politic, for example, allow General Motors, of all corporations, to build a money-making cheapy on our most prestigious plaza. Why else allow an English consortium to get rich by building Pan Am athwart our greatest boulevard, on a plot of ground which surely should have been a park. Sir Kenneth Clark calls the Pan Am the worst crime against urban beauty since the Victor Emmanuel Monument in Rome. These are harsh words but true. To think that for 34 million dollars, what the land is worth, the city would have had green space at its heart—2 dollars for each metropolitan citizen.

No, we respect money and the inalienable right of everyone to make as much as he can, especially in city real estate, whether it be the bankrupt Grand Central or the richest of the rich General Motors. In Rome and Paris if a speculator wishes to build a skyscraper, he certainly can, but outside—way outside—the old city. Sad to say, in the sacred city of

Athens, on the contrary, the American system has won out. We have succeeded where 2,000 years of vandals have failed. We have built a Hilton Hotel which violates the aspect through the columns of the Parthenon itself.

This materialist-industrialist philosophy also has brought with it our love, not to say adoration, of the automobile. There are many American families that spend Sundays polishing their cars rather than making their beds. And this worshipful attitude is reflected in our public appreciation of roads for the cars. We spend each year 20 billion dollars on roads, and tax ourselves gladly to do this. We build roads everywhere, through our very town centers, slicing them in two, destroying parks and waterfronts, but what do we do for the buildings these roads lead to? Nothing. We let buildings get built by anyone who wants to make the money.

Nor is the worship of money only an attitude of the rich or the would-be rich. It permeates the entire fabric of the nation. A taxi driver taking me across the upper level of the Queensboro Bridge, looking at the vast and inspiring skyline of mid-Manhattan, said did I realize I was looking at 2 billion dollars of real estate. The inspiration to him was financial, and he was not envious, but rather proud of living in the midst of all that money.

Strangely enough, however, we also love cheapness, or rather parsimony. It shows common sense and a good business head. When Con Ed, the much disliked utility company who had such bad luck last year, built a new plant so large that it dominates our East River and *must* be seen willy-nilly from everywhere, a most public monument, they built not an architect-designed structure, not a building of stone or even brickwork, but of corrugated asbestos, by far the world's ugliest and cheapest material. No one has objected. General Motors will be praised for building a cheap building on Central Park, while Seagram's was castigated from the bench by a judge who said the company used poor business judgment to build what most of us think is quite a handsome building with quite a handsome public plaza.

Perhaps it is lucky for New York that the robber barons were "public be damned" people. At least the great Vanderbilt gave us the Grand Central Terminal as a gateway to our city; our best these days is miserable Kennedy Airport, a conglomeration of cheapies with only one glorious but small exception. Are we no longer proud of the place we live? Only too obviously not.

A natural corollary to our money values is the high value we place on utility. If a thing be not useful, away with it. In building our cities, this rules out parks (expensive, useless), post offices (cheaper to rent space in office buildings), and now soon it will be churches. Yes, the argument now runs, and among Roman Catholics even, that a building should not be built for use once a week. Religion it seems is a private thing that can be celebrated in a garage or living room. It used to be that a once-a-week room was the spiritual culmination of that week, a culmination at which the services of great architectural space would be required to celebrate a great spiritual experience. But so far has our utilitarianism triumphed over our religion that the multi-purpose, convertible church is now "in."

Out in the town where I come from our biggest boast to visitors used to be the Carnegie Library (a monumental structure), the Post Office (granite steps) and the new High School (brick and limestone). The new town will obviously have none of these. There will be no symbol, nothing but raw utility; a vision of the future: the cheaper the better. My favorite Roman Emperor, Augustus, used to boast that he had found Rome a city of brick and left it a city of marble. Now we, on the contrary, actually are proud to say that we find a city of stone and brick and are leaving it a city of pre-cast concrete and corrugated tin.

I assure you we shall not be thanked by posterity. People are very apt to judge our ancestors by their buildings. Think of Williamsburg and Salem, the White House, the Capitol. Civilizations are remembered by buildings. They are certainly not remembered by wars, business, or utility. Think of my favorite civilization, that of Teotihuacan in Mexico. We know nothing of their language, their business or where they saved money. We don't even know their name. Yet they are an immortal people. Their pyramids are greater than those of the Egyptians; their great roads, plazas, temples are still witnesses to their artistic genius. Their art of building cities has made them great even today, a thousand years after they have been wiped out.

What can we leave our future generations to wonder at? To paraphrase T. S. Eliot, "one hundred thousand miles of asphalt paving and a million lost golf balls." Add a few twisted steel skeletons, and you have the lot.

So utilitarian are our ideas that when I proposed last year a huge sloping cylinder overlooking New York Harbor as a marker for the 16 million immigrants on Ellis Island I was violently attacked for building a tomb. We should think of the future, they said; we should build a mental hospital perhaps, a school, but not a monument. What use is a monument? What use, for that matter, my friends, is beauty? Why did the Athenians bother to take 30 years and the talent of every Athenian to build the Parthenon? Not much use. They lost the war to Sparta soon after it was finished. No, not much use.

Now, I do not propose that we appropriate tomorrow the 20 to 50 million it would take in today's money to build the equivalent of the Parthenon. It is not in the cards. But to be more modest, should we not appropriate some of our billions to make our houses, our cities beautiful, if not for posterity and immortality like the Greeks, then for ourselves for the same selfish reasons we dress well, decorate our bedrooms, and grow gardens? Call it beautification if you will, can we not be surrounded by beauty? Someone is going to remind me of the horrendous cost of all this. How about the cost of *not* doing it? The cost of our dirt, pollution, traffic jams, delay, mental anguish? They are immeasurable.

No, money is not the question. The question is, for what do we expect to spend our surplus. For surplus we have. How otherwise can we go to the moon for 50 billion, how fight a war for 60 to 80 billion *each* year or build roads for 20 billion *each* year?

The method of getting the paltry few billions we need for our cities I leave to the politicians who, after all, work for us. There are a few taxes I could suggest, of course. A thousand dollars on each car. If we can afford $2,000 for a car, we can afford $3,000. Inflation will soon make them cost 3 anyway. At 7,000,000 cars a year that will bring us in 7 billion a year which would help. Right now we pay 100% and more taxes on cigarettes and liquor, and surely cars are just as sinful and just as desirable as alcohol and smoking. A good tax. Another one might be a 10% tax on war. Another nuisance tax on one of our best-loved occupations. (It must be loved or we would not spend so much on it.) That would bring us in another 6 to 8 billion. Thirdly, we can take the 10 billion federal money for roads and spend it on places for the roads to go to. So we now have 26 billion a year. What dream cities we could build. What heaven on earth.

As you have guessed, I am being somewhat fanciful. But I am convinced Americans can do what they want. And I have it on the authority of Pericles, the leader of the fifth-century Athenians who built the Parthenon, who was proud that Athens (and we) could have guns and butter—and great buildings.

On the Great Architects

Schinkel and Mies

Speech, Congress Hall, Berlin, March 13, 1961; published in German in Schriftenreihe des Architekten- und Ingeneurs-Vereins zu Berlin, *XIII, 24; English text published in* Program, *Columbia University School of Architecture (Spring, 1962), 14–34.*

Johnson's admiration for Schinkel is profound, though necessarily less personal than his admiration for Mies. Johnson first went to Germany in 1928 to study the language; in the fall of 1929 he began to study the new architecture; in 1930, he focused on the work of Mies, and this, in turn, led him in 1930–31 to undertake a tour of the work of Schinkel, about whom he intended to write a book.

In this essay, Johnson does not give us a work of history along the lines he might have pursued in the thirties; rather, Mies and Schinkel are seen critically and a little iconoclastically at virtually the precise moment when Johnson is no longer content to operate within the confines of the Miesian vocabulary (he was known in the 1950's as Mies van der Johnson). In this light, the discussion of what might be described as Schinkel's "casual" composition, his eclecticism, and the emotional qualities of his space-making takes on particular significance. For Johnson, Schinkel's relaxed, inventive Neo-classicism seemed to offer a way out of the dilemma of the moment.

The closing remarks chide Hugh Stubbins for the structural exhibitionism of his Congress Hall design. By indirection they call to task a host of other architects then all equally adrift in the personal expressionism of the International Style as it entered its middle age. In this essay, perhaps more than any other, Johnson appears to be using history as a device to clear ground between his own views of current practice and the brashness bordering on philistinism that seemed so characteristic of the innovative design of the period. Johnson seems to be saying that it is not only that one cannot not *know history, as he stated so frequently in this period, but that only the architect who understands the "tradition of the modern architecture" will prevail.*

I have come 3000 miles to Berlin to pay a debt. All my architectural designing has been influenced by the work and example of two men, two men who both had years of their best work in this city. Two men, each of whom represented in their work and their thinking the greatest spirit of their very different centuries: Mies van der Rohe, for the 20th century, and Karl Friedrich Schinkel for the 19th. It is fitting that we meet on the birthday of the one which is only a few days separated from the birthday of the other.

Neither was a native of Berlin; one from the Mark, one from the Rhineland, both found Berlin a place to work. Both worked in a defeated capital after a disastrous war. They were born within five years of one hundred years apart.

These similarities, however, one would think, would be more than outweighed by the vast differences of the centuries, so much so, that the differences of their architecture would far outweigh the similarities. Yet, in spite of the death of the Greek column orders, in spite of the new technology of the 20th century, in spite of the changes made by the revolutions in aesthetics brought in the 20's of this century by Expressionism, Cubism and their architectural counterparts swept in by the Bauhaus, the similarities are more today than the differences.

I propose to show by a study of a few buildings of each what they have in common, and the lesson that at least one architect of the second half century (myself) has learned from both. Please bear with me if the discussion is slightly technical. The principles of both great Berliners are of sufficient importance for the whole continuum of architecture to deserve some careful study.

Behind the work of both men is the culture of the post-Renaissance Western world. Both centuries share the common culture with their continuing admiration of Greece and Rome. We can almost narrow the field and call both architects Romantic Classicists. Neither of them could possibly have removed himself from this continuum. Although both were also inflenced by the revolutions of their day, yet neither was himself a revolutionary. Schinkel's work is unthinkable without a consideration of Ledoux, Boullée and Gilly, Mies without Picasso, Mondrian, Lissitsky. And yet, each was primarily a builder in traditional lines, artisan-craftsman, not a theorist and an *avant-gardist*. In one sense, Gilly was more revolutionary than his younger admirer; Gropius and Le Corbusier, more revolutionary than Mies. Both men in one word were builders, men who loved to see construction going on, whose fantasies were best when disciplined into actual buildings.

This does not mean that either was a pedestrian designer. Both, on the contrary, are to be counted in the forefront of the imaginative art of their day. This famous painting shows Schinkel as a member of the Romantic school, almost as good a painter as Caspar David Friedrich, but with more

1

165

1

1. *Karl Friedrich Schinkel,* Medieval Town by the Sea, *detail, 1813. Munich, Neue Pinakothek*

2. *Mies van der Rohe, Drawing for Friedrichstrasse Office Building, Berlin. 1921–22. New York, The Museum of Modern Art (gift of Mary Callery)*

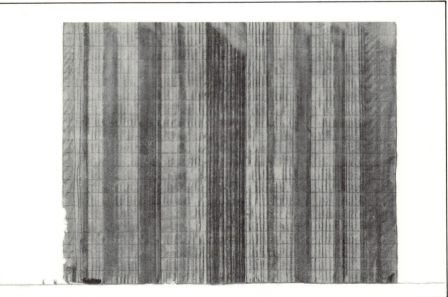

2

interest in architecture. Note that Schinkel has so reinterpreted Gothic that it is totally unbuildable, and so arranged the sunset that it permeates the stone itself. Schinkel's imagination was thoroughly "modern."

Mies's famous drawing of 1922 of his Friedrichstrasse Bahnhof is as *2* "Modern" for his day. It is Expressionist rather than Romantic. It is an elevation, not a perspective; the basic lines are even ruled. But, it is Mies's feeling for shadow and hollows of his faceted glass façade that makes it a drawing of value for itself. It is as unbuildable as Schinkel's Gothic towers, and as interesting in showing what Mies was dreaming of and what his generation was dreaming of: gossamer Gothic towers in one century; straight-line crystal palaces in another. And yet, the genius of both lay in the fact that they were both primarily interested in building buildings.

And both were founders of "schools." The word "Mies-Schüler" has not achieved the accepted status that "Schinkel-Schüler" has, yet his influence on his century is surely as great. Mies is still active in the sixties of this century, still the leading architect, at least of America, just as Schinkel (though dead by 1840) was in the sixties of the last century in Prussia. As to whether the followers of Mies are more able than Persius, Strack, and Stüler of the last century, we shall have to await history's verdict. Surely, however, New York is getting to be as Miesian a city as Berlin ever was a Schinkelesque one.

The analogy of the two centuries can be carried even further. In the 19th century, it was an English contemporary, Sir John Soane, who was a more original architect than Schinkel, more daring as an innovator, both spatially and decoratively, but who never affected his century as did Schinkel. Today, the exact contemporary of Mies is the elder genius of our time, Le Corbusier, who with vital originality causes the most excitement of the century. But Mies remains the central figure.

And so without having to decide between the geniuses of Schinkel and Mies, or deciding for that matter which of the two centuries was the more artistically creative, it will be interesting to compare the great giants.

It will be easiest if we compare a Classical building of Schinkel's with a "Classic" building of Mies, and then a more "Romantic" one of each. Our first pair of buildings will be the Altes Museum and the Seagram *3, 4* Building.

The most obvious relation is the symmetrical podium arrangement with the steps slightly more than one-third of the width of the building. Again, both plans are laid out axially symmetrical, but without any centralizing feature except the stairs themselves. Neither is a pyramidal design in the Baroque manner. Both are repetitive, columnar buildings. The Altes Museum has more columns, but both buildings have porch-like entrances.

The type of façade composition is also exactly the same in principle. *5, 6* We must allow for the fact that steel-cage construction has replaced

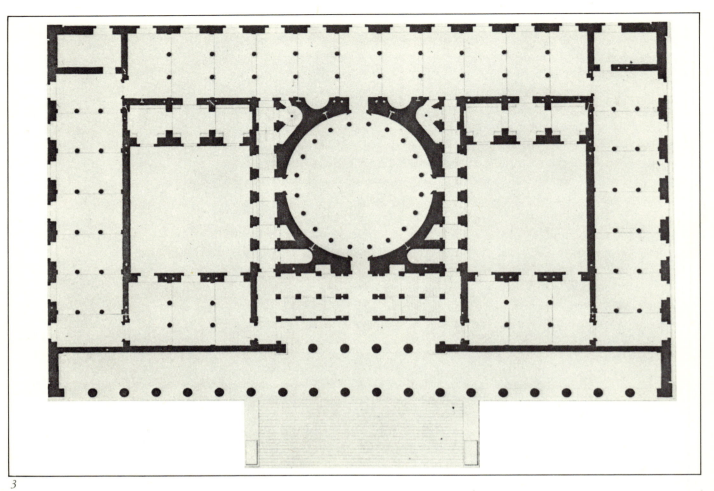

3

3. Schinkel, Plan, Altes Museum, Berlin
(Museum at the Lustgarten). 1824–30

4. Mies, Plan of Seagram Building,
New York. 1957

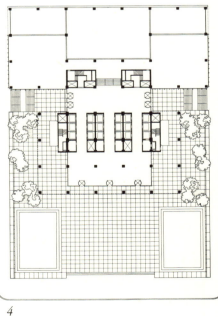

4

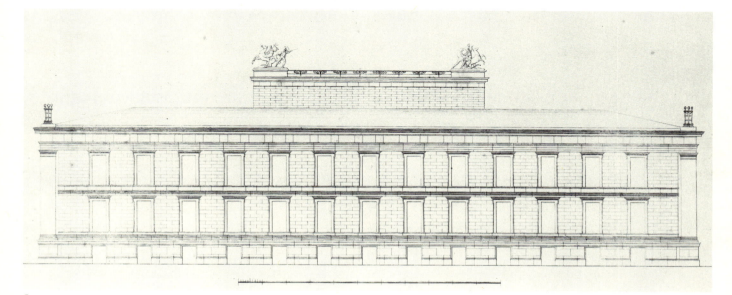

5

6

5. *North Façade of Altes Museum*

6. *West Façade of Seagram Building*

7. *Corner, Altes Museum*

8. *Corner, Seagram Building*

9. *Philip Johnson, Plan, Amon Carter Museum of Western Art, Fort Worth, Texas. 1961*

7

8

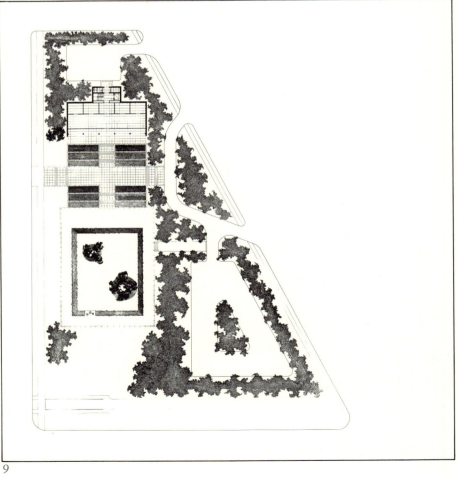

9

masonry as a structure system and that the 20th-century building is a vertical building. Nevertheless, we see the even repetition of windows without accent or change in rhythm, the whole distance. We see string courses in Schinkel's building, we see the vertical **H** mullions tying together the windows into vertical stripes. In both cases, the windows are organized into bands. They make no isolated holes in the wall, and compromise is not made with the unbroken repetitious rhythm. Both rely on good proportions, good shadows, and remarkably good corners.

In a sense architecture can be judged by corner treatment. It is, next to the cornice or top, the most senstive part of a design. Schinkel and Mies share the same approach: slow down your fenestration rhythm, introduce an element, a column, a pilaster, that will tie your building to the ground and at the same time cut off your horizontal elements.

Surely, the corner of the Altes Museum is one of the most famous in the history of architecture. The windows slow their rhythm. The last window is spaced far from the corner. The unique pilaster is of huge extra width. It is in the same plane as the wall, separated only by a groove or negative molding, and does not continue around the pilaster as do the base and the cornice. The eye is stopped, and at the same time, urged to go around the corner.

7

The corner of Seagram's is similar. The endless rhythm of the fenestration is slowed and one-half of the actual column is revealed, different, yet similar to the skin. It slows the eye just as Schinkel's pilaster; yet within the terms of steel skeleton structure. Since the column is inches behind the skin and windows, an extra plane, an extra shadow is introduced, to stop the eye from merely sliding around the corner. Also, this new plane is actually the plane of the exposed column on the ground floor, which leads the eye again to comprehend the totality of the building, just as Schinkel's corner pilaster reaffirms the size and strength of the whole Museum. None of Mies's imitators have been able to achieve this corner (nor indeed seem to want to!), nor am I familiar with a Schinkel-Schüler corner as strong, yet as subtle, as the Altes Museum.

8

But, there is more than just the outside design that ties the Altes Museum to our century. We have seen the symmetry, the repetitive fenestration, the method of framing corners continue through all the century-long revolutions, but it is the planning itself and the siting (*Lageplan*) which perhaps most closely shows the relation.

I take one of the museums I have built as an example because, though a Mies-Schüler, I still share his admiration of Schinkel. You will note that both museums are thought of as stoas, porticos, loggias, that are part of the public space they face. Both are open to the public square, though in mine, glass has been added out of deference to modern weakness and because of the revolution in glass manufacture. Both have unaccented, symmetrical column arrangements ending in, and similar to a *templum in*

9, 11

10. *Schinkel, Drawing, detail. Altes Museum, Berlin*

11. *Johnson, Amon Carter Museum of Western Art, Fort Worth, Texas*

12. *Mies, Cullinan Hall, The Museum of Fine Arts, Houston, Texas*

10

11

12

antis. They have different columns. The Ionic order has no meaning for us. It reminds us of academic or "Beaux-Arts" architecture; though actually Schinkel's use of the order is so personal, so very un-Greek, that it *10* no longer even reminds one of the Aegean, much less of Ionia. Today, the column shapes can be influenced by concrete technology, though they are of stone. (But surely, today one can copy concrete in stone, as the Greeks copied wood in marble.)

Missing in the 20th-century museum are the acroteria, the murals, the attic story with its horses, but surely the spirit is the same. And I show Mies's Houston Museum addition to illustrate another column system *12* executed in painted steel, but still a glazed portico to the street with heavy (in this case very heavy) corner treatment.

There was another side to Schinkel's work that we can look back upon these days with especial sympathy. In contrast to the ordered and classical simplicity of the Altes Museum, we can study the highly romantic Hof- *13* gärtnerei in the park in Potsdam.

It is unimportant in the 20th century to remark on Schinkel's Italian thoughts at this time. Where he picked up the grammar he used in this remarkable composition is of less importance today than it was at that time. Fritz Stahl wondered in 1912 if we were yet *Schinkelreif,* intimating that we were not. Maybe we are not yet. But is that really important? Can we of this generation not have our picture of Schinkel that is just as valid as that of 1900 or 2200 A.D.? Shakespeare, for example, has had as many different interpretations as there are generations since the 17th century. The Gothic style in architecture was admired for picturesqueness in the 18th century and for its religiosity in the 20th. It does not change the architecture, it merely shows how lasting it is. A 1960 view of Schinkel is worth just as much as any other. Perhaps some day the source of the Italian tower will be important again, but what I wish to bring out today is the extraordinary plan of the court. It has haunted me ever since I first *14* saw it thirty-two years ago.

Fundamentally it is a square centered on the water jet. Considered as a room, see how fascinating are its four walls. All sides are very different, yet harmonious. The lake to the south gives the romantic feeling of the unknown, as does the inaccessible shore on the other bank. The leafy tunnel over the canal to the east gives a hint of mysterious boats passing behind. To the north the Italianate arcade of the Römische Bäder. The *15* west is a grape arbor dominated by the villa itself. The arbor leads to the temple tea room, the colonnade of which faces east again, along the water. The court itself is sunken, emphasizing the intimacy and centripetal sense of the composition. The psychological accent of the space is the temple front with its court to the left, the water to the right; the view on the one side; the comforting sense of the enclosure on the other. The means Schinkel used to create this mood are simple, but I have always felt that

13. *Schinkel, Plan and elevation of the Hofgärtnerei, Potsdam, Sans Souci. 1829–33*

14

15

*14 and 15. Schinkel, Hofgärtnerei with
Roman Baths, Potsdam, Sans Souci*

16

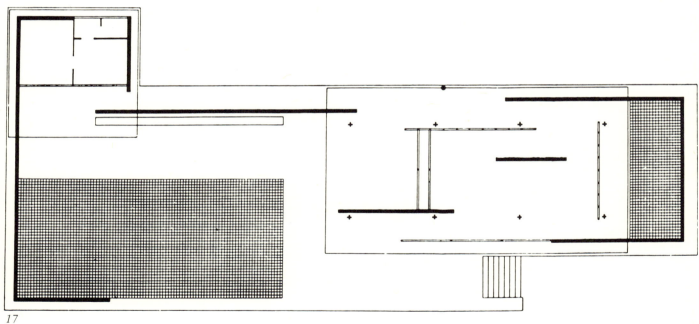

17

16 and 17. Mies, View and plan of German Pavilion, International Exposition, Barcelona. 1929

the projection of the temple on the south wall of the space makes an accent that no symmetrical Baroque *allée* could have emphasized as much.

This composition was impossible in any other period of architectural history; the creation of emotional space, by such casual and eclectic means. When Mies designed the Barcelona Pavilion he need not have been aware *16, 17* of this Hofgärtnerei with its romantic semi-enclosure of space, but nevertheless in his subconscious was surely the feeling of low-walled exterior space enclosed with various asymmetric means. No one does this quite as Schinkel and Mies. Mies's means, his grammar, are entirely 20th century: the sliding planes, the columns as dimensionless points, the walls and roof as two-dimensional planes only, the weightlessness of both walls and roofs, all are 20th century. The plan composition is post-Mondrian Cubist, but the podium, the space is Schinkelesque. Note the one open side with a partial return of the free wall similar to the temple in Schinkel's composition. Also, on another side, the inviting view into the main building like the arbor front in Potsdam. Peter Behrens in 1929 said of this building, "The Pavilion will someday be called the most beautiful building of the century." It expressed the very basic qualities of our century without thereby—and Behrens the 20th-century Neo-classicist must have felt this—defying the traditions of the centuries before.

A much more literal influence of the Hofgärtnerei is a house—the Boissonnas House that I designed in America. Again, the accent is on the *18, 19* outside space, the dwelling units being arranged around it. Again, one side of the outside space is a view, in this case, over a steep hillside. Once again, the accented unit, the arbor in the foreground looks both ways to the inner court and to the view.

A wonderful plan of Mies's shows his romantic side, the first suggestion for the campus plan at the Illinois Institute of Technology in Chicago. *20, 21* Although the whole enclosed plan is symmetrical around the main crossroad, the real axis is from the two facing large buildings which are by no means symmetrically placed. On the contrary, nooks and crannies, surprising half courts that melt into one another make the enclosed space lively and interesting. I like to think Schinkel would approve.

This then is the service that Schinkel and Mies have done for us in the young generation of our century. They have been the most modern designers of their respective centuries. But, their modern has not been fashion only, but always based on tradition.

Mies especially of the two was very much a contemporary of the peculiar revolution of the 20's in Berlin. Those were the years when I first came to find the Bauhaus in full activity (*in vollem Gange*). In those years, Berlin was the cultural capital of the world. All the currents in all the arts seemed to be centered there. In the theater, Piscator, in the dance, Wigman, in painting, Klee and Kandinsky, Lissitzky, Moholy, Richter, Eggeling, all seemed to end up (from whatever foreign country they came)

18

18 and 19. Johnson, View and plan of Eric
Boissonnas House, New Canaan, Connecticut.
1956

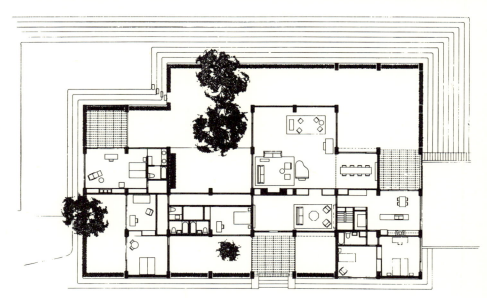

19

*20 and 21. Mies, Preliminary scheme for
campus, Illinois Institute of Technology,
Chicago, Illinois. 1939*

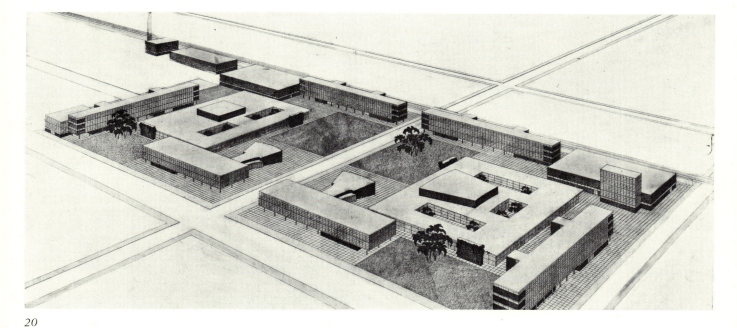

20

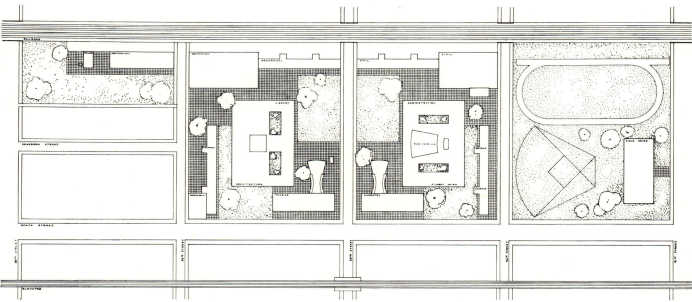

21

22 and 23. *Mies, Model and ground plan,*
Glass Skyscraper Project. 1921

22

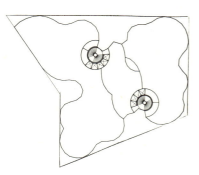

23

in Berlin. Mies with his early Expressionist designs for a glass skyscraper   *22, 23*
was typical of the post-war period.

After the Expressionists, in about 1925, came the *Neue Sachlichkeit*.
The angles and curves disappeared and everything was taken over by the
functionalists. Mies, of course, took part, but in a sense he remained
aloof. Many young architects of that time—and Mies was very young in
that decade—then considered that architecture was no longer an art, but
a functionalist technique to build for the minimum of cost with cheapest
materials.

Mies, I remember, was attacked because of the veining in the marble of
the Barcelona Pavilion. The *Neue Sachlichkeit* required artificial materials
and cheap painted surfaces. In addition to being rich, the marble was laid
symmetrically with the veining continuous from piece to piece. That was
thought to be arbitrary decoration and decoration was taboo. Mies was
attacked even for hanging raw silk curtains in his homes. The curtains
were considered unnecessary and silk too rich. The adherents of the new
Sachlichkeit felt Mies was terribly old-fashioned. But Mies never lost his
sense of traditional elegance. And today, the *Neue Sachlichkeit* is forgotten;
the Bauhaus time seems a long way in the past. The search for the
functional is no longer interesting and architecture is once more the art it
always was. The question now is—how can we design our surroundings
with beauty?

In this quest no one can help our generation more than the giants of
these last two centuries. There are many other directions besides that of
Schinkel and Mies. Indeed, speaking for us Americans, we have never
even heard of Schinkel. In America today it is fashionable to revolt against
all tradition, especially against the tradition of the modern architecture as
exemplified by Mies's work. The result is a centrifugal rage against order
of all kinds. Even in Berlin, this American revolt is seen in this very
building [Congress Hall] in which we meet. Architecture for the sake of
being different, for the sake of being interesting, is now the fashion. All
of us—and I admit to this heresy myself—are looking for new forms. It
almost seems to our friends that we choose any direction as long as it is
different or interesting enough to get attention in the architectural magazines. Attention, *à tout prix.*

To this attitude Mies (and Schinkel would give the same answer) has
given the proper rejoinder, "I don't want to be interesting, I want to be
good." This is a point of view that will always last in any art.

Is Sullivan the Father
of Functionalism?

From Art News, *LV (December, 1956),*
44–46, 56–57.

*Johnson's critique of Sullivan is highly subjective: an indictment based on a
literal reading of Sullivan's work in terms of the structural and functional
determinism of the Modern Movement. It should be contrasted with Vincent
Scully's far more sympathetic discussion in* Perspecta.[1] *It is surprising that
Johnson should regard as influential Sullivan's pronouncement on the impact of
the World's Columbian Exposition when it was, in fact, delivered not in 1893
or 1894 but in 1923 or 1924, near the architect's death, when the impact of
the Exposition on American architecture was everywhere manifest.*

1. *"Louis Sullivan's Architectural Ornament,"* Perspecta 5 *(1959), pp. 73–80.*

It is twenty-four years since I first made a Sullivan pilgrimage to Chicago to wonder at the Gage Building façade, the Auditorium Building and Carson, Pirie and Scott. Today, after almost a generation, what of his reputation? I am not scholarly enough to evaluate anew the work of one of America's great artists, but writing only as one of the architects under his influence and aroused by the present furor on the centenary of his birth, I want to examine his work once more.

I find I am by no means as sure as I was then. Apart from the Wainwright Building in St. Louis and the Guaranty Building in Buffalo, do I feel in myself any genuine respect for his work? Can I sense any influence? Quite honestly, no.

To me, the Sullivan story reads somewhat differently from the current encomiums. Here was a young Richardsonian designer, full of talent, who had a gift for Whitman-like prose that transformed the merest platitude of tautology into an aphorism. He was the second-best Richardsonian architect in the city in the great period of Chicago architecture. (John Root was the best.) As designer of tall buildings, he was (for a while and for only two buildings) great. But even in these two buildings the designs are all Richardson, i.e., in masonry terms, in contradistinction to the Reliance Building of Burnham and Root designed in terms of steel, which in the '90's was the emerging structural system.

We cannot today think of Sullivan as the "first to form fitting clothing for tall buildings." Perhaps the undecorated beauty of the Monadnock Block does not count in the tally of skyscrapers since it was pure masonry, pure form. Perhaps the Reliance Building, on the other hand, is no beauty; but it pointed the way more clearly to the future than did Sullivan's work.

After the Wainwright and Guaranty Buildings of the mid '90's, nothing Sullivan did ever could be called anything but second-rate. The ornament, which was always Sullivan's first love rather than structure or massing, became painfully ugly and the fenestration more and more arbitrary and ill-proportioned. He seemed not to have become aware of Wright's great revolution of 1900 in architectural form. Wright's "breaking of the box," which became the basis of all thinking in modern architecture, Sullivan never noticed. He remained a man of the "pencil" in his designs and a Richardsonian in his building.

History has been kind to Louis Sullivan. The alcholism, the sex troubles, his rejection by the public before he was fifty, the lonely death are all grist to the romantics' mill. In addition, being exiled in a sense from architecture by 1904, he had twenty years of life in which to write his apologia. Like Napoleon at St. Helena, he created his own myth while he was alive, but luckier than Napoleon, he was survived by his much greater pupil, his mythographer, Frank Lloyd Wright, who still calls him *Lieber Meister* (a phrase he can easily afford without loss of ego or arrogance).

Artists who write (was this always so?) have a great advantage, especially if they have a broad theoretical bent. (Le Corbusier, Wright, Neutra, and Mendelsohn are good architects, but their reputations are surely enhanced by their voluminous publications.)

An example of the power of the pen has been the invective Sullivan poured on the 1893 Fair. Not many of us now living ever saw that famous Exposition, but if one can judge from pictures, the White City was a far more unified and splendid sight than New York 1939 or Paris 1925. In fact Sullivan's little revolt in one wing of the Fair, the Transportation Building with its forty-seven kinds of ornament. "colored in gold, brown, green and crimson" (what a combination!) was not even a unified piece of design. Richardson would have integrated the great Saracenic portal into the total composition.

Sullivan's furious antagonism to the Classicist Revival, which swept into Chicago from the East, has been taken much too literally in the history books. Wright himself did distinguished Classical work in the '90's. It was in the air. Perhaps Sullivan's feeling was that everybody was out of step but himself.

Indeed Charles F. McKim of New York in his Boston Public Library, contemporaneously with Sullivan, created a design far purer, and much more inspiring to look at (at least for me) than nine-tenths of Sullivan's buildings. Any study of "Sullivan and His Times" must include the Easterners. We have Russell Hitchcock to thank for pointing out that as far as judging buildings of the '90's is concerned, whether Romanesque or Renaissance detailing or floral decoration was applied makes little difference. It is in the massing and over-all design of a building that the student must look for excellence.

There is, however, one field where Sullivan stands out: the tall commercial building. Richardson died before the problem existed, Root soon after, and Sullivan rose to the challenge. He was, as everyone agrees, the first to give architectural expression to the tall building of steel. And it seems to me personally that any architect facing the design of such a building truly cannot but be influenced by Sullivan's two great examples—the Wainwright and the Guaranty.

Let us analyze one of them: The Guaranty, now the Prudential Building, built in Buffalo in 1895. Sullivan saw that the problem of such a tall façade is somehow to unify it, make it a comprehensible whole, not a disjointed collection of floors and columns. The Reliance Building, for example, as skeleton-like as it looks, has no over-all design discipline. Sullivan, following as usual the basic elements of Richardson's Marshall Field Warehouse of 1885, which we know he admired, with great originality has stretched out the main arcade to include ten floors instead of the Marshall Field Building's three, or the Auditorium Building's four, and then confined the upper stories to an attic floor of *oeil-de-boeuf* windows that merge into a magnificent flaring cornice. He has extended the base story of the Marshall Field Building to two, making a more proportionate relation to the ten above. The corners of the building are thickened for visual stability as in the Marshall Field and Auditorium buildings. The piers project in front of the spandrels, thus creating a vertical accent similar to, but much simpler and grander than, the Auditorium Building.

It is a fine design and suited to a tall building. Some critics see a functionalism here which I fail to find. Sullivan said "form follows function," but he went on to define it very differently from today's architects, who mean either "suited to purpose" or "expressive of structure." Sullivan had a third meaning. An oak should look like an oak, a rose like a rose. Then Sullivan goes on to say what function means in a tall building. He felt it had a basic organic shape: at the bottom there are shop windows (naturally, but then why two stories? The second story of the base is useless). Then it has a middle section of repeated office units. Right. Then it has a top. Why? It seemed inevitable, "functional," to Sullivan; but hardly to us. We cannot escape the conclusion that Sullivan found a cornice inevitable simply because he was used to it and he liked it. That is a good reason, but let us not call him a functionalist or a proto-modern for clinging to cornices.

And most especially, let us not, as some critics do, call him a functionalist in a structural sense. The Guaranty is a steel-cage building, but its exterior is expressive only of masonry. A layman could never guess that only every other pier concealed a steel column no larger than the rest.

No; Sullivan's interest was not in structure, but design; and indeed, more and more, in the ornament which covers his later buildings.

At the time of the Guaranty Building, he had not yet reached the extremes he was later to achieve, but he had passed beyond the truly architectural phase of his ornamentation which had been so effective in the Wainwright Building of 1890. In that earlier building, only the spandrels and the cornice were ornamented; the piers and base stories remained magnificently plain. But by now everything is covered.

Any brief comment on Sullivan's ornament is difficult and bound to be subjective; and taste is hard to put into words. Nevertheless it has always seemed that there should exist at least two minimum requirements for architectural ornament: One, that it fit the structural expression; two, that it be self-consistent. But look at the details of a Guaranty Building capital.

The capital itself is similar in basic design to many medieval ones. The capital supports a beam, as all classic capitals support beams, but Sullivan spills some of his wriggly plant life from the capital on the beam, and then the beam is drenched in motifs by no means reinforcing the idea of beams in general or fitting these beams specifically. These beam decorations defy categorization. Sullivan was interested in overlaying again and again planes of geometric tracery and floral patterns, but what on earth did he intend by mixing the two in this particular way? It is hard to decide which is more shocking—the change in scale as the eye moves horizontally, or the shift from flat diagonal bands to the linear flora. Each square inch has motifs enough for a whole building, but Sullivan mixes his patterns in a totally inexplicable manner; note especially how the large-scale geometric diamond pierces to the heart a minute-scale curvilinear mandala. It is hard to see what we architects of the mid-century can learn from such a strange profusion.

On the other hand, I personally have learned much from Sullivan's one-man campaign for design, or DESIGN, in tall buildings. What courage in the face of the problem of building cheaply for the profit of the entrepreneur! What a triumph of art in the epoch of commercialism!

How, I wonder, could Sullivan compete in today's tall building scramble where rent per square foot is necessarily the dominant consideration. Sullivan made tall buildings into art. May we, fifty years later, be able to do half as well.

The Frontiersman

From Architectural Review, *CVI* (August, 1949), 105–10.

Johnson is one of the few architects of his generation to have anything important to say about Frank Lloyd Wright. Despite his polemically motivated efforts to justify his and Hitchcock's theories about the true, or at least proper, nature of modern architecture as they defined it in The International Style *in 1932 and their ambiguous attitude toward Wright, as evidenced by their excluding him from that book while simultaneously including him (at Hitchcock's insistence) among the "Modern" architects in their international exhibition of that same year, by 1949—as Johnson begins to emerge as an important architect—he seems self-confident enough to see Wright's achievement on its own terms and takes the opportunity to discuss "the greatest living architect [and] the founder of modern architecture as we know it in the West." Writing for an international audience in response to Wright's attack on The Museum of Modern Art,[1] he reiterates and justifies the fairly unique non-ideological, formalist, anti-functionalist bias of the museum's interpretation of the Modern Movement and begins to express his own dissatisfaction with the minimalist aesthetics of the canonical International Style of the 1920's. Johnson was probably the first of the American modernists to recognize in print that Le Corbusier was then rapidly moving away from that "flat-chested" minimalism with which Wright so often castigated the "International Stylists." In their book of 1932, Hitchcock and Johnson had already observed this shift in Le Corbusier's work as exemplified by the de Mandrot Villa and had resorted to an elaborate and rather convoluted argument in an effort to place its messages within the "International Style" canon as they defined it.*

Johnson's concluding remarks in "The Frontiersman," by seeking to return the discussion of modern architecture to a broader base than merely that of International Style modernism, reflect his belief in the inherent dichotomy between Romantic Naturalism and Romantic Classicism. How different this theoretical view is from Johnson's own life: Hamiltonian by day, as he sits in his efficient suite of offices high above New York's Park Avenue, Jeffersonian by night, as he rusticates in the exquisitely manicured landscape of suburban Connecticut.

1. *"Sullivan Against the World,"* Architectural Review, *CV (June, 1949), pp. 295–98, a chapter from his forthcoming* Genius and the Mobocracy *(New York: Duell, Sloan and Pearce, 1949).*

In my opinion, Frank Lloyd Wright is the greatest living architect, and for many reasons. He is the founder of modern architecture as we know it in the West, the originator of so many styles that his emulators are invariably a decade or so behind. All younger moderns—except perhaps Le Corbusier—acknowledge Wright's influence, though some may forget the debt in their later years. There can be no disagreement, however, that he is the most influential architect of our century. In the 1900's he originated the Prairie House, with its open plan, which through the Wasmuth publication of 1911 became the prototype of so much modern design. In the 20's he outdid the massiveness of the Mayan with a new kind of ferro-concrete structure. In the 30's and 40's he has been and still is inventing new shapes: using circles, hexagons, and triangles to articulate space in new ways.

But he is more than an inventor. No one understands the third dimension as well as he, the capacity of architecture to be an experience in depth, rather than a mere façade. His buildings can rarely be appreciated correctly except at first hand. A photograph can never relay the experience of being surrounded by one of them. Nor can a camera record the cumulative impact of moving through his organized spaces, the effect of passing through low space into high, from narrow to wide, from dark to light. (Taliesin, Taliesin West, Johnson Wax Co.)

Wright is also unique in his ability to adjust buildings to natural surroundings. Whether they rise from a hill (Pauson House, Loeb House, Hartford Tower) or hug the slopes (Taliesin, Taliesin West and Jacobs House) his structures always look rooted to the soil, in his words "organic."

It is of great importance, therefore, to listen to Mr. Wright's opinions—especially when expressed so violently—on the work of the architects whom he calls here "internationalists," "stencillists," "functionalists." Since he refers twice to the exhibition which I organized at The Museum of Modern Art in 1932 as the agent responsible for the introduction of these foreign "isms" perhaps a few notes on the intervening years would be appropriate.

Mr. Wright would undoubtedly include in his list of "stencillists" most of the architects in our 1932 catalogue. Besides himself, there were men like Le Corbusier, Mies van der Rohe, Gropius, Oud, Mendelsohn, Aalto, Neutra, Lescaze and Stonorov. According to Wright these are fascist-inspired, cliché artists, many of whom design two-dimensional flat-façade buildings because they are more interested in painting than architecture. Furthermore, they do not understand Nature; in fact, they are anti-Nature.

There is a lot of meat in Mr. Wright's castigations, but he is wrong in attributing a functionalist leaning to us at the Museum who have fought it for 20 years. There is also much doubt how many of these artists really believed in functionalism even though they sometimes gave it lip-service. Mr. Wright, for example, might better have remembered not only Le Corbusier's unfortunate propagandist *machine à habiter* but his beautiful definition *"L'architecture, c'est, avec des matériaux bruts, établir des rapports émouvants,"* to which most architects including Mr. Wright would subscribe.

When he writes that international architecture is "stencillist," and able to be repeated, taught and learned so easily that our universities have adopted it rather than Wright's own "organic" architecture, he is correct. Le Corbusier, and perhaps latterly Mies van de Rohe, have indeed been too superficially adapted for teaching; Wright's principles, on the other hand, are impossible to teach in the conventional, institutional way.

Again when he cites Le Corbusier for being two-dimensional in his approach he has a point. Le Corbusier façades are often flat, those of his followers flatter. And certainly the group as a whole has been distinguished by its extraordinary interest in painting. Le Corbusier, himself, is an active and accomplished practitioner of the art, but it does not necessarily follow, as Mr. Wright implies, that because he is capable of creating in two dimensions he cannot also create in three. A cube is undeniably three-dimensional. To raise it on stilts only serves to emphasize that fact. Such a purist concept is, of course, a far cry from the spatial complexity of a building by Wright, but the one does not necessarily negate the value of the other.

Mr. Wright has often attacked the slick box-like "negativities" of international work, the painted stucco, the boredom of repeated columns. But these objections have long since been met by the internationalists themselves. They no longer use stucco, nor rely on paint. The smooth flatness is gone. Mies projects his windbraces and columns to get shadow; Le Corbusier complicates his façades with Mondrian-shaped mullion patterns and *brises soleil*; Gropius, Breuer and Neutra now use native wood, pitched roofs and deep porch-like overhangs; Aalto curves entire buildings. The movement away from the "boxes" that Mr. Wright attacks brings the internationalists nearer to Wright's position and further from their own position of 20 years ago. How much of this enrichment is caused by a re-appreciation of Wright and how much to a natural reaction against bad material and lonely cubes would be hard to say.

When Mr. Wright claims that the international movement is fascist-inspired he uses the word in two senses. He argues first that the "provincial art elite," the trustees and visitors of The Museum of Modern Art, being rich are fascist-inclined because rich, and second that because Mussolini favored the *stile razionale,* therefore modern architects admired Mussolini.

The New York rich, however, are demonstrably Republican and as a class are the best clients for Georgian and Elizabethan mansions in the world. But more important, a large percentage of Mr. Wright's "foreigners" are refugees from Nazism and Fascism. It is hard to understand his argument. As a matter of fact modern architecture has never flourished in any totalitarian country whether Communist or Fascist. It is a true child of social democracy.

It is one the question of Nature and its relation to architecture that Mr. Wright is clearest. "We must learn to use the word Nature in its proper *romantic* (i.e., integral) sense" he writes (italics mine) and he is indeed romantic about Nature. He has proposed elsewhere that "the Tree should be the inspiration for American architecture of the Machine Age." He speaks of his new Johnson Laboratory Tower as having a tap-root and branches. His greatest objection to the "internationalists" is their anti-Nature stand.

In his eyes Japanese and Mayan work are "organic" while Greek and Renaissance architecture are inorganic, opposed to Nature. The internationalists, he correctly points out, admire the Greeks and consequently conceive their work as a contrast to Nature rather than a part of it. Like the Parthenon, their buildings are placed against Nature.

Mr. Wright's preference for regarding his buildings as identified with Nature has inspired him to produce the most remarkable architectural creations of our time, but does this in itself invalidate the other point of view? Rather, is not the contrast between Le Corbusier's *prisme pur* and Wright's luxuriant forms but another manifestation of the Classic-Romantic dichotomy? Does not Le Corbusier's work symbolize Mediterranean culture today: the bright, tight shapes of a static civilization, against a blue sky. And does not Wright's work typify the exuberant individualism of an ever-expanding frontier?

100 Years, Frank Lloyd Wright and Us

Speech, Washington State Chapter, A.I.A., Seattle; published in Pacific Architect and Builder *(March, 1957), 13, 35–36.*

This talk was delivered before the Washington State Chapter of the American Institute of Architects as part of its celebration of the 100th anniversary of the Institute's founding and was published by the Chapter in its own publication, Pacific Architect and Builder. *It is Johnson's most affectionate, most complete, and most candid discussion of Wright's work, presented in Wright's eighty-eighth year while he was very much alive and actively involved in the construction of the Guggenheim Museum in New York. Given the usual proscription of the A.I.A. concerning one architect's criticizing another, the publication of Johnson's remarks—which are in effect no more salty than the casual commentary about contemporary issues that Wright so regularly dispensed in numerous articles and interviews—was preceded by a disclaimer to the effect that the talk "is probably as provocative as any heard at centennial celebrations across the land . . . the views expressed in this digest of the tape-recorded extemporaneous talk are not necessarily those held by* Pacific Architect and Builder."*

Johnson and Wright enjoyed a love-hate friendship which began at the time when Hitchcock and Johnson were assembling materials for The Museum of Modern Art's "Modern Architecture" exhibition in 1932. When Hitchcock advocated Wright's inclusion in that exhibition, Johnson was said to have claimed that he thought Wright was dead. Whether he meant it literally or simply artistically is not clear; but news of Johnson's remarks got back to Wright, who was never reluctant to hold a grudge. Nonetheless, by 1945 the two were surely friends, and in the 1950's Wright visited at the Glass House several times. On one of these visits, he claimed that the asymmetrically placed Nadelman sculpture of two women was badly positioned; but after moving it to another location near the bar, he had to admit that it looked absurd there and should be restored to its original place.

You have to come to Seattle to get away from the hidebound East Coast, to get the wholesome air which is the essence of any new century in architecture. In general I can say that I have never been in a city where the level is so high and so fresh.

I spent the day before in San Francisco, which is a somewhat larger and much older city and has had a long history—what with Maybeck and all—of great architecture. But in relation to what is being done now, in the past three years at least, this is better.

You are newer; you aren't tied down by the traditions of San Francisco, which seems to be rather stuck with ordinary windows and ordinary walls. You do share the wood tradition, the great Maybeck tradition of using large enough wood so you can see it, unlike the Easterners who seem to prefer to use ¾-inch-thick boards or plywood. You do have that in common with Calfornia but I think you use it fresher and I think you mix it more with the strains that come from other parts of the world without fear for the future. But tonight I am not going to talk about the future.

I am very interested in Frank Lloyd Wright and would like to say a few things which have been on my mind for quite some time. I've known Mr. Wright for a number of years. I know he is still alive and I thought therefore that this in a sense is the right time to speak out because, were he dead, that old maxim of "nothing about the dead, but the good" would tie my mouth—and I don't want to wait until that time and have to make only pleasant statements.

Mr. Wright has been annoying me for some time. (I didn't say that he wasn't a great architect.) He says that my house, especially the Glass House that you may have seen pictures of, is not a house at all—it's not a shelter, it doesn't have any caves, it's cold and it doesn't give you a feeling of comfort; it's a box. He once said (he's much cleverer, of course, than all the rest of us so you can't say these things as well as he does) that my house is a monkey cage for a monkey. Then he came to my house the other day, strode in and said, "Philip, should I take off my hat or leave it on? Am I indoors or am I out?"

I don't hope to keep up to him in anecdotes but I claim that it is a perfectly beautiful house to live in. And I would like to counter with a few remarks about some of his recent houses. I claim that they lack a lot of other things that are very valuable for living: they lack elegance completely, they lack all sense of clarity, they are confused in design, they have no consistency structurally. In the last house he did down our way, he was going around so many corners that he didn't have time to hold up the beams, so he said to the boys, "We'll put a Lally column there." Unfortunately it happened to be in the living room.

He makes the strangest use of materials. He will combine cinder blocks, to which he has now taken a fancy, with mahogany: the roofs, the facias are all mahogany, the decorations all copper, but the house is made

Frank Lloyd Wright and Philip Johnson at Yale

of cinder block, an awfully unpleasant material in the evening with a silk dress.

Then there's his open plan. I like open plans too but then I'm a bachelor, I can stand it. He opened the plan so far on this last house that the clients had to get rid of him and put the wall in between the living room and their bedroom because the children woke them up in the morning. So I think I can say that all these things are very bad.

The worst thing I ever said about Mr. Wright was that he was the greatest architect of the 19th century. I thought it was a compliment but in a way if you think back, the houses that I'm speaking of are the recent ones. Think back, for instance, to the great Riverside Club of 1900: the clarity is there, the elegance is there, and only one material is used in the entire project. The great, brooding, shingle hip roof that became his mark at that time was extremely dignified and very clear structurally.

Then I'm annoyed by Mr. Wright's talking a good deal. He uses words in an unusual way. For example, he talks about cities thus, "Cities are vampires living off the blood of the countryside and the villages, sterilizing humanity." Then he says that skyscrapers are "mollusks." This is wonderful prose, pure 19th-century prose—"the mollusks erected for the exploitation of the man in the street."

He can have his opinions. Whitman had them; Thoreau had them. There's a quite good American tradition for having a hatred of the cities. But then why, in light of these remarks, does he intend to build the tallest, the largest and the most inhuman skyscraper in the world if he could (fortunately he cannot) in Chicago?

I find very annoying too his contempt for the history books, for all architecture that preceded him. Was he born full-blown from the head of Zeus that he could be the only architect that ever lived or ever will? I find it an undignified approach of our greatest living architect to talk about Michelangelo who, he says, created the greatest mistake of any architect that ever lived by building St. Peter's dome.

Then almost worse is the contempt for the people who are going to come after him—and this is where it hurts us most, we slightly younger, older architects. He is determined that there shall not be any architect after him. Have you ever heard him talk about his own disciples, those poor children who sweat over the garbage pails at Taliesin East and Tailiesin West year in and year out? Have you ever visited that place; and I am second to none in those who admire his architecture in those two houses, but he treats them like slaves.

I don't think there are any of us who can deny his position. I wonder if all of us realize exactly what we do get, and I mean from the earlier Wright naturally, in all our work. I wonder if we realize what it would have been had he not changed the course of architecture single-handed from 1900 to 1910. It was he, don't forget, who made roofs, walls, wainscoting and floor all independent of each other—independent elements of design.

But there is a gap which I still mean to point out and to me that happened in the architectural revolution of 1923, the internationalization of design which was based very much on Frank Lloyd Wright's own work. Of course I speak of the pioneers like Gropius and Corbusier and Mies van der Rohe who independently, after the First World War, came to a type of design which gradually has spread over the entire Western world. It was a great deal of synthesized Wright. The elements were Wrightian but they were something more: they regarded the structural elements more than Wright ever did or still does.

Mr. Wright is very careless about how his buildings are held up once he has the way of looking at them settled. We would not dare—even his admirers—to build a building as casually as he does. Fortunately his son-in-law is an excellent engineer and will see to it afterwards that there is enough steel put into the wood in houses to insure the cantilevers from drooping too much—but they still droop.

However, Mr. Wright is cavalier about that. The younger men coming along in 1923 were not cavalier about that. Mies, of course, is the most extreme. He insists that structure is the element, the essence of architecture, and the arrangement of the elements within that frame—to him steel, of course, since it is the most American material—is what architecture is all about. He takes a very strong stand against Wright's romanticism and I think that that has had an effect on every one of us; it has had its effect right here in the Northwest in spite of the much stronger influence of Wright here than anywhere else in the country.

Where are we now standing at this 100-year point? We ought to be standing at the threshold of the greatest architectural period in history; everything conspires to it. We have more buildings than the world has ever seen in a shorter time, more square feet. We have more money than any culture ever had at any time, within such a short time. We certainly have the architects.

Do we then have the principles that any of us can read in history books? Are we really convinced that right now are being designed the Taj Mahal, the Parthenon, the Chartres Cathedral? I don't think any of us will claim that we are in any such period, and yet what elements are lacking?

There is only one lack and that is that there is no will in our culture to build; there is no desire in our culture that building be of any great importance.

Where did we get off the track, as I believe we are? To me, it's to be blamed on commercial committees, not on us. We don't mind spending money; rather it's the timidity of our culture in which we live, the setting up of dollar values for things which cannot be measured by dollars and cents—beauty. Our great corporate clients, or government clients for that matter, give nothing for beauty.

One wonders sometimes if architects will be necessary at all. Because of the economy, look what happens. If you build schools what do the school boards say? "How many dollars per student, how many dollars per square foot and how many square feet per student"? And what do you spend your time doing: cutting costs or building beautiful things? It is now becoming so that if you build a religious building, they will say, "How many dollars per pew?" How many dollars per square soul, perhaps, as a starter.

I think maybe that we, as architects who shouldn't be, are getting a little bit influenced by the point of view of the world around us. We cannot be ivory-tower artists. We cannot sit it out if people don't like our designs. We've got to go on building. We've got to go on because of our office, because of our children.

Do you think we ought to be quite so businesslike in our approach? We make our firms the way lawyers make theirs, not the way artists make firms. McKim, Mead, and White are all dead. It's still a big firm because there's value in it, a dollars and cents value in writing Stanford White's name (he was shot in 1906), which is very strange—it's the only country in the world where this happens; it is the only civilization in which this has ever happened.

Now there are, of course, some architects willing to starve and sit it out.

There is a man like Louis Kahn of Philadelphia, of whom it was said in the recent *Harper's* magazine that if there is a genius in Philadelphia it's Louis Kahn. He's built one building there since the war. There is a man like Bruce Goff in Oklahoma. There is a man like Alexander Girard—all right, he doesn't have an architectural degree; I'm afraid I don't think that's terribly important. I think that what's important is how to mold space excitingly. Perhaps you have seen those magnificent colors he used to organize his own home in Santa Fe, N.M. Sure, that's the only work he's ever done but that doesn't mean he's not a great architect—well, let's not use the word "architect"; let's say "a shaper of space."

Because, after all, what are we here for? One wonders exactly what is the purpose of being an architect? It surely isn't only to put food in our mouths. There are other ways of doing that—a great deal easier and more remunerative.

But I wish to end with the same man I started with: a man that never gave up; the great American that perhaps we can admire at the same time we dislike him as much as I do—Frank Lloyd Wright. There is a man who creates space for its own sake and has never paid any attention to any other things.

Have you ever been to Taliesin in Arizona? I think that it is an experience which you can afford yourself. And I would plead with you to go before he is gone. He is 88; he is as brilliant and cantankerous and magnificent as ever. But the spirit will go out of the place when he is gone.

He has developed one thing which I will defy any of us to equal: the arrangements of secrets of space. I call it the hieratic aspects of architecture, the processional aspects. I would like to tell you about it briefly.

You drive up from Phoenix, about 20 miles out, up a dusty desert road, wondering why you came because it's terribly hot, and you go up a slight rise. Finally you turn into a piece of particularly dusty, nasty and ill-kept road. But there is a little sign that says "Frank Lloyd Wright."

You come to a conglomeration of tents and stones where the car stops. There is a low wall and you realize after you have been there and come back again, that he has been pushing out the spot where the car stops, further and further from his place. I'd like to recommend that to you and to me. The car, of course, is one of the deaths of architecture. It's out of scale, it makes noise, it doesn't please the eye. And you cannot, from a sitting position, even look at architecture. It has to be by the actual use of the muscles of your feet.

He now makes you walk about 150 feet, until you get closer to this meaningless group of buildings. You've seen the plans many times and I'm sure you didn't understand them any more than I did before I'd been there.

As you approach, he starts you off on a slight slope, with the mountains to your left, and so up the first steps you go, away from the buildings instead of toward them. And how he takes your eyes and makes them follow. You go down the steps this way but the buildings are over there.

Then the steps turn at right angles and you go between two low walls, very much narrower this time. You have the sensation that you are always changing your point of view on the buildings.

You turn, you pass his office, you climb four more steps and pass a great stone that he has put there with Indian hieroglyphics on it, which he found on his place. There is no door in sight. There is a tent roof on a stone base but no door; there is nothing in sight. You just begin to wonder.

Then the path takes you down a long walk, about 200 feet perhaps, with this tent room on your right, the mountains on your left.

You begin to wonder what is happening when, at your right, you pass the tent room, the building above goes on overhead. But the view separates—the two enormous piers—and you look again (a trick) through a dark room, a 6-foot room, out onto the terrace of Taliesin West: an enormous prow that sticks out over the mountains.

Now you've been climbing all this time and you never knew it because you never looked back; but for the first time, you realize you have been climbing and for 90 miles you look across the desert through that darkened hole. And again, of course, the steps start rippling. You go down three steps and then down three steps more and you are pulled out onto this prow of the desert. He calls it his "ship of the desert." That's where Frank Lloyd Wright is usually standing to greet you with his purple hair, his cape, and you say, "Now I've arrived at this magic place."

But you've just begun the trip. He then leads you through a gold-leaf concrete tunnel that turns three times and you are pushed out into the most single exciting room that we have in this country. It is indescribable except that you can say that the light, since it all comes from the tent above, has infiltered and mellowed.

You are just beginning to absorb this room when he opens a few of the tent flaps and this is when it really hits you. You look out—but not onto the desert. You look out this time on a little private secret garden that he has built beyond this room, where water is playing unlike any water in the desert. The plants are 20 feet high in this garden, and there is a lawn such as you have seen only in New England.

You say, "Now I see what I've come to Taliesin for"; you have not. He makes one more turn, two more turns. This time the door is 18 inches wide and you have to go through sidewise. It is entirely an inside room, no desert or garden. One wall is of plants. To be sure, you cannot see them; that is, you can't see through them, but that gives you the jungle light that comes into the room. There is a shaft of light that comes from 12 or 14 feet above (this is a very high room now). The room is 21 by 14 feet, all stone. One entire length of it is the fireplace; on the other long wall is a table and two chairs—and that is where you have come to be. You sit down with Frank Lloyd Wright and he says, "Welcome to Taliesin."

My friends, that is the essence of architecture.

Correct and Magnificent Play

Review of Le Corbusier, Complete Works. V. 1946–1952, edited by W. Boesiger. From Art News, *LII (September, 1953), 16–17, 52–53.*

Philip Johnson at Chandigharh, 1965

Volume 5 of Le Corbusier's Complete Works *brought to focus for a relatively wide professional audience what had already become well known—if not necessarily understood or appreciated—among the cognoscenti of the Modern Movement: that in the immediate post-World War II years Le Corbusier almost completely reversed himself with respect to his buildings, though not necessarily his theories, of the 1920's. Johnson takes the normally slight occasion of a book review to formulate a major assessment of Le Corbusier's work, dealing not only with the obvious shift in the work between the two periods, but also with the more subtle and complex inter-relationship between Le Corbusier's urge to build rationally ("the house is a machine to live in") and his urge to build monumentally ("architecture is the play of forms, correct and magnificent, under the light"). In his characteristic way, Johnson sees these objectives as pretty much mutually exclusive and finds the latter "much more satisfactory."*

Le Corbusier's post-war work is discussed, perhaps for the first time, in relationship to that of his contemporaries. It is not seen simply as a variation on more or less established themes, as Giedion and other apologists for the canonical International Style of the 1920's tried to make it seem, but rather as an idiosyncratic, personal style permissible in an existentialist world where every man is for himself. Though Johnson is enthusiastic, his recognition of Le Corbusier's achievement is not given without certain ideological reservations: it is not "interior architecture" (a phrase Johnson takes from Matthew Nowicki and makes his own over the years), and it is crude, especially in its use of exposed concrete ("what an ugly material concrete is").

Johnson's discussion of Le Corbusier's work at Chandigarh tempers enthusiasm with distrust; he seems to be trying to convince himself as he tries to convince the reader. Surprisingly, given his characteristic erudition, Johnson makes no mention of Sir Edwin Lutyens's work at New Delhi, a project which is an obvious point of reference in such a discussion and one of which Le Corbusier himself speaks admiringly in the volume under review. And his admiration for Le Corbusier's plan for Chandigarh is also surprising. Johnson's acceptance of its separation of pedestrians from motor traffic and its concept of self-sufficient neighborhoods is unquestioning and rather matter-of-fact; it in no way connects with the serious analysis of similar themes in "The Town and the Automobile" (see pp. 81–83), nor does it seem to connect in any significant way with the town he was commissioned to design for Joseph Hirshhorn in Canada or such later projects as "Third City," Harlem, and Roosevelt Island.

Johnson had not visited India when he reviewed the Corbusier book (an uncharacteristic situation for him; like Hitchcock, he almost never discusses in writing buildings he has not seen firsthand). In December 1965, Johnson visited India and came back with opposite views about Le Corbusier's government complex, which he found interesting as architecture but a disaster as an urban ensemble. Lutyens's complex, on the other hand, "bowled him over," and he admired even more the work of Lutyens's followers.

The trouble with great men is that one never knows what they are up to. Le Corbusier, for example, never designs a "LeCorbu" building. It is always a design that refuses categorization that any architect and any lay critic could ever dream of. This fact often angers them. I have heard otherwise intelligent architects say: "But these latest things," the buildings in this book, "are really crazy." For "crazy" read, of course, "unexpected."

These buildings are unexpected. Le Corbusier is now sixty-five and just now at his prime. After being known for thirty years as the leader of the international school of design, what Alfred Barr christened the "International Style" (although Holland and Germany helped to start the International Style in about 1922, Le Corbusier was the man they all looked to), he now in full vigor steps out into space sculpture, breathtaking and unanalyzable.

With whom can one compare this giant? Comparisons with living artists are invidious. Frank Lloyd Wright belongs to another generation. Mies van der Rohe's greatness lies in another field. Perhaps with some temerity, with Michelangelo; the sculptor sculpting space as if with his hands. But Le Corbusier does not enjoy chipping away in the quarries of Carrara; he enjoys imprinting his message in soft concrete—which he calls the most accommodating of materials. More so even than bronze. (Curious, what an ugly material concrete is. All the more wonder what beauty Le Corbusier creates out of its ugliness.) Like Michelangelo, Le Corbusier enjoys decorating space violently with immense and odd punctuations. The apse of St. Peter's (a piece of grandeur that Le Corbusier much admires), with its over-scaled pilasters, diagonal rhythms and under-scaled niches, has its counterpoint in Marseilles. (How high is a man on one of Le Corbusier's great balconies?) The Capitoline Hill is tricky in spite of its regular march of colossal-order pilasters; Marseilles, in spite of its utter simplicity as a box, is loaded with tricks of scale—on its roof, underneath and on the sides.

The late Matthew Nowicki once wrote: "All architecture is interior architecture." Perhaps. The Parthenon then must be sculpture, but the Acropolis as a whole is a work of architecture. So with Le Corbusier's great roof at Marseilles, spatially his greatest work yet executed. One is outdoors to be sure, but surrounded with bits and pieces that create architectural space. It is banal to say that the ventilation pipes, the elevator towers, the stairs, the artificial mountains, the children's *crèche* on its pilotis, the hall for physical culture (unpleasant title), are *well proportioned and well related to* each other! One aspect can be emphasized perhaps: the high parapet around the roof cuts out the surrounding country except the mountains which, because they are seen *through* objects and *over* the wall, become somehow terrible and close, quite different from their aspect viewed from the ground.

"L'architecture, c'est le jeu correct et magnifique des formes sous la lumière." Le Corbusier writes under a picture of these shapes and these mountains—"the play of forms under the light." No other architect is quite as concerned with light. On an early page in this book he reproduces a sketch he made in 1910 of Hadrian's Villa, showing the mystery of light which penetrates from unseen sources to a dark room. Mediterranean light—hard, blue, dark—is his specialty. The roof shapes at Marseilles revolve, cut, shadow, flatten under the light, and the mountains advance and recede.

It is annoying to hear quotations taken from Le Corbusier's early period, such as: "A house is a machine to live in." Maybe it is under one aspect: Bacon said, as early as the seventeenth century, "A house is intended to live in, not to look at." But *"architecture* is the play of forms correct and magnificent under the light." Much more satisfactory.

Other architects as well as Le Corbusier have their proverbs which are just as personal and which illustrate just as much their penchants and prejudices. Frank Lloyd Wright says that he proposes the Tree (capitals his) as the inspiration of American architecture. His Fallingwater house and his Johnson Wax Tower are proofs that he is right (for him). Mies writes: "Wherever technology reaches its real fulfillment, it transcends into architecture." Again, "Less is more," revealing a superb "builderly" interest in clarity of structure, the maximum of effect from the minimum of aesthetic fuss. This is Mies's "art that conceals art" which results in his understated majestic buildings. Every architect should have his own definition of architecture.

The *"lumière"* Le Corbusier writes of he understands very well. The apartments at Marseilles are marvels of daylight. The rooms are two stories high, but only 12 feet wide, and glass fills the space at the end; but halfway up at the intermediate-story level a flat plane is introduced outside the glass which cuts the glare, that enemy of tall buildings (try working on the fortieth floor of a New York office building without lowering the shades) and reflects the strong high light back to the ceiling. One is bathed in light from the floor, from the narrow walls, from the ceiling.

The influence that this man has had! When in history, I have been asking myself, has any architect become so much admired and so much copied, and during his lifetime? It is true that Palladio had quite an effect in England and Ireland, and perhaps some nameless master in Classical times started a Mediterranean trend, but today—what with literacy and photography and individualism and the world dominance of Western culture—Le Corbusier has spread around the globe. There is no country (Franco's Spain perhaps excepted?) which has not some example of his work or the work of his followers (whether they admit being followers or not). Our country shows perhaps the least, yet in New York City alone, the United Nations building is inspired by his designs directly, and Lever

House indirectly. Japan ranks Le Corbusier first of the Westerners and copies him. In Latin America modern architecture is synonymous with Le Corbusier's forms.

Yet no architect has been so attacked as has Le Corbusier. In 1930 he was "a strict functionalist who made boxes—*machines à habiter*"—without aesthetic merits or even artistic pretense. Today he is the "impractical artistic dreamer of Marseilles" who sacrifices economy, modern plumbing and the comfort of his tenants to an iron and expensive aesthetic theory. Neither, of course, is true. His early, simple, but highly colored "boxes" were really paintings translated into three dimensions. And his Marseilles apartments are lived in and eminently livable dwellings.

How often dislikes of aesthetic form can engender meaningless rationalistic criticism on quite another plane. Do we all "think with our prejudices"?

Wherein does Le Corbusier's greatness lie? Perhaps one clue is his handling of fantasy versus discipline. He has ever been the admirer of the pure cube—*le prisme pur*—(the most difficult of shapes to handle), yet, on the other hand, he is the leading fantasist among his contemporaries. It was he who so admired the pure volume that first raised his cubic buildings on "pilotis" to show, I presume, the sixth and most difficult side of the prism. Then on the prism against the sky he fashioned strange shapes: inverted cones, curved roofs, cylinders, boxes, and even artificial mountains.

At Marseilles (it is difficult to judge from the pictures in the book) the pilotis are shaped like giant hands which hold up the great weight, with the effort of an Atlas holding up the world—like the vaudeville weight lifter who strains in his effort of holding so that the very effort increases the beholder's feeling of mass. Like Michelangelo's colossal orders, these "hands" set up a strong rhythm which orders the rest of the building. Yet Marseilles is essentially a *prisme pur*—a box floating in the air and highly decorated, but—a box.

Chandigarh: the capital city of the Punjab. Le Corbusier's career in this year, 1953, is still ahead of him. His masterpiece (his St. Peter's) is now under construction in India. To build a city is the dream of every architect—the lot of practically none. Since Filarete and Leonardo, architects have dreamed and planned and still no great plan exists in stone or steel. Yes, there is New Delhi, there is Haussmann's Paris, there is Canberra, but when the dreamers of today look for actual cities for models, it is to none of these lesser places but rather to Greece and to Venice, or to small spots like San Gimignano or the Crescent at Bath.

It is a real proof of our greatness as a cultural period that such an architect as Le Corbusier was given the job of building on such a scale. (Should the Western world get the credit since the city is in the Orient?)

One looks for some antecedents for such a tremendous design. The

Renaissance was too little, the Baroque too axial. Even Ledoux, the first great Romantic architect, planned his cities rather stuffily. the Middle Ages were too interested in tight enclosure to suit our times. The nearest that comes to mind is the Acropolis at Athens and some of the Roman forums, where buildings and cult statues were spaced asymmetrically according to impressiveness and angle of approach. Looking at these models, as I believe he did, the painter-sculptor-architect Le Corbusier has conceived his monumental city-center plan.

The art of the plan—it is a pleasure to see merely the plan of Chandigarh. How balanced the masses, how surely tied together by roads and paths, how well anchored by the great Ministries Building in the lower left; how cleverly accented by the great monument placed in the upper right.

Yet this is not the "plan beautiful" merely. It works. For the first time, for example, the curse of the automobile has been overcome: vehicles are relegated to side roads and back entrances (there is no crowding, however, since the plan is vast), the pedestrian is king. Le Corbusier knows well that vehicular traffic divides space instead of unifying it. Compare Venice and Times Square. Every practical need is taken care of in this plan. All the buildings are buildable, they are all reasonable in cost.

Nonetheless, the space is magic. There are walks above the traffic, looking into gardens over water, at artificial mountains; the directions frequently change, the view varies. Most exciting (in plan still) is the walkway to the Governor's Palace: a sort of broad wall on each side of which, far below, are pools and stairs and gardens and trees; and the wall (which seems to be about 100 feet wide) does not go straight, but rather gets thin and thick and at times changes axis. This, Le Corbusier explains, is to add interest to the approach to the palace, which at this scale might be boring.

"For the first time in history" is a strong phrase in architecture, an art which has Parthenons and pyramids in its past. Yet the organization at Chandigarh of vast and emotional space such as this has never before happened. Angkor Wat is tiny, the Forbidden City is small. The pyramids are massive, but they are not a city. The danger, and Le Corbusier has seen it, is that the vastness could be too vast. It could cause a terrible ennui. It is a mark of his genius that it does not.

The Law Courts Building is nearly finished. It will be as great as Marseilles. Here the *prisme pur* of Marseilles is turned inside out like a glove. The tricks of the Marseilles roof are put inside the volume, the pilotis are inside. Outside is a box, but a box that is solid on the ends and top only. Seen from the two long sides it is but a vast shelter, or as Le Corbusier calls it, an umbrella and a parasol. Under this shelter there are grouped three buildings with their own roofs and dripping with Mondrian-like sunshades and screens. Above the three, the vaulted shelter rises free and the space left open among them is as impressive as any space in Western architecture.

This book is difficult to read. The lay reader should concentrate on two sections: on the Marseilles apartments, which are finished and occupied, and on Chandigarh. These two great works are his masterpieces to date. Architect readers, on the other hand, must read *every* drawing. If the text is read it should be read in French (it is only fair to state that the text is intended to be trilingual).

No formal review of the book is needed. It is the fifth of the living record that publicist Le Corbusier is writing for architect Le Corbusier. The publicist includes selections from painter Le Corbusier's murals and pictures of sculpture executed with the help of the cabinetmaker Savina for sculptor Le Corbusier. There is no doubt that these multiple and vast artistic activities enhance Le Corbusier's mastery of architecture.

Speech Honoring
Mies van der Rohe on His
Seventy-Fifth Birthday

Speech, Chicago, February 7, 1961;
previously unpublished.

Mies van der Rohe, Philip Johnson, and
model of the Seagram Building.
Photograph by Irving Penn, Vogue, August
1, 1955. Copyright © 1955 by The Condé
Nast Publications, Inc.

Johnson's early advocacy of Mies's architecture and his subsequent emulation of it in his own work are virtually without parallel in recent architectural history: Wright may have called Sullivan Lieber Meister *but that was about all; and Wright in turn spawned imitators among his weaker apprentices and disciples, while the stronger among them, including his son Lloyd, as well as Barry Byrne and Bruce Goff, went off on their own very oblique tangents. Though Johnson, on the other hand, has earned the fierce loyalty of many younger architects, including Howard Barnstone, Hugh Jacobsen, Hugh Hardy, Richard Meier, Charles Gwathmey, and the two commentators in this book, he has not spawned disciples, possibly because the direction of his work in design has been so diverse.*

The speech about Mies included here takes on particular interest. In his 1947 monograph, Johnson wrote about his mentor from the point of view of an historian and propagandizer. In the speech delivered in April, 1961, at the Columbia University School of Architecture and included in the book Four Great Makers of Modern Architecture,[1] *Johnson exudes a self-confidence in his own importance as an architect that he could not have had in 1947; moreover, because he is in the throes of shedding the overtly Miesian influences on his work, his remarks are undercut with not a little irony. It is also a "serious," "correct," and important revaluation of Mies's achievement, rather too much directed to the history books.*

Such is not the case with the tribute delivered in Chicago on the occasion of Mies's seventy-fifth birthday. With the great man present, Johnson's remarks are personal and affectionate.

1. "A Personal Statement," Four Great Makers of Modern Architecture, *New York, 1963, pp. 109–12.*

Mies needs no praise or homage from me. It would be too egotistical of me to praise him, since I would bathe so deliciously in the reflected glory of having helped, though so little, in bringing him to this country and to the attention of the world.

Rather, therefore, than a speech, I shall give Mies the greeting on his seventy-fifth year that is written with exquisite calligraphy on this scroll. It is the greeting from a handful of his out-of-town admirers. Here around me I see hundreds of his colleagues who would be eager to join me. But I have chosen here a few who do not see Mies daily, who came from differing ways, a few to represent from among the hundreds that I might have selected. Please, Mies, accept this scroll as representative only, and the signatures as representing in turn the thousands who even outside this city look to you with such admiration.

I first met Mies in 1929. I had first heard of him in 1928 in a Propylaean book called *Baukunst der neuesten Zeit*. I said to myself then (bright boy Johnson) that this man with the strange name looked like the best. The only other names I remember were Le Corbusier and J. J. P. Oud, the young Dutch genius, but I thought Mies was much better, much the best. And then Mies was hardly forty, an age at which here we think an architect is just beginning to get started. Mies's position in Berlin in the twenties was unique. He was a leader of revolutionizing modern architecture and the arts. He was the owner and publisher of *G*, the most avant-garde paper in an avant-garde age. But he was at the same time a professor at the Prussian Academy and head of the Deutscher Werkbund, neither organization being anywhere near as advanced in the arts as they might have been. Mies was "way out" modern, but he loved Schinkel, and he even told me once with some pride what an excellent Beaux-Arts architect he could be if he wanted to.

The Bauhaus crowd, and especially the functionalists, the literal-minded believers in what was called *die Neue Sachlichkeit,* rather suspected Mies's modernity. They felt (and it sounds a little strange now, thirty years later) that architecture was now at last purely functional: it was a technic, a technic only, of building buildings. Art was a word not to be used—it was even banned for a while at the Bauhaus. They agreed with Henry Ford that history was bunk. It was not studied at the Bauhaus. After all, how could history help solve technical problems?

Naturally, the architects who talked this way created much more interesting architecture as art than they would ever admit. But Mies stood apart to defend the art of architecture, saying that architecture merely as a tool was the business of the engineer. The architect's duties were of a higher order. They were questions of space arrangement, the fulfillment of the spiritual needs of the day. This argument filled the air those days. One was terribly old-fashioned to believe in art as the primary aim of our profession.

Mies was much attacked. I remember Kiesler's telling me that they criticized Mies because he used wall-to-wall curtains in his interiors—and silk curtains at that. The functionalists felt curtains unnecessary. I also remember Mies's being criticized for laying up the marble sheets in the Barcelona Pavilion book-matched, and Mies felt he had to defend this to me by saying that only photography shows this symmetry of veining, and that anyhow marble is always laid this way. That he would be called on to defend himself seems absurd today.

Yet so out of the mainstream did Mies seem to his contemporaries that Sigfried Giedeon, in commenting on the book *The International Style* that Hitchcock and I wrote thirty years ago, said it was a good book except that there was a terrible over-emphasis on the work of Mies van der Rohe.

History came to Mies's rescue. He was one of the few, as we look back, who kept his head, who saw most clearly the nature of the era he was in. He also had the strength and the leadership to put over his convictions in the otherwise committee-ridden Werkbund. Nothing is more amazing or more typical of his ability than the Weissenhof Exposition in Stuttgart in 1927. It is comparatively easy for us with 20/20 hindsight to decide who the great architects of 1927 were—the names are still familiar: Gropius, Le Corbusier, Mart Stam, J. J. P. Oud, but it took remarkable foresight in 1927 to select them and get them all to do similar work next to each other so that the world could see what the new international architecture was really like. We have only to imagine a Weissenhof Exposition with today's younger architects participating to imagine the chaos: Saarinen, Yamasaki, Pei, next to each other, all similar designers. Just look at Idlewild, if you will!

Yet Mies put together his group, had them each build a freestanding house, made them build with flat roofs and with stucco, the material of those years. Even today it would fascinate each of you to make the trip as a part of your history course to see how great the great already were a generation ago.

The culmination of these years was, of course, the Barcelona Pavilion, which I did not see. In one design, Mies confirmed the thought of decades. He summed up the new attitude to structure: the free column, the skeleton, the cage, the new wall—freestanding—independent of support. The new design-art, with space flowing into space with asymmetrical juxtapositions, with axis-less space sequences. The new decoration, marble with its own inherent richness. The building is more than the twenties, however; it is timeless. I can do no better than quote the tribute to it that was uttered at the time by the dean of early modern architecture, Peter Behrens, under whom Mies had worked. This Pavilion, Behrens said, will one day be considered the most beautiful building of the twentieth century. I must say today, a generation later, that I find no reason to change in any way this prophecy.

On His Own Work

House at New Canaan, Connecticut

From Architectural Review, *CVIII* (September, 1950), 152–59.

Johnson's decision to publish his first major work of architecture in the self-annotative manner of T. S. Eliot's The Waste Land *is, for an architect, an act of unparalleled daring. The iconoclasm of the acknowledgment that the Glass House is a "frankly derivative" work cannot be overstated, given the pseudo-functionalism and anti-historicism of the leading modern architects of the period. And the extent of the historical references convincingly brought to bear on this very modestly sized suburban domestic grouping, not to mention the breadth of the erudition, is dazzling. Not only are the more-or-less predictable ancestors drawn upon — Mies, Ledoux, Schinkel, van Doesburg, and Le Corbusier — but also the principles of Greek site planning and architecture as articulated by the Beaux-Arts theorist and historian, Auguste Choisy. Despite Le Corbusier's acknowledgment of these principles in his* Towards a New Architecture, *it was not until Johnson cited them that they were openly discussed by a confirmed adherent of the International Style in direct relationship to new work. Johnson's iconoclastic use of history does not go beyond the realm of organizational principles; that is to say, he vigorously eschews anything which might be construed as eclecticism. He is not yet the "functional eclectic" he will later claim himself to be. Interestingly, Johnson's progress toward the final design of the Glass House shows in a fairly overt manner his reliance on forms borrowed from history (figs. 1, 4–7, 10), and his renovation of the interior of the Brick Guest House in 1952 includes the now famous guest bedroom with its plaster vaults that not only are based quite closely on the work of Sir John Soane but also recall some of the early, discarded schemes for what was to become the Glass House.*

In citing Miesian precedent as justification for the structurally based decoration of the exterior, Johnson, despite what appears to be a daring reference to mannerism, is only elaborating a point he made with Hitchcock in The International Style; *and his invocation of "stock structural elements" smacks more of influence from the Charles Eames House at Malibu than of the daring plea for richness and luxury that had characterized his earlier discussions of Mies's work.*

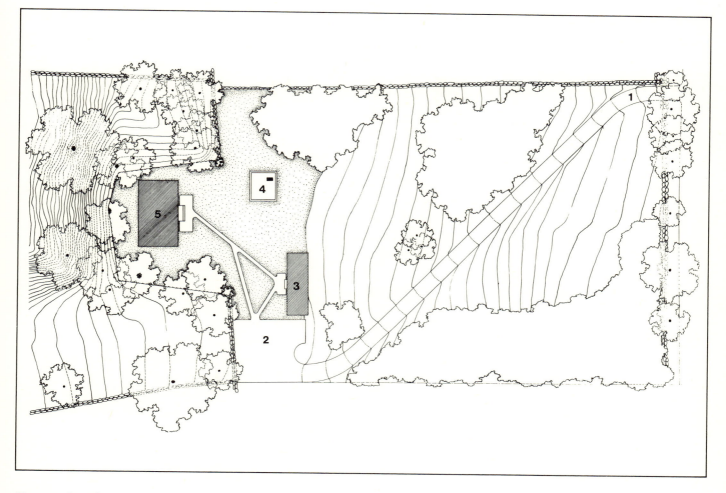

Key to site plan:
1. Entrance to site. 2. Car park. 3. Guest house. 4. Sculpture.
5. Glass house.

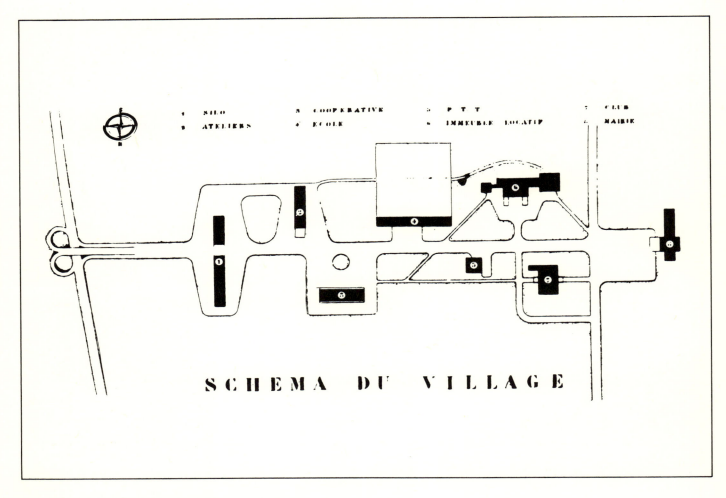

1 Le Corbusier: Farm Village Plan—1933.

The approach to the house through meadow and copse is derived from English Eighteenth Century precedent. The actual model is Count Pückler's estate at Muskau in Silesia. The driveway is straight, however, like the pathways in the plan above. The footpath pattern between the two houses I copied from the spider-web-like forms of Le Corbusier, who delicately runs his communications without regard for the axis of his buildings or seemingly for any kind of pattern.

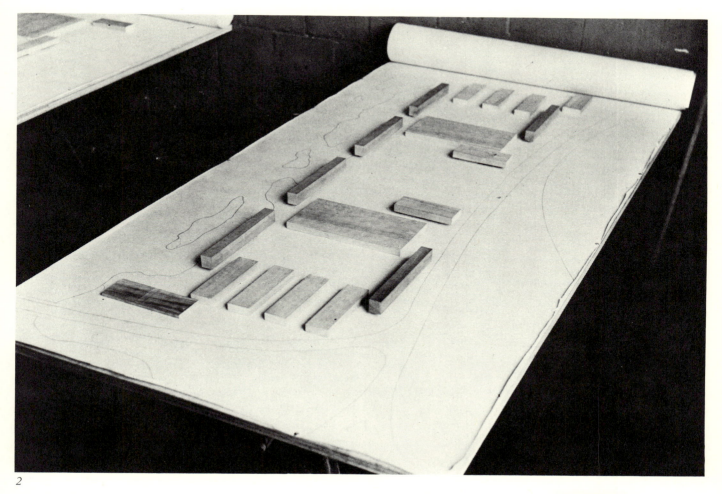

2

2 Mies van der Rohe: Ideal arrangement of Illinois Institute of Technology Buildings, 1939.
The arrangement of the two buildings and the statue group is influenced by Mies' theory of organizing buildings in a group. The arrangement is rectilinear but the shapes tend to overlap and slide by each other in an asymmetric manner.

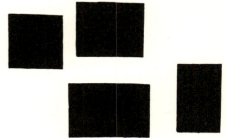

3 Theo Van Doesburg: The Basso Continuo of Painting. (Published in "G" an *avant garde* magazine by Mies van der Rohe in 1922).
The idea of asymmetric sliding rectangles was furthest developed in the De Stijl aesthetics of war-time Holland. These shapes, best known to posterity through the painting of the late Piet Mondrian, still have an enormous influence on many other architects besides myself.

3

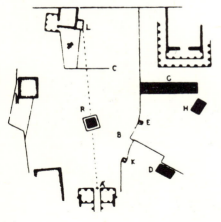

4

4 Plan and Perspective of the Acropolis at Athens from Choisy: *L'Histoire de l'Art Grecque.*

Choisy proved that the Greeks restricted the angle of approach to their buildings to the oblique; also that they placed their monuments so that only one major building dominated the field of vision from any given point. The grouping of my buildings follows Choisy: from the focal point at the beginning of the footpath near the parking lot, the brick house (Propylaea) is passed and forms a wall on the right hand. The statue group (Athena Promachos) is in full view slightly to the right. The glass house (Parthenon) comes into view (from an oblique angle) only after the pine tree at the angle of the promontory is circumnavigated.

5 Karl Friedrich Schinkel: Casino in Glienicke Park near Potsdam, c. 1830. Entrance façade.

The site relation of my house is pure Neo-Classic Romantic—more specifically, Schinkelesque. Like his Casino my house is approached on dead-level and, like his, faces its principal (rear) façade toward a sharp bluff.

6 Karl Friedrich Schinkel: Casino in Glienicke Park near Potsdam, c. 1830. Terrace overlooking the Havel.

The Eighteenth Century preferred more regular sites than this and the Post-Romantic Revivalists preferred hilltops to the cliff edges or shelves of the Romantics (Frank Lloyd Wright, that great Romantic, prefers shelves or hillsides).

5

6

7 Claude Nicholas Ledoux: Maison des Gardes Agricoles, at Maupertuis, c. 1780.

The cubic, "absolute" form of my glass house, and the separation of functional units into two absolute shapes rather than a major and minor massing of parts comes directly from Ledoux, the Eighteenth Century father of modern architecture. (See Emil Kaufmann's excellent study Von Ledoux bis Le Corbusier.*) The cube and the sphere, the pure mathematical shapes, were dear to the hearts of those intellectual revolutionaries from the Baroque, and we are their descendants.*

7

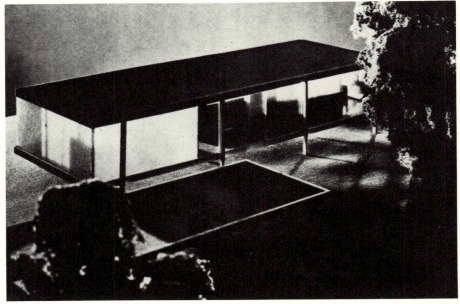

8

218

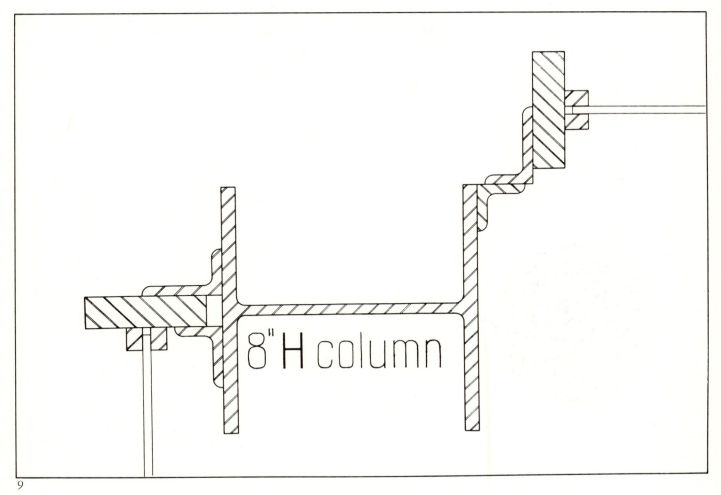

9

8 Mies van der Rohe: Farnsworth House, 1947. (Now under construction near Chicago).

The idea of a glass house comes from Mies van der Rohe. Mies had mentioned to me as early as 1945 how easy it would be to build a house entirely of large sheets of glass. I was sceptical at the time, and it was not until I had seen the sketches of the Farnsworth House that I started the three-year work of designing my glass house. My debt is therefore clear, in spite of obvious differences in composition and relation to the ground.

9 Philip C. Johnson: Johnson House, New Canaan, 1949. Section at corner.

Many details of the house are adapted from Mies' work, especially the corner treatment and the relation of the column to the window frames. This use of standard steel sections to make a strong and at the same time decorative finish to the façade design is typical of Mies' Chicago work. Perhaps if there is ever to be "decoration" in our architecture it may come from manipulation of stock structural elements such as this (may not Mannerism be next?).

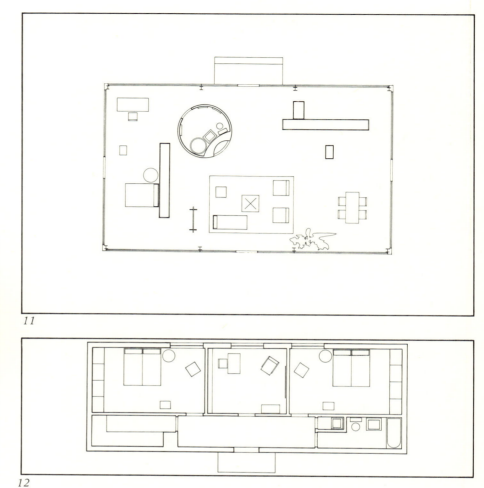

10 Kasimir Malevitch: Suprematist Element: Circle—1913.

Although I had forgotten the Malevitch picture, it is obviously the inspiration for the plan of the glass house. Malevitch proved what interesting surrounding areas could be created by correctly placing a circle in a rectangle. Abstract painting of forty years ago remains even today the strongest single aesthetic influence on the grammar of architecture.

11 Johnson House: Plan of Glass Unit.

North end, sleeping and writing; brick cylinder, washing and w.c.; south-east, cooking; south-west, eating; west, sitting.

Except for the cylinder, the plan of the house is Miesian. The use of 6-foot closets to divide yet unite space is his. The grouping of the furniture asymmetrically around a coffee table is his. The relation of cabinets to the cylinder, however, is more "painterly" than Mies would sanction.

13

12 Johnson House: Plan of Brick Unit.
Two double guests' bedrooms with study between; combined entrance hall-picture gallery with storage room at one end, bathroom and shower at the other.

The guest house with Baroque plan central corridor and three symmetrically placed rooms, was derived from Mies' designs. The three round windows in the rear of the façade are a Renaissance approach to a Miesian motif. Mies uses the round window as a method of admitting light in a long brick wall in a manner least to disturb the continuity of the wall. A rectangular hole would compete in direction with the shape of the wall itself. I used the round windows for the same reason, with a totally different compositional effect.

13 Johnson House: North End of West Wall.
The multiple reflections on the 18' pieces of plate glass, which seem superimposed on the view through the house, help give the glass a type of solidity; a direct Miesian aim which he expressed twenty-five years ago: "I discovered by working with actual glass models that the important thing is the play of reflections and not the effect of light and shadow as in ordinary buildings."

221

14

16

15

14 Johnson House: General View of Brick and Glass Units.
The bi-axial symmetry of each façade of the glass house is as absolute as Ledoux and much purer than any Baroque example. Opposite sides of my house are identical and the "minor" axis is almost as developed as the "major." (Is there a slight leftover of Baroque in the fact that the front door is in the long elevation?)

15 Johnson House: Entrance Façade of Glass Unit.

16 Johnson House: Entrance Façade of Brick Unit.
The guest house with central door and severely axial plan is jointly descended from the Baroque and from designs by Mies. (See 12.)

17 Johnson House: Glass Unit at Night.

The cylinder, made of the same brick as the platform from which it springs, forming the main motif of the house, was not derived from Mies, but rather from a burnt wooden village I saw once where nothing was left but foundations and chimneys of brick. Over the chimney I slipped a steel cage with a glass skin. The chimney forms the anchor.

18

18 Johnson House: Interior looking South.
Mies van der Rohe has not only influenced the concept of the house. He has designed all of the furniture—some of it a quarter century ago, none of it later than 1930.

19 Johnson House: Sculpture Group.
The papier-mâché sculpture by Nadelman provides the type of foil which this kind of building needs (Mies again established the precedent in his Barcelona Pavilion).

19

20

21

22

20 Johnson House: Interior looking West.
The view of the valley, with its repoussoir *of giant trees, is contrived with the aid of many Baroque landscapes. A view without a frame seems impossible after the Seventeenth Century.*

21 Johnson House: Cooking Unit.
The kitchen I reduced to a simple bar so that it would not close off any space. I have no idea what precedent I followed on that.

22 Johnson House: Interior, North-east Corner.
Bed and writing desk, with strips of pandanus cloth hanging from the ceiling — the only screening I felt to be necessary.

Whither Away—
Non-Miesian Directions

Speech, Yale University, February 5, 1959; previously unpublished.

This is the first publication of a talk given at Yale in February, 1959, on the occasion of the opening of the first, and to date only, one-man exhibition of Johnson's work. In no other talk or essay does Johnson so clearly articulate his views about the characteristically Modern distinction between Weltanschauung *and* Zeitgeist; *nowhere else is he franker about the inexorable hold that the Modern Movement's puritanism has over him.*

As Johnson points out, the title of his talk and of the exhibition it relates to is a misleading one. Though at first glance Johnson's distinctions between being "non-Miesian" and "anti-Miesian" seem mere semantic hairsplitting, on second inspection the differences reveal themselves as very important. Even to this day, and in some ways despite Johnson's own intentions, Mies's work remains the basis of Johnson's: the highly innovative skyscrapers of the late sixties and seventies would be impossible without Mies's two projects for tall buildings in 1919 and 1921; the Crystal Cathedral at Garden Grove, California, with its vast interior space uninterrupted by intermediate structural support, is unthinkable without Mies. To Johnson's exhortation that one "cannot not know history" must be added, in his case at least, that, to design, one cannot not know Mies.

Johnson's use of the word "traditionalism" to characterize the historicism of much of his work of the 1906's is important. His is certainly not the radical eclecticism called for by Charles Jencks and others. That Johnson does not wish to revive old forms is odd, given his view of history as both "a background of ideas" and a corpus of forms. It is understandable, however, in light of his continuing bias toward the Modern Movement's passionately moralistic commitment to the idea of architecture as the will to new form.

I don't like the title of my show. Somebody in the school thought it was cute and called it "Non-Miesian." I am just as Miesian as I ever was. The fact that it has to be called Non-Miesian shows you Mies's strength. Pick up the new issue of the *Architectural Forum* with all those little pictures of things to come; there was one Wrightian influence, all the rest were Miesian. In other words, Mies stands out so far today that one must stand for him, against him, underneath him, on top of him, on his shoulders if you can get there. My stand today is violently *anti*-Miesian. I think that is the most natural thing in the world, just as I am not really very fond of my father. It is all very understandable; in these days of change, you have to thumb your nose as you can in order to exert your own poor little ego. Mies said it beautifully on that record you all heard, "I'd rather be good than original." I suppose the rest of us aren't quite that great; and we all have our little egos, and we are damn well going to express them, and I think that is what's happening.

I want to give you tonight a few of the reasons why I am doing what I am, and what direction I am taking. I happened to bring with me the announcement of this exhibition, which you can read later at your leisure; it's a very important manifesto. I printed it large. In the twenties, it was always the passion to have manifestos. No, this is not a manifesto of a movement; this is a personal expression of—Paul Rudolph in his introductory remarks called it doubt; you know, I don't think I doubt, but if he says I do, well maybe that's what it is.

I have always been delighted to be called Mies van der Johnson. It has always seemed proper in the history of architecture for a young man to understand, even to imitate, the great genius of an older generation. Mies is such a genius. But I grow old. No respect, no respect. This one-sided exhibition of mine is unfair, unfair to my work as a whole but maybe amusing to Yale undergraduates. My direction is clear: traditionalism. This is not academic revival; there are no classic orders in my work, no Gothic finials. I try to pick up what I like throughout history. We cannot not know history. Then it goes on to buildings you haven't seen yet. How could the Roofless Church exist without Bramante, or the Lincoln Center Colonnade project without St. Peter's, or the Amon Carter Museum without the Loggia dei Lanzi, and so forth and so on? I have gone back to my own little way of looking at things, which is purely historical, and not revivalist but eclectic, as you will see as time goes on, and I want to describe a little bit the background for this strong current. In the first place, it's impossible to do architecture without a background of ideas. I mean, of course, the forms are important, but the ideas that compel architects to do something are also important. Most important to us in your generation and mine is the revolution in form—not in ideas, mind you, but in form. What happened in 1923, and why did it happen? Why did the International Style arise—do I dare use that word? I think you have heard of the Style; it lasted quite a while, from 1923 to 1959, perhaps; but why did that revolution suddenly happen, and why were the shapes that were formed at that time the way they were? Well, it was the final reaction of forms overtaking ideas. Sullivan said that form follows function. Of course it doesn't. Forms follow ideas in people's minds, if they get strong enough to come out. But the ideas that formed that revolution were much earlier than the creation of the International Style, with its credo of simplicity, structural clarity, and functionalism—both structural and social. That is, the building had to be based on its own structural clarity of members. All the buildings that you see around you in the Style are still today among the better buildings. All Bunshaft, all Rudolph, up till recently all mine, have all been in that style. To you people it is all recognizable. To you it has not been new since we wrote the book twenty-five years ago. But I'm interested tonight to go further back, to the ideas behind the men who founded the movement. Mies was of course one of the great leaders of that famous year 1923—Mies, Gropius, Corbusier, Oud, van Doesburg, Malevitch, and the rest.

And they had ideas coming from much further back in history that finally did turn into form. You have all been exposed to them, perhaps, in a great university like this: the ideas of Viollet-le-Duc or Ruskin, who felt such a moral strength about structural expression, and such hatred of the Renaissance in its fakery, and love of Gothic in what they considered to be its truth. The preference for Greek simple columns over Roman forms and shapes, the puritan reaction against the nineteenth century, were very old things by 1923. This idea that architecture had something to do with morals, and that there was a right and wrong way of handling steel and handling stone, had a history way back; and the only funny part of it is that it didn't come out until 1923. Really, I sometimes think Goethe was the founder of Modern architecture, although the forms came a hundred years afterwards. In his famous sentence, "the pilaster is a lie," you can see his resentment against everything that's happened since the Greeks. A pilaster to him was just a projection in the wall that was made to look as if it were a column. It looked like a column, and it wasn't doing the work of a column; therefore it was dishonest, therefore it couldn't be great architecture. That line of thought was of course underlying, along with the discovery of concrete and steel, and Japanese prints, and painting; of course we can't omit the rest of the great themes that come into the creation of the International Style.

What is the mental composition of the men who made that revolution, and how was it done? Well, now that we are all over at the other end, it's rather interesting what this all led to: it led to the great work of the twenties, to the great work of Mies van der Rohe. What a man's *Weltanschauung* is, is really immaterial; I mean, he can believe in devils or gods or genies out of the sea and still do good buildings. But when a whole generation takes over, as we all did (Rudolph, too, in spite of his youth), takes over these principles of clarity, simplicity, and expression of structure, that's quite a general acceptance. We all have individual differences within this morality, but we are all moral. You take Lou Kahn: Lou Kahn's interpretation of modern architecture doesn't look much like Mies's, you might say, but the morality is there. My engineer tells me that when the ducts were put under one of his new buildings, the easy way to run the ducts was diagonally across under the ground, like this, from this corner to that; but Kahn wanted the ducts to go under the corridors, so he put them around that way, costing another few thousand dollars. It's the moral principle that the duct work for the air-conditioning should follow the paths of the people. Take Lou's moral attitude on structure, his triangle. Now, triangulation of structure is of course an eminently practical principle. We ran into it in the Seagram Building, when we had to put many thousands of tons of concrete where we didn't particularly want them, merely to create stability in the lateral direction. Kahn took that principle and erected it into a poetic fantasy; but the attitude is still one of morality, like Mies's theory of "less is more"— when it's obvious that more is more. We don't have to discuss that, but the fact that he would think the simpler the better is a very strong moral line that runs through his thinking and colors all his work. Of course, he escapes from his principles whenever he wants to. I once asked him a stupid question, the type that students ask. I said, "It is true, is it not, that if a girder runs this way and the beams run into it perpendicularly, the girder is deeper than the beam?" "Yes." "Then why on the facia of your building, Mr. van der Rohe, is the girder expressed the same depth as the beam? It should be deeper, because it's carrying more weight." He said, "Don't be so literal-minded." He doesn't worry about things like that. Quite rightly; his theory is a much deeper one than that.

Then you have architects like Paul Rudolph, who is now doing boxes all over his buildings. I refer to his school now under construction in Sarasota. All Yale will have to go down there next year and take a look, because those violent shadows are going to be something that we haven't seen since Furness of Philadelphia; I doubt there has been anything that strong since the 1870's. The interesting part, though, is that these seemingly arbitrary shapes are related to structure; these forms on the roof create the beams, as he no doubt explained to you a hundred times. I think sometimes they are *not* structural; I'm not sure, but I don't care. The whole point is that it is related to structure; structure is, as with Mies, still a point of departure. Structure, clarity, clear planning, help you in your design; they are the things that start your creative juices running. Today, this belief is running thin.

The idea that clarity, simplicity, logic, and honesty is the best policy, that these "virtues" will get you anywhere, falls down in many ways, and in other fields than architecture. The emergence of existentialism, for instance, with its noble philosophy that cuts across Christian and atheist thought, has changed some of our most cherished values. The existentialist basic assumption in life is also mixed up, in the beat generation, with Zen (I am a natural Zen, they tell me; since I know nothing about it, it's easy to believe in it, you see). But the main point about Zen is that you don't have to be going anywhere: no more purposes in life, no more "higher things." You just do what you want to do; that's all right, just go right ahead. The lack of the old puritanism is very refreshing. In architecture this attitude leads to what Rudolph calls doubts, and doubts can get mighty fundamental; and then there follows the question: "Whither away?" What handles are you going to grab on to? It was easy when I went to school. Several generations had it simple because there were very simple criteria: if an entrance was off, it was very easy to put straight again, because of the clarity of the underlying conception. It's fun to take this latest copy of the *Forum*. The things that are to be built "International Style" can be criticized easily from the basis of a rule of book. I have done it on many a jury myself. It was very simple, but it's not so simple anymore when you are creating new things.

Tonight I shall show you just a few of my slides to illustrate what the new currents are that the International Style and the puritan *Weltanschauung* simply can't cope with. That is, there are problems today that simplicity doesn't solve. I am talking purely architecturally now. You have got to get away from the straitjacket of the thought processes of the early part of the century. My particular answer, that history is the answer to everything, will naturally be disputed by every other person, but I think that is fine. I think it's grand to have blinders so that you only see the direction you are going in. I have never heard of an architect who was broad-minded, because that means shallow, and you just cannot design without convictions. I don't know how many Moslems there are present, but I am sure that faith would help just as much as being a Marxist or an existentialist. I don't think it makes any difference. My passion is history. I pick up anything, any old point in time or place. I couldn't design without history at my elbow all the time. Maybe some of you don't want to do that, and that's just fine, but I would propose it as a substitute for the debacle of the International Style, which is now in ruins around us. History is a vast and helpful discipline.

For instance, an interesting intellectual exercise in this regard is the Seagram Building, which was conceived by Mies within his philosophy of "less is more," as of great trabeated clarity, a simple design. I don't see it that way at all. Through my blinders, it looks quite different; it is a great exercise in Schinkelesque classical design. Regard its corners, for instance. Note how very, very heavy they are, in relation to the five-inch-wide mullions of the rest. The change of pace at the top of the glass: how cleverly the mullions go right on up through to the roof, but the glass all changes to the dark hundreds of linear grilles; little lines, every one of which Mies personally drew, because he knew the cornice was the most important part of the building. This is the old historian getting in on the act. I don't know how conscious Mies is of that, and I don't know how much I am reading in. I don't care, I just think it is amusing that a building is great, although you can look at it in many different ways. Winckelmann and Goethe looked at the Parthenon one way; I look at it another. I find it highly—well, I'm not going into the Parthenon, I have enough trouble with modern building. But Mies and I don't agree at all on what's good history. He thinks Berlage is a great architect, and I think Richardson is. Well, so what! Mies is a great architect. He thinks Berlage is a great man who understood the nature of brickwork. Well, Mies certainly understands it, and if he learned it from Berlage, more power to him. You take the Seagram cornice, you take the Seagram base. Did you ever see a stylobate more carefully worked out? The three steps—not four, not two steps, not five, but three; and Mumford caught the reaction perfectly well by saying, "I feel as if I had gone up an enormous flight of steps as I step up to the Seagram Plaza." Well, I don't know how "less is more" helped Mies on that, but whatever it was, it came out a classically satisfactory stylobate. You take the corner treatment that the Greeks had trouble with. The Greeks had to push their columns in and tilt them to make them go around their corners. Mies didn't tilt the corner columns of the Seagram Building, but he spent many a long day, and I have seen him at it, deciding just where those corner mullions occur. They could have occurred anywhere. The column itself, you'll notice, is revealed all the way to the top of the building, which gives a continuity between the base and the mass of the building; but that corner (as it is in all great architecture), is of the essence. If you can't solve that, you can't build a building. I suppose it is simple, but it is the art that conceals art. So simple that you (and maybe he himself) think it just came naturally. Believe me, it didn't—"from my historical point of view," I'll have to add; because maybe it did. Maybe Mies just said, "Hell, let's build any old building," but I find these refinements hard to explain merely on the basis of the International Style.

I must explain that my past is peculiar. I have spent much more time as a critic, an historian, than I have as an architect, because I didn't start architecture, as Rudolph so kindly points out, until I was thirty-five years old; so naturally my historical sense is over-developed. I think I am right, or I wouldn't be up here defending myself. I see no reason to have a Thirty Years' War among the various groups that are now going to take over the remains of the International Style. After all, it is going to be rather hard for you young people to build an office building without regard for the Seagram Building. I am very glad no one has asked me to do one in the last year or so. Exactly where would you start? I see in the classrooms today buildings of the size of City Hall in New Haven, with extended fronts in the Rudolphian manner of very deep shadows. That's fine; but you go up five hundred feet with those, and you are going to have piles of pigeon nests. There are all sorts of problems involved that lead you back to a rather simple vertical. Somehow or other, if you've been talking to engineers a little while, and then you add the fact that New York streets are straight, you can't start doing curves. The Seagram Building is going to exercise a very strong influence, because there is something in the Miesian way of looking at things that does fit extraordinarily well with the way we actually build. That's where Mies got it. Mies has transformed ordinary building into poetry, but his theories, as far as theory goes, would also fit half the factories in this country. It's awfully hard to design a factory. I tried to last year; it cost only three times what it would have if it had been built without "design." I did not get to build it, needless to say. In other words, economy, which Mies considers terribly important, is important. Mies based his art on three things: economy, science, technology; of course, he was right. It's just that I am bored. We are all bored.

What I think it really comes down to are the four things that I am now going to discuss. There are four areas in architecture in which I think the puritanical religious background of the International Style has failed me. This failure has driven me to a renewed study of history. The first is the theater; the second is the façade; the third is religious building; and lastly, the plaza.

The theater I shall take up in a minute. Second, the façade. Even the word was anathema to the International Style. There were no façades. Façades were merely the expression of what went on inside. Paul Rudolph has said so well that the worst thing the Bauhaus ever did was to denigrate the word "façade." The façade exists as something you look at; it is an important part of a building. Ideologically, for the past thirty years, it has been considered the least important.

The third thing that I find the International Style can't help us with is the religious building. There is no way for a perfectly straightforward structural system to give us emotional satisfaction. And the fact that they didn't know that back in the twenties, thirties, and forties shows how different their ideology was from the one that is coming up today.

And the fourth area is the plaza. In International Style days, you put a clean-cut building all by itself, isolated here, and one here; but you couldn't enclose space as in St. Peter's Square or St. Mark's. The attached group of buildings leaving an architectural "room" as a plaza was foreign to our thinking. Look at housing developments. None of us has ever, recently anyhow, seen a housing development by any authority that has used the plaza—maybe because it would be so substandard from the point of view of light and air that it couldn't be tolerated. But it isn't that so much; it is the ideological rejection of the plaza as an organizing room, as an organizing theme in architecture.

And those four things are illustrated with four pairs of slides which will illustrate what I have been discussing. This is the New York State Theater at Lincoln Center, illustrating the first of the four problems the International Style couldn't solve. The problem of the theater is extremely old, and I have had a lot of fun going back and tracing its history up through to the puritan revolution; and I think I will start with the puritan revolution because that's what was so interesting. It started long before 1923; it started in 1850 with Semper, who reacted against the royal court theaters. The State Theater is an adaptation of such a court theater. Eighteenth-century theaters are good! But in 1850 they thought they were terrible, because you couldn't see from the boxes. You still can't. You can imagine in 1850 a new generation coming in with a sense of order and asking the moral question, "Who would want to make a theater where you could not see the stage?" So the result was a whole movement ending up in Bayreuth and the Munich theaters, with the fan shape you are familiar with from your books, the fan without surrounding balconies, just a great slice-of-pie shape. These earnest revolutionaries completely forgot that if you sit in one of the corners of the fan, you might as well, emotionally speaking, have stayed at home.

Then came the twenties and the Corbusier design for the theater, Gropius's design for the theater, and Mies's, all of which were single-pitch fan-shaped houses. The Salle Pleyel in Paris carried the sight-line passion further to include acoustical considerations. The shell (as in Le Corbusier) drops toward the stage in a giant curve—the pseudo-science of acoustics of the period. They curved the ceiling down to the opening of the proscenium, you have all seen that. I feel you might as well stay away from the theater if the theater is going to bow at you like this. It is as if I were trying to talk to you with blinders on, when you have to look at the stage through these dippy things. But that shows the ideology that was at work: the idea that science can give us a lift (the crutch of science).

In the theater, they say, we no longer have to think about the *royal* court and the *royal* box. That's true, we don't. So that's left out; so what do they put in its place? Acoustics and sight lines. They will tell you absolutely nothing about architecture as attractive space, and there isn't a structural trick that will give you any help. The only thing that will give you any help is the memory, the history of how you feel in enclosed theaters, and there is absolutely no substitute for that. You have to use your imagination too, but the lessons are perfectly clear from actual buildings you visit. Study the reasons the court theaters got that way within a great period, the sixteenth, seventeenth, through the eighteenth century; and they built eighteenth-century theaters right through the nineteenth century (the old Metropolitan Opera House in New York was an eighteenth-century theater). The court theater makes it possible to make the theater small enough, appearing to give you a sense of intimacy in the theater; and the curtain is gold, and the ceiling doesn't bow down for the acoustics, and the whole thing is simply delightful! That tradition was started when there were many fewer people going to the theater, and when sight lines were not nearly so important as were social events. And now we are so scientific we think we have to see the show.

You have to give in in some way, of course, and I have in the State Theater. I have tried to do both: to see and to be intimate. The continental seating drives a lot of people crazy, but obviously it is the only way to get the feel of a hall, when you have continental seating and five balconies rising around you. If you sit somewhere in the back, you do see the stage, but around you, crowding around the proscenium, are people; the walls are paved, covered, wallpapered with people. You can see the catastrophe of not doing that in most New York theaters, where they shut off all the boxes and cover them up. Your angle of vision from the rear includes much more than the proscenium; it takes in a lot of the side wall. And people sitting up there sometimes can't see well (it's not as bad as all that, some of them can see), but at least you say, "I'm in the midst of a wonderful place where something is going on." You get a sense of participation; the curve around the back doesn't have any corners (like the fan) where you could get the feeling you were not in the theater at all. And the five balconies contain as many people vertically as possible. The proscenium of course goes the full height, a sixty-foot high opening. The full sixty feet are not used. There is no theater in the world that goes higher than forty, but you hang a false front in front of that so it makes you think you are seeing something on a stage that is sixty feet high. Of course that's cheating; isn't most art? Before the curtain goes up, you say, "My goodness, a sixty-by-sixty-foot performance is coming on," and then you forget it. Well, you have all been to the Met, and none of you ever realized that the curtain rises only thirty feet. That's the only way it seems to me that you can approach the theater.

I'm not sure what historical precedent I used for the exterior of the State Theater. This façade is not concrete; I hope if we can afford it, it will be granite, which is much prettier than concrete pre-cast. But the cost is staggering, so we are in a little trouble. What I wanted to express here was the tension potentiality of concrete with the beauty of granite and still get the scale and shadows of the ins and outs that a bay fifteen feet wide and sixty feet high would give you. You can't understand scale from any model. Eighty feet is higher than The Museum of Modern Art. I would like to build a full-scale mock-up to understand it. Well, it's what Mies did. Remember Mies built that house in canvas (it's in the first chapter in my book) in 1912 in Holland. That's how you find out whether the building fits the site or not: you mock it all up in canvas. But you have to do that to get the scale of the fifteen-foot-wide thing going up eighty feet high. That's a glass wall, but it is gold glass, gold-flecked glass. You can look in but not out at night. It would glow (as the model glows in the office). This glass is almost opaque, so you get a gold-mirror effect at night from the inside, and from the outside you get the speckled light coming through the glass, but it is not clear vision.

The next slide shows two façades: the one on the left is a house for a Mr. Mann on Rittenhouse Square in Philadelphia, which he didn't build when he heard the price. The building on the right is the rejected version of Asia House. The accepted version is now halfway up, and it is a perfectly straightforward International Style building. You see, we are licked by progress or anti-progress. This first version was so expensive that we saved a hundred thousand or so by not doing it. I doubt if that was the real reason; the real reason was that I showed this to the client, and he said, "Philip, that looks like a church, and I can't build it." You see, to him modern building meant "that bank." (If you don't know what I mean by "that bank," it's that one on Forty-somethingth and Fifth Avenue, and that represents modern to New Yorkers.) This building to me is pure façade; there is nothing behind it. You could build it first and build something behind it some other time. I was interested in having a solid base, a solid cornice to cut down the glass, to emphasize the mullions. The surface is pre-cast, each piece faired into the next, rounded and curved. The entrance door is curved. To cap the composition at the top I did what many an architect in cast iron did in the forties and fifties of the last century. They trabeated up to the top story and then ended with arches. It's a perfectly sensible way to end the top. It may make a funny sort of room, if there are a lot of offices back of those curves, but that does not interest me very much. Two people use these offices for every hundred thousand that walk by the front door. It does seem to me that shadows are much more important than whether somebody has a round-headed window or not, and I thought it was quite a modern building. I meant to cover it with broken tea cups (like Gaudí), but that turned out to be impractical in New York, so we would have made it out of pre-cast concrete.

The Mann House is an attempt to set things back from the street, to get more plasticity into the façade, to introduce the loggia. I was also fascinated, and I still am, by heavy stone piers with thin, completely semicircular shells on the top, and bronze spandrels kept quite independently of the front piers. You drive your car right through to the garage behind; the *piano nobile* was on the second floor. A consideration intimately connected with the façade is the problem of the loggia or the stoa—a device that has been much neglected since Roman times. It is a marvelous device; a one-sided, arcaded front can be added to a perfectly normal building. It doesn't make much difference what building you put behind it; the point is that any one-sided building is grateful for any type of arcade or porch. (Remember the Feldherrnhalle in Munich and the Loggia dei Lanzi in Florence. I was very interested in those two buildings.)

Next, two buildings now under construction. One is the front (only the front façade) of the Brown University Computer Center, a type of building which is as near to a religious building, perhaps, as we can get these days. Where the altar should be, there is the computer. It is a memorial to Mr. Thomas J. Watson. The arcade is entirely freestanding in front of the actual façade. The glass is behind that, with its own frames, simply a shield. The arcade is decoration in front of the building. But it didn't look well when I made it cut out the sun. Have you ever been to South America? I advise it strongly; you never have to worry about sun shades (*brises soleil*) again. They don't work at all. Behind them you feel you are in prison. Oscar Niemeyer, who is one of the better-known architects down there, told me on my last trip that he'd done his last, and indeed he has never designed one since then. So the sun is less important. After all, they made air-conditioning to take care of the heat. So let's not worry about the sun. But we must worry about plasticity; we must worry about monumentality. I didn't just take a classical column and clip off the corners; I did something you can't do except in concrete. You can't make those shapes except in pre-cast. It is not a stone form; so I have my own little way of bowing to the nature of the materials. (As much as I resent other people paying attention to the nature of the materials, I pay some attention myself.)

This portico for the Amon Carter Museum in Fort Worth is made of real stone. (I know it looks like concrete, but it isn't.) The arches are curved, each curve carved of Austin stone, the most beautiful stone next to travertine that I know. Every square inch or so is a fossil. The color is cream, which stands up beautifully in the fantastic light of Texas. In this case, the portico does a very good deed by keeping off the sun, because the glass is set way back of it. The use of gray glass, the great overhang, and the east exposure I hope will combine to help against the sun. The shapes here are purely visual, but it also is a great satisfaction to build in stone. Maybe none of you knew George Howe when he was here; we used to sit over a Scotch and dream of the days of stone; once again to be able to build in solid stone! He had regretted so much that the Philadelphia Savings Fund Society granite was not over three inches thick. We dreamed of using a nice solid block to hold buildings up. The Fort Worth museum is solid stone; the arch is a stone arch from which go concrete beams, but at least the entire arcade and the building around are built of solid stone. I don't think that since the Morgan Library there has been anybody doing that, but merely knowing that a stone this wide and this long and that deep will be in place is a wonderful feeling for an architect.

The subject of religious feeling never got expressed in the older modern period. I don't know what you were supposed to have instead of religious feeling. In the last thirty years, puritanism took over to a degree. Simplicity was emphasized the same way it was in Puritan America. Both Modern architecture and Early American used white paint and clear windows; the white meeting house was almost as anti-religious as modern buildings. We are so used to seeing a "lovely" eighteenth-century church that we forget how anti-religious the atmosphere is in those bare white rooms with the glaring windows. There shouldn't be windows in religious buildings. If you want to heighten religious feeling with light, then certainly the Gothic and the Baroque knew best. You don't want just white paint! And in modern times, think of the churches, starting with the bare concrete of Perret's Raincy to the Karl Moser Church in Basel, then J. J. P. Oud's church in Rotterdam, which was a box with a window in it, then still further to Mies's strange chapel at I.I.T. Mies's logic would say that a bank is a church is a golf club is a house: I mean, the structural clarity, the style, carried through no matter what the purpose of the building. He has a wonderful new saying in *Time* magazine: "The building lasts much longer than its function." He has just built a museum in Houston where some people complain that there is no place to hang pictures, and he answers, "But the building will outlast that function." And of course in Houston, Texas, it certainly may. But you see that drive enables him ruthlessly to be able to build a chapel of brick walls with a flat roof. He also had an economic factor that simply could not be got around there. You and I couldn't have done it half as well, so let's not laugh-at that church. But the fact remains that it doesn't quite satisfy us today.

This room in my Brick Guest House does five or six things besides providing for sleeping. It does something to cradle the spirit to be in a curved surface, and I have never minded the fact that the dome is hung from the ceiling; the idea of its falseness never crossed my mind. (Why should a dome *not* be hung from the ceiling? It is a normal way to hang them.) The fact that the colonnettes go to the ground is a visual element to keep you from the walls, to keep the light and the lighted walls outside the room that you are in. The room is small up to the columns, and then the great outdoors takes over with the light on the pink walls.

The Roofless Church is the building I am working on now: the Shrine of the Rose. This is a shrine out in Indiana for a Texas lady, and the symbol of that town is the rose, so it is the Shrine of the Rose; and that's the Lipchitz statue in the center. This idea comes from many historic sources, primarily the Indian stupa. It is about sixty feet high, fifty feet across, and it is built of shingles, which comes from the stave churches of Norway. The circular shape comes from central planning in any period. A circle has magic meanings, which after I had designed it I found in Jung, in his description of primitive shapes. It is amusing that I was designing according to Jung; it is a good feeling to be connected with the super-unconscious or whatever it is. The bases are megaliths ten feet high of limestone, and the roof is open to the sky. It is Kelly-lighted at night, needless to say. It is surrounded by a high wall forming a temenos broken only by the portico at the right which looks out over the landscape connected to the fertile Wabash Valley. But I couldn't start on the design of the structure without computers, and the cards are getting stacked this high on the floor of the office. In other words, there is nothing simple or direct in the forms of these very strange compound curves.

In this building we are still designing religion in a way, although it houses a nuclear reactor instead of an altar. My two important religious buildings are the one at Brown for the computer and this Nuclear Reactor, which is now half up on the Mediterranean Sea in Israel. The religious overtones were also very conscious in the minds of the clients, when they came not to an engineer but to an architect to do their reactor. Of course, straight structural simplicity would have dictated cylinders, something like a gas tank. A gas tank would probably be the cheapest shape to build, the most direct and simple. After all, you want no windows; there is no problem inside except of housing the machine. Actually, no interior space is possible, because the monster is so big that you don't get space feeling around it. It is an "outside" building. Now what we have done there is to use hyperbolic paraboloids vertically, which shape the building. It has a monumental presence in the desert that I don't think you can get out of straightforward engineering shapes. This was about my sixth try; because of course in this kind of a building in raw concrete you have to make it as cheap as you possibly can. You enter through a court like the narthex at St. Ambrose, and as at St. Ambrose, the church (reactor building) looms over the court.

Now we will get to the last type of buildings that seem to me too difficult for the International Style to handle. This is my plaza design (an unpublished and unpublishable and practically almost already rejected version) for the Lincoln Center Plaza. With six of us architects sitting around the table, you can imagine what happens. What fun my co-architects would have with any such design! Each one of us thinking that he alone was descended from God and able to dictate what this plaza should look like. And the arguments have been fantastic, based on a good deal of differences in the *Weltanschauung* that I spoke of, because among us there are architects of the modern persuasion, architects who would never place buildings on the three sides of a plaza, and then cement them into a single outdoor room, the way I would do. There is one of us who would compose the building into a tower block and circle. You can see that is a good old 1928 method of conglomerating into a composition all those vast things that have to go into this seventy-five-million-dollar project. My idea was quite simple: forget all the buildings, *all* of them, and build a plaza; then you bring up whatever you have to, whenever. Anyone can see that there is no way of building all these buildings at once. There are going to be lots of holes for many, many years, and nobody knows how big the buildings are, because nobody knows where the money is coming from. Yet we have to start building. It is much like Yale University having to add, and all of a sudden they have to add twice as much before they finish the first. The result is a mess.

This Lincoln Center has to start with some magnificence. This is the place in which New York sets out to prove itself culturally, and so all of us architects are desperately anxious to compromise and to arrive at some solution.

The advantage of a plaza physically, as I told you, is the fact that you could put any buildings onto it and it doesn't affect it. I am building a campus like this in Houston, Texas. It is a Miesian arcade, and as their needs change at the university, they tack on whatever buildings they want, much as in the University of Virginia. Now in "modern" colleges, of course you can't do this. You are not supposed to build a plaza and tack things on behind the façades. Every building is supposed to have its own existence. The best example I know of International Style planning is, of course, the campus at the Illinois Institute of Technology. There are buildings of extremely subtle and modulatory relations. The buildings, no matter what the size, or the size of the neighboring building, are somehow modularly related and slip by each other in Mies's famous way of slipping rectangles. The result is a magnificent plan. But it doesn't satisfy. It does not do us emotionally enough good anymore just to see buildings well related in blocks. Here again, what history can do for us! Think, for example, of the plans of Roman army camps (Timgad), Hellenistic squares (Assos), St. Peter's, St. Mark's. You can't talk about American examples, except Jefferson's, alas. Why don't we, why can't we have a court approach?

In my plaza, I didn't design the opera house because it is not designed yet. All I was interested in was an arcade that would give dignity, and where one could see through from the city into the court to the important center building, which of course has to be the Metropolitan Opera. My theater and other theaters would be on the side, merely tacked on to the arcade. The whole plaza would be closed, so you couldn't get out except through the front way.

Now as to the details of this plaza. I designed this system of concrete pre-cast columns which I now realize only today that I got from flamboyant cathedral façades. I can't use stone today; I don't know how they ever held stones together then. Today we would have to reinforce them with rods, but in those days, they were real stones, lacy stones! We would build of concrete. My columns would be easy and very, very cheap to make, if we use concrete, and I see no way in this generation to use stone in a monumental enough way to make any sense.

Now I don't know where all this is leading to. History is the thing I always start with. I mean, I would rather start with the street pattern of Rome and work from that to modern. I am not sure where we are going. Some of you will be doing blocks; some of you will be doing just ins and outs; some of you can go on doing "Modern" if you want to. I think we are getting to a splitting up that is fantastic. I think we are all galloping off in all directions, and all I can say is, "Here we go! Let's all go to the races and have fun!" My own particular thing is, "Hurray for history, and thank God for Hadrian, for Bernini, for Le Corbusier, and Vincent Scully!"

Johnson

From Perspecta 7 (1961), 3–8.

Perspecta 7 *is a key document of the second generation of the Modern Movement's International Style as it came to be practiced in America. As such, it can be regarded as the formalist counterpart to the socio-functionalist* Team Ten Primer. Perspecta 7 *not only contains innovative work by principal form-givers of the day—including John Johansen, Louis Kahn, Paul Rudolph, and Eero Saarinen, as well as Johnson—but also carries with it critical assessments of their work, and of the then-current situation in American architecture, written by journalists and historians (Peter Collins, Walter McQuade, and Sibyl Moholy-Nagy), as well as two provocative views of American practice by English architects then little known to American readers, James Gowan and Colin St. John Wilson.*

In Perspecta 7, *Johnson is represented by some of his most daring if unresolved work of mid-career, including the miniaturized pavilion for his garden at New Canaan, and projects for the Benedictine Priory at Washington, D.C., and the Sheldon Memorial Art Gallery, Lincoln, Nebraska. The text, which the editors title with ironic equivocation simply "Johnson," needs little comment. What does bear remarking upon is Johnson's relationship to* Perspecta, The Yale Architectural Journal, *an occasional publication edited by the architectural students at Yale, which he has supported to the fullest extent since its inception under the patronage of George Howe in 1951. Johnson has reserved for* Perspecta's *pages some of his most interesting buildings and projects and some of his most carefully articulated essays about architecture. In the 1950's, when he was a pivotal figure on the Yale scene, he participated in the after-hours discussions organized by the students. Some of these sessions were tape-recorded, transcribed, and collated to constitute a "conversation" with other key figures, notably Louis Kahn and Vincent Scully, and published in* Perspecta 2 *as "On the Responsibility of the Architect." In* Perspecta 1, *Johnson, along with Buckminster Fuller and Paul Rudolph, was singled out as a representative of "New Directions" in architecture.* Perspecta 3 *contains his "Seven Crutches of Modern Architecture" (see pp. 137–40), as well as a presentation of his Wiley House, accompanied by a brief essay by him explaining the house.* Perspecta 7 *includes the material in this section.* Perspecta 9/10 *was privileged to benefit from Johnson's generosity to what had by then become an established, if erratic, publishing venture. Not only did he write "on commission"—and, of course, without fee—the essay, "Whence and Whither" (see pp. 151–55), but he also permitted me, its editor, to rummage through his files and select a number of hitherto unpublished and unbuilt designs that I was anxious to present in order to "flesh out" the story of his struggle against the formal straitjacket of the orthodox International Style—a story I then regarded and continue to regard as critical to setting the scene for the emerging style which has since come to be described as post-Modernism.*

In an intellectual atmosphere of casual heaviness in design, of careful not-design, or at least a look of to-hell-with-it, it is difficult to write of my work. It seems I cannot but be Classically inspired; symmetry, order, clarity above all. I cannot throw around cardboard boxes, or make a pseudo-functional arrangement of air-conditioning ducts into a *trouvé*'d type of design.

In the opposite direction, I can no longer build glass boxes—the pleasant glass box for all uses!!—the general purpose universal box. We live in another era. Like the old Beaux-Arts men in my youth, yearning for their *partis* and *entourages,* I now look back with pleasure, and yes, even some nostalgia, on the days in the twenties when the battle line was clear, the modern versus the eclectic, the dreams of universal panaceas, standards, types, norms, that would "solve" architecture.

Now we know that we cannot "solve" anything. The only principle that I can conceive of believing in is the Principle of Uncertainty. It is a brave architect that can possess convictions and beliefs, and keep his tongue out of his cheek. Personally, my desire for order and clarity will have to suffice. I cannot find any shapes to copy, and forms like the good old Malevitch or Mondrian 1920 ones to fit in. Nor do my contemporaries give me a clear lead. The very best known of my own generation do one building in one day and the very opposite the next. It has got so that a critic can hardly say "This must be a Zilch building; it has the earmarks of his style or manner." We seem, even more than even in that much maligned 19th century, to be making a new architecture every day. Where are we at?

My own manner is in these three buildings. It seems an architect is only inarticulate about his own work. It is much easier to write about Saarinen and Rudolph than about Johnson. I really don't know why I designed these the way I did. Others will tell me.

The three projects represent two poles of my present tendencies. The clearest and furthest developed (the Pavilion is under way) is the direction of the Pavilion and the Sheldon Art Gallery. It is clear from the pictures that the grammar is the same, the buildings only are different; one is symmetrical with infill—making pilasters out of the columns. (How long ago it was that Goethe said the pilaster is a lie! One would answer him today—"yes, but what a delightfully useful one.") The other is sporty, open, and only hiddenly symmetrical. One is hand-carved travertine, the other pre-cast concrete.

The grammar is rather Classical and yet the idea of it came from looking at the Delaunay St. Séverin series. His toed-in Gothic arcade suggested the widened bases. The concave sides of the columns came from the wish to vault in four directions without the use of imposts or soffits. Also a High Gothic wish. The problem, as usual, was the corner column. A concave curve at the cornice was unthinkable, so it is convex, warping toward the typical concave base. The arch itself is a hit-or-miss ellipse, created freehand, and calculated afterward. The modularity, so un-Baroque, is probably modern. (Greek revival modularity is usually strengthened at the corners, this is not.)

The importance of the Sheldon Art Gallery lies in the central court which divides the functions into four clear spaces and itself forming the fifth; the Grand Salon, the stairwell within, focuses all the subsidiary spaces. This focus is intended to destroy museum fatigue at the same time giving a lift to the spirits. The coffered ceiling "vaulting," again carved travertine, should make a monumental room. (Classical or neo-Gothic?)

The Pavilion is a sport. First, it is underscaled. Each square unit which appears first to be scaled at 12 × 12 feet is in actuality only 8 × 8. The idea is to make giants of the visitor (an idea borrowed from the dwarfs' chambers in Mantua). The intention is to place underscaled concrete furniture within some units. The central little pool (higher than the surrounding pond) with its radiating canals is a barrier from unit to unit and at the same time an accented feature. The water from the canals falls on thin metal, to tinkle gently. The ceilings which look 9 feet high are 6 feet, very unsettling. A hundred-foot-high *jet d'eau* will play in the pond in full view.

The design is aimed at the amusement we all feel of the miniature and the complicated; the pleasure of hiding among a forest of columns (Córdoba?); the sense that one of us is in one pavilion and can't reach the other except by a long circumambulation; the feeling of an island and the little pool on the little island.

The composition itself is a casual assembly of squares, roofed, open, or water, the roofed elements being symmetrically laid out. Again there is no Baroque accent, hence quite "modern," but certainly not Chinese in spite of the moon-viewing implications. It merely seemed to me as I was working on the design that architecture has room for pleasure domes, even if somewhat reduced in scale.

The Benedictine Priory is something else again. It is certainly historical in plan—a narrow, long and high (90 foot) barrel-vaulted basilica, sans transept. But it is also purely functional since the shape was developed originally for conventual liturgy. Why change? This is the very tradition (along with the Gregorian chant) that must be preserved in the architecture. But the preservation of the shape—the processional length, the height, need not interfere with contemporary forms and materials. It is to be concrete—*béton brut* throughout, columns, buttresses, infill and vault. The walls are partly vertical, partly canted, depending on whether they follow the column or the buttress. Both column and buttress are *plissé;* that is, V's of thin concrete, and the buttresses alternate with rather than support the columns. The cross section is rather like a gantry crane. The indescribable terminations of the nave and apse are flat and should be stained glass, but only dimly translucent, since the main light source comes from skylights on the side aisles, which wash the walls. There is no light directly into the chancel.

The competition for the Idlewild Union Air Terminal, which I lost to I. M. Pei, is more or less in line with the Benedictine Priory. Like the column sequences there, the column clusters are the main point of the design, making humanly apprehendable spaces out of a building, which, because of the program, was very, very long—1,100 feet. The main problem was the very low ceiling necessary for so large a room—47 feet. To make it seem higher, rather than using a 12-foot-deep truss lowering the ceiling to 35 feet, we (Lev Zetlin, engineer) developed a sine curve, double-waving roof, emphasizing, like the column clusters, the eleven bays. The design of the façade of each bay is symmetrical and classically or Classically mounted: The ground floor, solid stone, with the door in the middle; a glazed *piano nobile;* small panes of glass with heavy mullions turning at 45° at the cornice line where the roof dips. The feature of the exterior (impossible to draw) is the 35-foot overhang.

The plan is different from most new airports in that the de-planing passenger proceeds through the Great Room to buses or taxis. It is the fashion today not to allow de-planing and en-planing passengers to mix. I am glad the genius who designed the Grand Central Station lets me come from the train into the same Great Room where others are about to en-train. What good is a great gateway room if the visitor is not to see it?

The great airport of our age has yet to be designed. Forty-seven feet high is the limit at Idlewild. In the cause of sacred monumentality, we should get up a public subscription to raise the height of the Idlewild central tower, which controls the height of all the buildings of the group. Why should the air age not have the glow of the Renaissance Age? The Grand Central and the Pennsylvania Station, before they fell on evil days, were spaces that made the heart sing, spaces that never got too small as traffic expanded, as do our airports. What we have lost is a public passion for greatness. No cathedrals? Not even any great public nuclear plant? What is our generation going vicariously to enjoy as in old days the palace, the church, or the Acropolis? We cannot all of us enjoy slum clearance and parking lots.

The questions are rhetorical. There are no answers. A culture gets the monuments it desires.

Article for the *Kentiku*

Dated January 25, 1962; *from* Kentiku, V (May, 1962), 21–23.

Perhaps a sense of frustration over the incredibly difficult cultural barriers that must be surmounted by Americans and Japanese in order to achieve genuine mutual understanding, perhaps simply the occasion of the first important retrospective publication of his work, inspired this, Johnson's most concise and measured philosophical statement of the period. In any case, through a consideration of the emergent Pop Art movement —of whose works Johnson was a pioneer enthusiast and collector—Johnson finds a mirror for his own struggle with modernist abstraction. His contemporaneous mocking evocation of pre-Modern Movement form in his so-called "ballet school" phase reveals itself to be for him a reflection of his boredom with the limited gamut of the International Style, just as Andy Warhol's serial depictions of Campbell's Soup cans were as much an act of contempt for the Abstract Expressionism of the prevailing New York School as they were a new way of seeing familiar things.

Ever since Le Corbusier, architecture has become a total worldwide phenomenon. We can no longer speak of Japanese influence or German. We architects are all artists of the world.

But what are we doing? The history books of the future may know more than we do at the moment. But today we can only see centrifugal tendencies more or less interesting or original. Indeed, the whole concept of originality is getting new emphasis. Boredom is the negative side. A few years ago I was proud to be tagged with the sobriquet "Mies van der Johnson." I thought that certainly "style" in the old sense of the word was an important and valuable attribute of architecture. The Gothic, the Classical, were strong periods. The example of architecture of the Far East was equally strong. In Japan my favorite architecture is the complex at Nikko and, though far developed, represents the culmination of style the idea of which was clearly traditional and derived from the temples of previous centuries. A continuity with changes within a framework seemed to me ideal. Great works of architecture, I thought, could only be created in a period such as those with a strong style sense, and that I could feel in the International Style of 1920–1930, a new and lasting "Great Style" within which I would be glad to work.

But in the last ten years all is changed. I remember meeting Kenzo Tange in São Paulo in 1957. We were both surprised at the thoughts in each other's minds. Both of us, though we had never met and never spoken publicly about our problems, were very, very bored—restless.

I think we both still are, though heaven knows in different ways. Both were bored with the "less support the better" themes of the International Style. Both were most admiring of Le Corbusier, his heavy concrete originality, and both of us greatly admired the history of our different cultures.

After these common thoughts, however, we go off on different paths. The fact that I admire as I do Tange and many great living Japanese architects, and still go a different way seems to me significant of the movements all over the world. They are centrifugal; they vary from the Brutalism of the younger English to the lace work of Yamasaki. And yet we do not hate or condemn each other's work. No, the field is too strewn with failures and tentative, even timid, designs for any of us to attack the others.

That is just what is wonderful about today's position in the arts. There was very shortly ago for instance in New York, a New York School of painting, Abstract Expressionism it has been called, which in the last year or two has lost its grip. Once more people paint the way they want to, jokingly, terrifyingly or merely decoratively. But no one movement has become an academy as strong as Abstract Expressionism. No academy can exist in these times of violent atomization of thought, of values, of ways of life. There are no hidden valleys where an artistic "school" can develop.

Rather we all live in the near-total chaos of the whole planet waiting more or less patiently for some end.

And—while we wait, I venture to say we are having more enjoyment in the field of art than many a generation before us.

True, we are having next to no effect on our cities—we artists. True, commercialism and Communism are both anti-aesthetic movements that control our cultures. Tokyo is hardly more beautiful than New York. Nor is it going to get more beautiful any sooner than New York.

Yet my colleagues in your country are doing as much—more than we are—and they enjoy it. Life is absurd—life is chaos, there are no rules—enjoy it.

Up till now there has been a moral attitude toward design. A romantically moral attitude. Frank Lloyd Wright always considered himself a moralist. Lewis Mumford does still. Architectural design somehow had to be based on honesty, social improvement, sound structure, functional consideration of the problems of our day, etc. Walter Gropius is the greatest teacher of our day of this philosophy. The last generation came by this attitude naturally. Ruskin and Morris in England, Viollet-le-Duc in France, Sullivan in America—preached the moral nature of our art. Painters were luckier. No one told them they had to be moral.

The International Style must be considered the end development of the Modern Movement which the great 19th-century founders started. The end of puritanism and false morality in architecture.

And when we became bored with it all, chaos came back. I am not sure that chaos is all to the "good." But the question now is not "What is good," but "What is actually the present state?" Certainly it is chaos, and we shall work with it.

My particular, individual, not-to-be-copied method is to search for the re-establishment of elegance. I would, within the confining limitations of our era, create some tiny oases of marble and gold wherever I can. They would not be large, but the halls, the suites, the fountains, the terraces would be as grandiose as the confining mores of our century will allow.

It is obviously not for me to make the awesome piles of Le Corbusier nor have I the splendid discipline of a Mies van der Rohe. Nor can I imagine who in the second generation can fill their shoes. But for one I do not need to care what they do. The problem of our generation is ours. And I would like some tiny place in the search for the answers.

Full Scale False Scale

From Show *magazine, III (June 1963),* 72–75.

Johnson's garden folly is considered by many critics to mark the nadir of his "ballet school" phase. The pavilion does not seem to satisfy: not because it is frivolous, but because it is not frivolous enough; not because it is a rich man's plaything, but because the rich man was not rich enough, using earnest pre-cast concrete where only either lath and plaster or marble would do. Johnson's essay, on the other hand, is rather a different matter. It does convince one of the art and intelligence that conceived of the pavilion, while the Saul Leiter photo that accompanied it in the ill-fated but physically glorious Show *magazine is a most accurate photographic mirror of the Johnson we know.*

Every little boy should have a tree house—every little girl a dollhouse. Every grown-up child should have his version of a playhouse, and this pavilion in a pond is mine.

If it be more than a little absurd to build playhouses today, will someone please tell me what is not absurd today?

My pavilion is full scale false scale, big enough to sit in, to have tea in, but really "right" only for four-foot-high people. Change of scale like this is a harmless and pleasant joke on serious architecture. And yet it is serious architecture, if architecture is to be defined as the art of making pleasant enclosures for people to be inside of. It is pleasant to be in a false scale—to feel big or feel small. How small you feel in St. Peter's false-scaled nave in Rome; how big in a doll's house. In my pavilion you feel big and important. When you sit for tea, you reduce yourself to child size and romantically enjoy the view through the seemingly countless arches, isolated from the world on a small island in a pond.

I designed and built the pavilion for two reasons: one, the place needed a gazebo and, secondly, I wanted deliberately to fly in the face of the "modern" tradition of functionalist architecture by tying on to an older, nobler tradition of garden architecture.

Both reasons gave me inordinate pleasure. In 1963, we are, I should imagine, thoroughly sick of Utilitarianism in all its forms, but one of the most banal effects of this philosophy has been its effect on the art of architecture. Usefulness as a criterion condemns our art to a mere technological scheme to cover ourselves from the weather, much as to say that shoes should be practical, not hurtful and handsome. Actually, there exist shoes designed just for comfort and we all know them for the hideously ugly monstrosities that they are. But somehow the idea has come about that mere functional (cheap) buildings are good enough for Americans. We no longer need beautiful buildings. But I say, just as in footwear, we need beautiful, in addition to mildly useful, buildings. My pavilion I should wish to be compared to high-style, high-heel evening slippers, preferably satin—a pleasure-giving object, designed for beauty and the enhancement of human, preferably blonde, beauty.

Fortunately, my place needed a gazebo badly. I had a pond—two years ago the place needed a pond—which looked rather empty. Something interesting to look at from the house was necessary. Contrariwise, some place to walk to from the house—from which to look at the house—was also necessary.

These "necessities" are, of course, meaningful only on the assumption that "gardens" constitute a vital part of the art of architecture. By "gardens," naturally, I do not mean places to grow flowers, but landscapes that have form and incident much as a great interior space must have form and incident. As a highboy gives emphasis to a gracious Colonial room, so a gazebo gives focus and meaning to an outside "room." "Gardens" in

Full-scale architect: false-scale arch

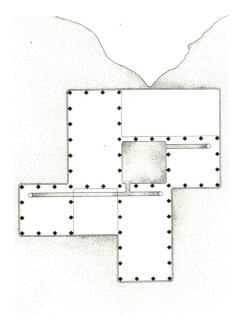

Plan and model of Philip Johnson Pavilion, New Canaan, Connecticut

this sense are more important, bigger, more meaningful as works of architecture than even the greatest interior spaces.

Great ages have known this. Lenôtre in France and the English 18th-century Romantics all knew it. We are ignorant, but need we be, in an age—they tell us—of affluence? In any case, it is time someone started outdoor architecture on its way again. The William Morris—Walter Gropius cult of the useful must be overthrown. Grandeur we must re-establish.

My pavilion is too small to be grand I know, but the intent is there. If Louis (of any number) would give me the commission, or a Fouquet or a Burlington, what good big follies (*folies*) we could build! Follies in gardens—or arbors—or pavilions—or teahouses or summerhouses (as they were apologetically called in my Edwardian youth) must go on.

My moon-viewing pavilion (some still think of the Chinese tradition) is unusual for more than its peculiar scale. In the picture of the model you will see that there are four rooms placed around a small fountain. You will see canals which run in and out of the rooms—and an uncovered terrace. The rooms have names—for romantic association: the Entrance Hall, the Library, the Living Room, the Boudoir. It is the conceit that people in one room—all of eight-foot by eight-foot squares—cannot communicate with those in the adjoining one. Doors and walls are easily imagined. The tiny fountain is easily imagined, big and important.

The form of the design—the grammar—is frankly "modern." It seems useless to me to imitate past forms just because I wish to join a "noble" historical tradition. Forms always remain modern. The arcades are whimsical and most unclassically terminated; each interior corner, for example, holds up two different roofs at once. If the forms are modern, however, reminiscences abound: Moorish, Chinese, Palladian; traditions which are parents to all our design today.

The idea of the arch is, of course, contrary to "modern" design, the modern of the age of usefulness, because it is obvious these arches are not truly structural—not honest. But to me they are handsome and comforting. I use them often, at all sizes. The domes in my guest room are ten feet high as against the five-and-a-half of the pavilion. They have a calming, quieting effect on the guests—most enjoyable. The big 40-foot arches of the Sheldon Art Gallery in Lincoln, Nebraska, are monumental and should make the observer elated and give him heightened awareness for the fine arts within the building.

Arches big and small, carved or cast, with vaults or without, freestanding as in the pavilion, or engaged in the flat walls as in the Sheldon Art Gallery, are basically fascinating.

Arches on islands in a lake, doubly fascinating. Arches in full scale false scale, triply fascinating. Long live arches, long live follies.

Review of *Philip Johnson: Architecture 1949–1965*

From Architectural Forum, *CXXV (October, 1966), 52–53.*

How much like a lunch with Johnson at his "corner table" at the Four Seasons this magnificent piece of chutzpah seems! At top speed, running with the hare and hunting with the hounds, thinking and proclaiming, Johnson reviews his own book, and frankly bares his own intentions to make as certain as possible that history recognizes his achievement, that it looks at his oeuvre in the context of contemporary practice as well as in the context of the grand tradition of Modern architectural history taken as a whole.

It is always good in our decadent world to see a well-designed, sumptuous book come on the market. This is one. Paper heavy, lots of color, generous type, excellent cover design. Elaine Lustig at her best. Cocktail tables look handsome with it.

The importance of the book, however, is other. It is the latest in a line of architects' books on their own work. The genre deserves propagation. Perhaps because Johnson was an architectural historian before he became an architect at the age of 36, he thought it important for some of his public (the few who buy books) and especially for the future to have a record made by the architect's hand. How right he was.

All of which has nothing to do with the quality of Johnson's architecture. Plenty of second-rate architectural works are also grist for the architectural historian's mill, as anyone going through Avery Library can judge. The value of this book, for example, is the new way of showing architecture. Color photography beats heliotype any day. And think of the impossibility today of the beautiful line drawings of Schinkel's works or Frank Lloyd Wright's 1910 *Ausgeführte Bauten.* No one would ever do it. Marcel Breuer's half-tone photos and Saarinen's fuzzy gravure seem pale next to Technicolor.

Whether color catches on or not is less important than that here is a book which by its very existence shows that someone (publisher?, architect?) cares about the position of architecture. Architecture becomes as important a branch of knowledge and life as, say, Beautiful Meissen, or Wild Life in Africa. And anything that will raise the level of public estimate of our hitherto lowly art is very, very welcome.

The text is faultless. Henry-Russell Hitchcock, the dean of architectural historians of the 19th and 20th centuries, has produced a lucid, critical essay that well might stand as a paradigm for the monographs on living architects. Although commissioned by Johnson, he indulges in no hyperbole. He *says* something in each sentence, and what he disapproves of, what he finds positively ugly, he mentions not at all. He accentuates the positive without flattery or sycophancy. A difficult piece of tightrope walking. The result is packed, objective, interesting.

Concerning the quality of Johnson's oeuvre, I shall have to hide behind what Furneaux Jordan wrote. Personally I feel too close to the trees to see the forest. Contemporary architecture is too near to let us judge. Mr. Jordan wrote in the London *Observer:* "Whether the work of Johnson will eventually be looked upon as a culmination, a climax, in modern architecture, is for the future to decide. It is certainly difficult to see how his kind of architecture can be taken further. There is more than one facet, more than one technique, in modern building."

Whatever Johnson's place in history may be, it is a plus for the historians to have a book on his work. Without any invidious comparisons to the great self-publications, starting with Ledoux and Schinkel down to

Otto Wagner and Frank Lloyd Wright and the incomparable *Oeuvres Complètes,* it might be said that Johnson's book may encourage architects to bring out their own books. For a minor reason, it is fun to see what the artist picks out to illustrate, also how he wants to show it (think of the difference between Le Corbusier and Frank Lloyd Wright in methods of self-advertising!). Also interesting: Why did they choose the buildings they chose? Also, why did they change styles when they changed? Also (alas, lacking in Johnson's book), why does what they say differ from what they do?

What Makes Me Tick

Lecture, Columbia University,
September 24, 1975; previously
unpublished.

*"Modern Architecture Symposium," Columbia
University, 1964. Above: Philip Johnson,
Henry-Russell Hitchcock; below: Philip
Johnson, Henry-Russell Hitchcock, Edgar
Kaufmann, Jr., Sybil Moholy-Nagy,
Vincent Scully*

In the 1950's and early 1960's, Johnson was a frequent visitor at the leading architecture schools. He gave generously of his time as a visiting critic, a juror for studio projects, and a platform lecturer. While it would be convenient to say that the pace of his work in the office in the period after 1965 or the temporary decline of his energies in the early 1970's forced him to cut down on these activities, such would not be an honest account of the case. The reality of the matter is that in the unintelligible brutalizing of educational goals and standards which accompanied the, for me, rather more intelligible protests by university students and faculties over political situations at home and abroad in the time between Vietnam and Watergate, Johnson became persona non grata at most campuses. While architecture students mindlessly groped through a period of virulent anti-professionalism, of street-corner surveys, and courses in "how-to-build-your-own-yurt," Johnson came to be regarded as the enemy. All that articulate intelligence, cutting wit, and a much too substantial corpus of work alienated him from a generation of students who believed that those were precisely the most irrelevant attributes and achievements an architect could possess. Willing though the students of the late sixties were to sit for six, eight, nine befogged hours before a Buckminster Fuller, they would not offer even a quarter of an hour to Johnson, because they sensed in advance that Johnson knew about Fuller and knew about architecture, and could and would tell them about the differences between the two.

It is ironic and, for me, gratifying that Johnson's comeback to the university circuit was on the platform at Columbia in 1975. Johnson prepared his talk carefully, writing it down in advance, a most unusual thing for him to do. The message it imparts—the by-now eternal verities of his beliefs—is as clearly and convincingly stated as ever. One thing that is new and wonderful is the personal note, the willingness to talk about his own work not only in terms of the predictable list of predecessors and contemporaries, but also in terms of the younger generation.

After the miscalculations about the direction architecture was taking in the mid-1960's, as manifested in his review of Robin Boyd's book (see pp. 129–33), Johnson began to look very carefully at the situation in design as it was emerging around him. The work of the Venturis, Moore, and Giurgola began to interest him and provoke him to serious response. The firm of Hardy/Holzman/Pfeiffer fascinates him, and he has written an unpublished essay about it; he admired Gwathmey enough to write an introduction to a book about his firm's work; and he also wrote a postscript to the second edition of the book Five Architects: Eisenman, Graves, Gwathmey, Hejduk, Meier. *He has been a faithful member of the audience at every occasion of importance when the work of young architects would be subjected to serious scrutiny. He knows the new scene very well, and while I don't think he likes all that much of what he sees— "likes," that is, in the sense that he is about to borrow from it—I do believe he can discuss it more intelligently than most.*

So we come almost to the present: Peck's Bad Boy is still bad; the rules are still there to be broken, the pretensions of architects to be stripped away, and the work of other architects freed of its protective camouflage of justifications and excuses and subjected to serious scrutiny. Only Johnson among our established architects can be counted on to provide this necessary criticism, and he can be counted on to do it for us because he cares so much for architecture. He continues to do it at this very writing and, one hopes, forever.

What I would like to talk about today is what makes me tick; what goes through my mind when that awful moment comes in which I have to face the blank paper on the desk; what determines the direction of my thoughts; what makes the shapes of the buildings that come off the board.

I know what it used to be: the strict disciplines of the old International Style, a period I can look back on with less loathing, let me say, than you, or rather than Robert Venturi, the current brilliant guru of anti-modernism. I am nearly the last, Breuer and I perhaps, of the generation brought up on Le Corbusier-Bauhaus aesthetics, the aesthetics of the 1920's: Breuer as one of the young founders, myself as epigone.

We may not see a period like the twenties again for some time—the birth of a style of architecture built on commonly held beliefs in a few seemingly simple "truths." We really believed, in a quasi-religious sense, in the perfectability of human nature, in the role of architecture as a weapon of social reform, in simplicity as a cure-all ("less is more"). We believed in expressing honestly the structure of a building, we believed with Laugier, Ruskin, Viollet-le-Duc, and Emerson in usefulness as an aesthetic criterion. Remember the early Museum of Modern Art exhibitions called "Useful Objects"? Not Beautiful Objects; Useful Objects. If something was useful, then a sort of halo descended upon it. The puritan ethic triumphed at last: only simplicity was allowed—straight lines, narrow supports, cheap materials; only flat roofs, flat walls, and cubes were permissible. A style easier to describe with negatives.

There were, nonetheless, masterpieces. In spite of Le Corbusier's "*machine à habiter*," he built the Villa Savoye. In spite of Mies's "less is more," he built the Barcelona Pavilion. In spite of the fact that the word "Art" was forbidden at the Bauhaus, Gropius built the most artful Bauhaus building in Dessau.

But the beliefs of these leaders of fifty years ago sound quaint indeed today. I re-read with excruciating embarrassment a piece I wrote in 1931 defending our upcoming exhibition of architects at The Museum of Modern Art [see pp. 29–31]. (In those days "Modern" had a meaning.) Functionalistic clichés are laid end to end. Yet it was through those clichés that we hoped to sell what we really believed in: the coming utopia when everyone would live in cheap, prefabricated, flat-roofed, multiple dwellings—heaven-on-earth.

The utopia did not arrive. But beliefs are not related to actual results. And there have been many faiths in modern architecture. Besides the patent absurdity of *machines à habiter* and "less is more," recall Frank Lloyd Wright with "the horizontal line is the line of life" and Lou Kahn's "I ask the brick what it wants to be."

The day of ideology is thankfully over. Let us celebrate the death of the *idée fixe*. There are no rules, only facts. There is no order, only preference. There are no imperatives, only choice; or, to use a nineteenth-century word, "taste"; or a modern word, "take": "What is your 'take' on this or that?"

Not that there are not some diehards. The Communists of the thirties have been succeeded by advocacy planners who still believe in salvation by architecture. There is the alternative culture whose members "do their thing" with faith in the results. There are technolators who believe with Bucky in salvation by the maximum of coverage with the minimum of materials, a Frei Otto who believes—and beautifully—in tension. There are some, mainly in England, who believe in the future of 4-by-8 panels that can be fitted by anybody, anywhere, for any purpose.

I can't honestly believe that all these are not a minority. I would like to hear from you on the subject provided that you want to be that articulate. (Parenthetically, there is no reason you should be articulate. Architecture is built with bricks and stones, not with words. But should you have beliefs, I would like to hear them.)

I am of the opinion that we have no faiths. I have none. "Free at last," I say to myself. However, shapes do not emerge from a vacuum. There are currents in the air. For example, historical architecture is "in" after almost a hundred years of neglect by the various "moderns" of the late nineteenth and twentieth century. True, we don't build in the Gothic style or the Renaissance style, but we are not averse to inspiration at least. A Stirling with his dockyards, a Stern with his Lutyens, a Venturi with almost everybody, a Meier with his "take" on Corbu. So what—we cannot not know history.

Philosophically, it seems to me we today are anarchistic, nihilistic, solipsistic, certainly relativist, humorous, cynical, reminiscent of tradition, myth-and-symbol-minded rather than rationalistic or scientifically minded. What makes a building satisfactory—the word "beautiful" is more than ever treacherous—to Stern or Venturi, for instance, is bound to be different from what is satisfactory to me. *Vive la différence,* we live in a pluralistic society. So it is sometimes hard for me to understand what makes splendid architects like Chuck Moore or Aldo Giurgola (to pick at wide random) tick.

I can only talk about me. Maybe what makes me tick is unique. I don't mind, but it may be of interest to know how different my tick is from yours and yours.

Whenever I start a building design, three aspects—as I might call them—act as a sort of measure, aim, discipline, hope for my work.

First, the Aspect of the Footprint—that is, how space unfolds from the moment I catch a glimpse of a building until with my feet I have approached, entered, and arrived at my goal. In a church, the aspect of the footprint is simple; the hieratic procession to the altar itself. In a home, from the automobile the footprints may lead to a seat by the fire; in an office building, from the street to the elevator door. (The elevator, of course, being the death of processional architecture, my mind stops at its door.) The processional for most buildings, including homes, is complex, and in different eras is differently complex. At Ur in Mesopotamia five thousand years ago, the processional was also the architecture. Three enormous staircases that ascended eighty feet without landings, from three different directions, but all visible from the approaching visitor's path.

In Egypt it was a straight line, but what a straight line! very high, very low, wide, dense, straight to the holy of holies.

Most complex, on the Acropolis at Athens. You ascend on foot (the only tourist attraction that cannot be reached by auto, thank God) through the stark gateway. The colossal Athena Promachos on the right, near the back wall of the Pantheon, then the Erechtheum on the left, until in the full face of Mount Hymettos you make a 180° turn to face the unenterable Parthenon.

The medieval approach was a small diagonal street leading to a small square, where, facing nothing at all, usually off center in the piazza, stood the church. The bursting into the Piazza San Marco in Venice is a huge example.

The Baroque processional was symmetrical, straight, and grand; Versailles or St. Peter's, the grandest of all.

In modern times, at Taliesin West, Frank Lloyd Wright made the most intriguingly complex series of turns, twists, low tunnels, surprise views, framed landscapes, that human imagination could achieve.

In urban street and plaza design, we find the same differences of processional in different periods: the Greek, the interrupted gridiron street system, the medieval diagonal, the Baroque *allée*.

It is with this richness of processionals in mind that I try to imagine buildings.

Second, the Aspect of the Cave. All architecture is shelter; all great architecture is the design of space that contains, cuddles, exalts, or stimulates the persons in that space. It is the design of the cave part of a building that overrides all other design questions. Like Lao-tse's cup, it is the emptiness within that is of the essence.

There are lots of "insidenesses" to be studied besides the obvious interiors like Chartres Cathedral or the Grand Central Terminal. Nowicki once said all architecture is interior architecture—the Piazza San Marco in Venice, even the Acropolis in Athens, since walls that descend around you can hold you as securely as walls rising around you.

A plain box can hardly be an exciting cave; visit your local auto factory building. Nor does size alone count; once more visit your local auto factory. The modulation of interior space must have complexity: the side chapels of Brunelleschi's Santo Spirito, Michelangelo's transepts in St. Peter's, the spiral walks in the Guggenheim, the aisles of a hall church in the thirteenth century, the polychrome columns of Le Corbusier's High

Court in Chandigarh, the scale-shifting boulders floating in the Ryōanji Garden of Kyoto, are all tricks of molding caves to excite and thrill the observer. Spaces go in and out, up and down. They overlap, they cheat or suggest, all the time enriching the architectural experience. With all these noble paradigms in mind, I still like to try my hand at caves.

The third aspect, the most difficult, is the Building as a Work of Sculpture. Architecture is usually thought of as different from sculpture and indeed not much great architecture is sculpture, Pyramids, yes; Taliesin West, no. Stonehenge, perhaps; Versailles, no; the Guggenheim Museum, maybe. The Parthenon, certainly not. (Columns and entablatures see to that.) Frank Lloyd Wright roofs, arcades, colonnades, all speak architecture, not sculpture.

In the last few years, however, it seems to me sculptural forms, not necessarily geometric, have become a mark of architecture. As we have become impoverished in our external architecture by the lack of decorative motifs our forerunners could use—steeples, pointed and unpointed arches, and the like—we have turned to other modes of expression. Since there are no structural limitations today like the lintels of Stonehenge or the Parthenon, we can warp or carve or tilt our buildings the way we will. A wonderful example comes to mind: the fantastic gouges and the slithering angles of I. M. Pei's National Gallery addition—majestic, playful, abstract sculptures. Or take Kevin Roche's nine stelae at Indianapolis (only three have been built): desert megaliths serving as an insurance company's headquarters.

These three aspects, the Footprint, the Cave, the Work of Sculpture, do not in themselves give form, but they are what I think about in the night away from the boards, when I try to brush away the cobwebs of infinite possibilities and try to establish some way out. Very frustrating.

By no accident, the best illustration from my own work of the three aspects is a building I built for my own delectation in 1970 in New Canaan: the Sculpture Gallery, which many of you have seen, at least in magazines. First, the Footprints. Here the exterior approach is straight down a three-hundred-foot *allée* of maples. No diagonal, no steps, no space warp. The interior, on the other hand, is a play of changing directions.

The main entrance, the "gozinta" I call it, is the key to any building. What is your first impact? How does it prepare you for the future experience? Do you stop in wonder? Do you perhaps enter in a low tunnel as at Taliesin West to burst into a great space? The "gozinta" here is a glass door giving a glimpse of a room of Don Judd sculptures to the right. The left is cut off by a wood partition above eye height, which gives you a six-foot space to reveal to you the glass roof, the white walls, but conceals the surprise view down to the main pentagonal space twelve feet below. The way then proceeds along a parapet (twelve inches high to create tension and fear), a right angle to the left. The room (the building is only one room; Mendelsohn was right—an architect is remembered for his one-room buildings) changes radically a few steps further with Robert Morris's sculpture at the right. Seven steps down, then a 45° turn, seven more steps, a new view of the room. You are now on a bridge—below to the left, still the focal space below; on the right, the Flavin sculpture room. A 90° turn and seven more steps, and you have curled around the focal space and landed at the bottom. You carom off the entrance wall and settle down a turn and a quarter from the entrance door like a dog which has sniffed out a room and settles circularly into his place.

The gallery also illustrates the second aspect, the Aspect of the Cave. Although it is one room, the four peripheral bays facing four of the five sides of the central area each form three-sided rooms, the fourth side opening on and enlarging the main space, like open-sided chapels of a church. The glass roof covers all four of these bays as well as the focal space, sheltering the entire complex. You sit or stand in this focal space, the stairs slicing and around you, but beyond and above you stretch the four bays on the four sides of a pentagonal focal space, the fifth side being the entrance wall. The space is broken into sub-spaces. All of its three thousand square feet are visually usable, though each of the five sub-spaces is intimate within its own perimeter. This doubling of the spaces, or rather the borrowing and overlapping of the four side bays with the focal space, is what I was trying to learn from Frank Lloyd Wright's great lobby of the Imperial Hotel in Tokyo.

Let us now talk of the third aspect—Sculpture. On the outside the building has the shape of a southern Spanish white barn gone awry. The ridge beam is set diagonally to the main rectangle, suggesting many 45° and 135° angles jarringly juxtaposed.

The most successful sculpture that John Burgee and I have built is Pennzoil Place in Houston. Two trapezoidal buildings each composed, if you can imagine it, of a square plus a right triangle, that almost meet at a point in their corners, each roof sloping 45° toward each other. In plan, each building of course has a 45° point at the triangle. The ridges of the buildings, however, are also broken to slope away to a corner, giving the rather absurd impression of a twisted parrot's beak. At the base there are two courts, again with roofs that pitch 45° up a hundred feet high, tapering in plan to ten feet wide.

The work of sculpture sounds more complex than it is. Straight walls, or 45° slanted walls; no roof at all. The plan is orthogonal, with occasional 45° elements. All is play of simple angular volumes. But these simple volumes meet at the all-important ten-foot slot which is the key of the design—a non-volume which makes the sculpture. The gap is visible, but only sometimes; the rest of the time it is a mystery known about, but unseen. Parenthetically, it must be admitted that the processional element of Pennzoil is really automobilistic. The parrot's beaks, the surprising slot, are best seen from the freeways that surround the city.

Another building of John Burgee and mine which illustrates the processional and cave aspects of our work is the I.D.S. complex in Minneapolis. The Crystal Court tnere has become the "living room" of the city. The crowds are huge. They come to buy Baskin-Robbins ice-cream cones and to watch the girls—and our balconies and our processional make it easy, nay, inevitable, for them to enjoy the experience.

Luck we certainly had. Bridges on all four sides bring in more people than the four entrances on the street level. Minneapolitans are trained by their Siberian climate to bridge their streets to keep warm. So we had our two-level city to start with—a dream situation for an architect. To help our luck, however, we were very careful about our "gozintas." On each of the four sides, a zigzag funnel pierces the façades, narrowing often twenty or thirty feet to an eighteen-foot wide entrance. The visitor then bursts after a short tunnel into the Crystal Court: a room covered with clusters of glass cubes that pile asymmetrically to a hundred-foot-high apex. Again asymmetrically placed against a diagonal wall, we placed a high-speed escalator to the balconies, which wind their way around the Court and lead in turn out over the lower funnels to four buildings across the streets.

Thus, we like to think, the eight entrances to the cave, the enforced diagonal of the balcony, the clarity of four entrances, four compass points, make pleasant processions. We like to think that the design of our cave, mounting to a crazy high point, decorated with the balcony ribbon and its slanted escalator and its peculiar pentagonal shape, with no two sides the same length, making an odd centrality with its surrounding walls constantly zigging and zagging in 5-by-10-foot orthogonal modules creating a basic rhythm, helps the excitement that all people seem to feel in the room.

John Burgee and I have had fun the last few years with shapes and funnels, plazas, "gozintas," indoor streets, sloped sides and/or roofs, making processionals, spaces and sculptures. We have even finished a 1930's ribbon-window, round-cornered, setback building in Houston. What a grand period for us to live in today!

Contrariwise, what will all this sound like in ten years?

Afterword
Philip Johnson

It is strange to recall my Saul/Paul conversion to modern architecture almost a half century ago. I was, before that, a student of philosophy and the classics, interested—but only interested—in architecture. Also, however, in painting (Simone Martini on my dormitory wall), and in music; and I had illusions of becoming a concert pianist! To me, architecture at the time was the usual undergraduate enthusiasms: the breathtaking experiences of the Parthenon, of Chartres, of Bernini's colonnade, of St. Mark's Square. The moment of conversion came in 1929 when I read an article by Henry-Russell Hitchcock on the architecture of J. J. P. Oud. From that moment, it was only modern and only that kind of modern architecture which enthralled me—not de Klerk, not Berlage, not Poelzig, or Lutyens, or Perret, not what Hitchcock has variously called the half-modern or the New Tradition. Not the expressionists Taut or Mendelsohn, or early Mies van der Rohe; nothing but the "pure" direction of Oud, Le Corbusier, Gropius (the Bauhaus), and Mies.

There were two directions that in the early thirties I especially and contemptuously discarded: the Modern Movement and Frank Lloyd Wright. The Modern Movement, with capital letters, is a British expression that, to me, has always had undertones of Ebenezer Howard, William Morris, and the good, the moral, and socially aware Fabians of England. Frank Lloyd Wright I threw out as a nineteenth-century figure. In mitigation of my misjudgment, remember that at that moment in 1930 Frank Lloyd Wright was doing precisely nothing, and it was precisely the decade up to 1930 that was my period.

In 1929 I met Alfred Barr, and very much under his influence I became a propaganda bureau for what he (with Hitchcock and myself) named the International Style. In re-reading the Hitchcock and Johnson book on that style today, it sounds, shall we say, dated; and why not? What theoretical work of architecture could stand that half-century gap? Remember what we were describing was the history of the decade from the point of view of what we considered to be the great architects of the period. In retrospect, we were right.

There has been much discussion of the title of our book: The International Style. *Few have objected to the word "international"; the style was never parochial, regional, or nationalistic. The chauvinists of the period disliked it; Stalin, Hitler, and Roosevelt all condemned it. The sobriquet "style," on the other hand, has connotations that still raise hackles. The more socially conscious critics of the Modern Movement—especially Lewis Mumford, our lone American architectural social critic—found it a term too artistic, too restrictive, too prescriptive to allow for the natural development of social architecture.*

But if "style" is to refer quite simply to architectural forms that look amazingly alike during a certain period, then the International Style is a style. Remember that the subtitle of our book was "Architecture 1922–1932"; our intent was to offer not a prognosis, only a history. Certainly, this was as much a style as Gothic. The Duomo in Florence does not look very much like the brick hall churches of the Hanseatic cities of the North, but no one says they are not both Gothic.

What is so strange about The International Style *is our definitions, our rules, our "how-to" recipes for design. It would be interesting—and equally beside the point—if someone were to write a comparable "how-to" book on the Gothic by attempting to isolate its elements. Even the pointed arch itself is not necessarily Gothic. Plenty of critics have pointed out the inconsistencies of our book; for instance, that Le Corbusier in 1930, in the de Mandrot House, was hardly dealing with a skin-covered Citrohan architecture, and that Mies's Barcelona Pavilion was not volumetric in the way that the Villa Savoye was. A foolish consistency, however, is what Emerson said it was, the hobgoblin of little minds. Our failure nicely illustrates one of the hazards of trying to capture the visual arts in inadequate words.*

Alfred Barr introduced us to the word "style" in his role of a scholar trying to further the study of art history by the normal taxonomy necessary to any academic discipline. And there was the precedent of the Gothic of about 1400, which scholars have long called the International Style—descriptive only, and easy for art historians to refer to without long definitions.

It still seems to me that Barr was right. The work of the twenties does strike one as similar—all over the world there appears to have been no other movement of that time that could be a logical rival. When Wright began building again, he paid the Style the ultimate compliment. Fallingwater of 1936 was Wright's answer: he showed he could do flat roofs and horizontal ribbon windows better than anyone.

My Glass House of 1949 is, of course, a very late example of the style— inspired as it was by the Farnsworth House that Mies had already designed. By that time, much had happened to change the sensibilities of the twenties. I myself made many sketches for the future Glass House in which the main theme was a series of low—almost Syrian—arches cut into a blank stone façade. And there are anomalies in the house as built that Mies would never have tolerated: the round brick element that "anchors" the design, and especially the chair rail that ties the house into an enclosed composition rather than an indoor-outdoor Mies design.

Besides the scholarly, there was another side to Alfred Barr, and consequently another influence on my youthful enthusiasms. He was a preacher's son, than whom there is no one more puritanical or evangelical. This suited me. We were to save the architecture of the world at The Museum of Modern Art. We would show by exhibitions and by publications the inevitability of "modern" and rout all the philistines.

To understand this evangelical campaign, however, we must analyze the contemporary "enemy." In 1930, the International Style was unheard of in this country. It was "foreign," and foreigners were—well, foreign. The enemy was what we called the "moderne" or "modernistic" much more than it was the eclectic or revivalist. It was a hydra-headed monster—the existing 1920's modern.

There were three separate strains that, in combination, drove us to do battle for "our side." With the benefit of fifty-year hindsight, those former "enemies" now look more interesting, more rich in associations, in metaphor, in decorative abundance, than the Style which we espoused. The "modern" of the twenties that looks best to me now is the "skyscraper style," crystallized by Raymond Hood and Eliel Saarinen in the early 1920's, and lasting through Rockefeller Center in the 1930's—a vertical, Gothic-inspired piling of elements that still gives New York its New York look.

Second, there was the "moderne" styling of the streamlining designers: Raymond Loewy's railroad trains, everybody's three linear moldings on all movie marquees, the round-cornered projections of many a Greyhound terminal, and the like. Fascinating richness (but lumpy when applied to pencil sharpeners and refrigerators!). In revolt, we at The Museum of Modern Art called an exhibition of useful objects "Machine Art."

Third, there was the decoration derived from the 1925 "Exposition des Arts Décoratifs" in Paris. This movement we puritans found shocking, but at least there was ornament; and there are books and books illustrating, in technicolor, its glories. These pictures today have far more glamour than any picture of the Seagram Building! But as nostalgic as these movements are today, to us in 1930 they were only surface treatments, often self-contradictory. They also turned out, even with the help of the 1933 Chicago Fair designs, to be ephemeral. By contrast, the International Style swept the country, and even today, in 1978, flat-topped glass boxes for office buildings are the characteristic marks of the new, proliferating city centers all over the world.

But now for the counter-story. The flat-top boxes had triumphed, but for a whole generation there have grown theoretical and practical objections. The Bay Region style of California in the late twenties was billed as a new regionalism. Churches and houses, especially, being almost impervious to box architecture, were designed by some great men like Bruce Goff and Frank Lloyd Wright the way they wanted. Junk architecture flourished. Historical eclecticism raised its head again. The culmination among the theorists has been quite recent. Charles Jencks, Robert Venturi, Arthur Drexler mount counter-drives.

In my own design work, the story of the mid-fifties led me through a sporadic, superficial historicism mixed lightly over an International Style base. My dissatisfaction with the International Style was chiefly with its simple straight lines and simple geometric shapes and boxlike forms. It struck me, as one interested in history, that much good architecture paid no attention to Ruskin, Morris, Semper, Viollet-le-Duc, Laugier, or Gropius. In the 1940's my favorite theorist was Geoffrey Scott, who in The Architecture of Humanism of 1914 had inveighed against Morris, Ruskin, et al. The designs of the past that struck closest to my senses were those of Romantic Neo-classicism, beginning with Ledoux and going through to 1845 with the death of Ludwig Persius. Soane and Schinkel, for no conceivable theoretical reason, touch me closer than do Borromini, Gaudí, or Brunelleschi, no matter how enthusiastically I react to *their greatness. All this Romanticism led me in 1947 to work with many arches for my house.*

A little later, in the 1950's, trying to find out where I stood, I called myself a "functional eclectic." All such terms are part true, part fictional, part self-serving, part earnest attempts at self-knowledge. The "functional" meant, and means, that I cannot free myself from starting designs with the program as outlined by me or by my clients. I know that other periods have begun with shapes and only later shoehorned the uses into shapes. I am too "modern," too puritan for pure form. I am, in spite of speeches to the contrary, a functionalist; but, perhaps in contradiction, also an eclectic. "Eclectic" means to me that I am free to roam history at will, and that brings with it a new sympathy for the "style-to-suit-the-job" attitude. (I can almost believe that a bank should be Doric, a home should have a sheltering-roof look; almost, but not quite. I am not sure that an airport should look like a bird.) Further confusions come in what might be called applied eclecticism; for example, I often find myself trying out ideas from McKim's Boston Library and Mies's 1921 glass towers as crutches to an identical urban program.

Another new development is architecture for the "place." Along with everyone else in the practice of architecture, I am constrained to study anew the genius loci, *in approaching any design. What look does the ambience call for? What do the surrounding buildings look like? What is the local scale? Today's sensibility is toward preservation, not radical innovation. In New York, for example, the omnipresent work of McKim, Mead & White of the 1890's and the office towers of Raymond Hood of the 1920's set a tone for the city that needs re-invocation.*

We live in a time of flux. There seems to be no consistency of style in the architecture of the seventies. Sensibilities change fast, but in what direction? There are no regional prides, no new religions, no new puritanism, no new Marxism, no new socially conscious morality that can give discipline, direction, or force to an architectural pattern. Today we know too much too quickly. It takes moral and emotional blinders to make a style. One must be convinced one is right. Who today can stand up and say: "I am right!"

Who, indeed, would want to?

Chronology

Philip Johnson was born in Cleveland, Ohio, July 8, 1906. He received his A.B. from Harvard University, Class of 1927, and his degree as Bachelor of Architecture from the Harvard Graduate School of Design in 1943. From 1932 to 1934, he was Chairman of the Department of Architecture, The Museum of Modern Art; he returned to head that Department in 1946 and from 1949 to 1954 served as Director of the combined Department of Architecture and Design. He has been the recipient of many professional honors, the most recent being the 1978 Gold Medal of the American Institute of Architects.

Listed below are all buildings completed by Philip Johnson, or under construction, as of December 31, 1977. Designs for unrealized projects or for those not yet begun are not included. Beginning in 1973, all works have been in partnership with John Burgee; partners in previous projects are as indicated. Associated architects have been: for the University of St. Thomas, Howard Barnstone & Partners; for the Hendrix College Library, Wittenberg, Delony & Davidson; for the Bielefeld Art Gallery, Cäsar F. Pinnau; for the WRVA Radio Station, Rudina & Freeman; for the Art Museum of South Texas, Barnstone & Aubry; for the I. D. S. Center, Edward F. Baker Associates, Inc.; for the Boston Public Library Addition, Architects Design Group, Inc.; for Pennzoil Place, Wilson, Morris, Crain & Anderson; for the Fine Arts Center, Muhlenberg College, Coston, Wallace & Watson.

Dates given are those of completion.

1942
Philip Johnson House, Cambridge, Massachusetts

1944
Barn, Townsend Farms, New London, Ohio

1946
Mr. & Mrs. Richard E. Booth House, Bedford Village, New York (incomplete)

1947
Mr. & Mrs. Eugene Farney House, Sagaponack, Long Island, New York

1949
Philip Johnson House ("Glass House"), New Canaan, Connecticut
Mr. & Mrs. G. E. Paine, Jr., House, Wellsboro, New York
Mr. & Mrs. Benjamin V. Wolf House, Newburgh, New York

1950
Mr. & Mrs. John de Menil House, Houston, Texas
Annex, The Museum of Modern Art, New York, New York
Mrs. John D. Rockefeller 3rd Guest House, New York, New York

1951
Wing, Mr. & Mrs. Henry Ford II House, Southampton, Long Island, New York
Mr. & Mrs. Richard Hodgson House, New Canaan, Connecticut (Landes Gores, partner)
Mr. & Mrs. George C. Oneto House, Irvington, New York (Landes Gores, partner)

1952
Mr. & Mrs. Richard C. Davis House, Wayzata, Minnesota
Schlumberger Administration Building, Ridgefield, Connecticut

1953
Mrs. Alice Ball House, New Canaan, Connecticut
Alteration, Philip Johnson Guest House, New Canaan, Connecticut
The Abby Aldrich Rockefeller Sculpture Garden, The Museum of Modern Art, New York (James Fanning, Landscape Architect)
Mr. & Mrs. Robert C. Wiley House, New Canaan, Connecticut

1955
Joseph Hirshhorn House, Blind River, Ontario, Canada
Pavilion, Meteor Crater, Coconino County, Arizona
Wiley Development Company House, New Canaan, Connecticut

1956
Mr. & Mrs. Eric Boissonnas House, New Canaan, Connecticut
Kneses Tifereth Israel Synagogue, Port Chester, New York
Mr. & Mrs. Robert C. Leonhardt House, Lloyd's Neck, Long Island, New York

1957
Dormitory, Seton Hill College, Greensburg, Pennsylvania
Auditorium and Classroom Buildings, University of St. Thomas, Houston, Texas

1959
Asia House, New York, New York
Four Seasons Restaurant, Seagram Building, New York, New York

1960
Museum, Munson-Williams-Proctor Institute, Utica, New York
Nuclear Reactor, Rehovot, Israel
Roofless Church, New Harmony, Indiana
Dormitories, Sarah Lawrence College, Bronxville, New York
Robert Tourre House, Vaucresson, France

1961
Amon Carter Museum of Western Art, Fort Worth, Texas
Computing Center, Brown University, Providence, Rhode Island

1962
Philip Johnson Pavilion, New Canaan, Connecticut

1963
Museum for Pre-Columbian Art, Dumbarton Oaks, Washington, D.C.
Monastery Wing, St. Anselm's Abbey, Washington, D.C.
Sheldon Memorial Art Gallery, University of Nebraska, Lincoln, Nebraska

1964
Mr. & Mrs. Henry C. Beck House, Dallas, Texas
Mr. & Mrs. Eric Boissonnas House, Cap Bénat, France
Kline Geology Laboratory, Yale University, New Haven, Connecticut (Richard Foster, partner)
East Wing, Garden Wing, remodeled Sculpture Garden, and Upper Terrace, The Museum of Modern Art, New York, New York
New York State Theater, Lincoln Center, New York, New York (Richard Foster, partner)
New York State Pavilion, World's Fair, Flushing, New York (Richard Foster, partner)

1965
Epidemiology and Public Health Building, Yale University, New Haven, Connecticut
Mr. & Mrs. James Geier House, Indian Hills, Ohio
Philip Johnson Painting Gallery, New Canaan, Connecticut
Kline Chemistry Laboratory, Yale University, New Haven, Connecticut (Richard Foster, partner)
Kline Science Center, Yale University, New Haven, Connecticut (Richard Foster, partner)
Henry L. Moses Institute, Montefiore Hospital, Bronx, New York
Hendrix College Library, Conway, Arkansas

1966
John F. Kennedy Memorial, Dallas, Texas

1968
Bielefeld Art Gallery, Bielefeld, Germany
WRVA Radio Station, Richmond, Virginia
Mr. & Mrs. David Lloyd Kreeger House, Washington, D.C. (Richard Foster, partner)

1970
Philip Johnson Sculpture Gallery, New Canaan, Connecticut

1971
Albert & Vera List Art Building, Brown University, Providence, Rhode Island

1972
Tisch Hall, New York University, New York, New York (Richard Foster, partner)
Façade, André and Bella Meyer Hall of Physics, New York University, New York, New York (Richard Foster, partner)
Art Museum of South Texas, Corpus Christi, Texas (John Burgee, partner)
Burden Hall, Harvard University, Cambridge, Massachusetts (John Burgee, partner)
Neuberger Museum, State University of New York, Purchase, New York (John Burgee, partner)

1973
Elmer Holmes Bobst Library, New York University, New York, New York (Richard Foster, partner)
Hagop Kevorkian Center for Near Eastern Studies, New York University, New York, New York (Richard Foster, partner)
I. D. S. Center, Minneapolis, Minnesota (John Burgee, partner, for this and for all succeeding buildings)
Addition, Boston Public Library, Boston, Massachusetts

1974
Niagara Falls Convention Center, Niagara Falls, New York

1975
Fort Worth Water Garden, Fort Worth, Texas
Morningside House, The Bronx, New York, New York

1976
Pennzoil Place, Houston, Texas
Post Oak Central I, Houston, Texas
Interior, Avery Fisher Hall, New York, New York

1977
Century Center, South Bend, Indiana
Fine Arts Center, Muhlenberg College, Allentown, Pennsylvania
General American Life Insurance Company, St. Louis, Missouri
Thanks-Giving Square, Dallas, Texas

Under construction:
Apartment Group, Isfahan, Iran
Brant House Building, Greenwich, Connecticut
Crystal Cathedral, Garden Grove, California
Façade, 1001 Fifth Avenue, New York, New York
National Centre for Performing Arts, Bombay, India
Post Oak Central II, Houston, Texas
Studio Theater, Kennedy Center, Washington, D.C.

Bibliography

Prepared by David Whitney
and David White

This bibliography is composed of all available published and unpublished statements by Philip Johnson on architecture and architects, with the exception of some very minor quotations. Published speeches or lectures are generally entered under the date of publication rather than of delivery.

Every item listed in the bibliography may be found in the Library of The Museum of Modern Art, New York, either in its catalogued material or in a complete archive deposited there by Mr. Johnson. Grateful acknowledgment is made to Pearl L. Moeller, Supervisor of the Library's Special Collections, for her assistance in the preparation of this bibliography.

1931

Built To Live In. New York: The Museum of Modern Art, March, 1931. 14 pp.

"The Architecture of the New School." *Arts,* XVII (March, 1931), pp. 393–98.

Introduction to catalogue of the exhibition "Rejected Architects." New York, 171 West 57th Street, April 21–May 5, 1931.

"The Skyscraper School of Modern Architecture." *Arts,* XVII (May, 1931), pp. 569–75.

"Rejected Architects." *Creative Art,* VIII (June, 1931), pp. 433–35. Reprinted in *Oppositions 2* (January, 1974), pp. 83–85.

"In Berlin: Comment on Building Exposition." *New York Times,* August 9, 1931, art page.

"Two Houses in the International Style." *House Beautiful,* LXX (October, 1931), pp. 307–9, 356.

1932

"The Berlin Building Exposition of 1931." *T-Square,* II (January, 1932), pp. 17–19, 36–37. Reprinted in *Oppositions 2* (January, 1974), pp. 86–91.

With Alfred H. Barr, Jr., Henry-Russell Hitchcock, and Lewis Mumford: *Modern Architecture: International Exhibition.* New York: The Museum of Modern Art and W. W. Norton, 1932. 199 pp. (Philip Johnson wrote the sections on Mies van der Rohe and Otto Haesler, and part of the introduction.) Arno Press reprint, 1970.

With Henry-Russell Hitchcock: *The International Style: Architecture since 1922.* Preface by Alfred H. Barr, Jr. New York: W. W. Norton, 1932. 240 pp. Paperback edition, with a new foreword and an appendix, "The International Style Twenty Years After" by Henry-Russell Hitchcock, New York: W. W. Norton, 1966.

1933

"Architecture in the Third Reich." *Hound & Horn,* VII (October-December, 1933), pp. 137–39. Reprinted in *Oppositions 2* (January, 1974) pp. 92–93.

Foreword to catalogue of the exhibition "The Work of Young Architects in the Middle West." New York, The Museum of Modern Art, April 3–30, 1933.

1934

"Architecture and Industrial Art," in catalogue of the exhibition "Modern Works of Art: Fifth Anniversary Exhibition." New York, The Museum of Modern Art, November 20, 1934–January 20, 1935. 2nd edition, emended, 1936.

Machine Art. Foreword by Alfred H. Barr, Jr. New York: The Museum of Modern Art, 1934. 115 pp. Arno Press reprint, 1970.

1942

"Architecture in 1941." Unpublished article for encyclopedia.

"Architecture of Harvard Revival and Modern: The New Houghton Library." *Harvard Advocate,* 75th anniversary issue (April, 1942), pp. 12–17.

1945

"War Memorials: What Aesthetic Price Glory?" *Art News,* XLIV (September, 1945), pp. 8–10, 24–25.

1947

Mies van der Rohe. New York: The Museum of Modern Art, 1947. 208 pp. 2nd revised edition, with added chapter, 1953. 3rd edition, revised and enlarged (forthcoming). German edition, Stuttgart: Gerd Hatje, 1956. Spanish edition, Buenos Aires: Victor Leru, 1960.

1948

With Peter Blake: "Architectural Freedom and Order: An Answer to Robert W. Kennedy." *Magazine of Art,* XLI (October, 1948), pp. 228–31.

1949

"The Frontiersman." *Architectural Review,* CVI (August, 1949), pp. 105–10.

1950

"House at New Canaan, Connecticut." *Architectural Review,* CVIII (September, 1950), pp. 152–59.

1951

Opening remarks as chairman, symposium on "The Relation of Painting and Sculpture to Architecture." New York, The Museum of Modern Art, March 19, 1951.

1952

With Henry-Russell Hitchcock: "The Buildings We See." *New World Writing,* I (April, 1952), pp. 109–30.

Preface to *Postwar Architecture,* edited by Henry-Russell Hitchcock and Arthur Drexler. New York: The Museum of Modern Art, 1952. pp. 8–9. Comments, pp. 72–75. Arno Press reprint (together with *Built in U.S.A.: 1932–1944*), 1968.

1953

Speech, symposium on "Art and Morals." Northampton (Mass.), Smith College, April 24, 1953.

"Correct and Magnificent Play." *Art News,* LII (September, 1953), pp. 16–17, 52–53. Review of Le Corbusier, *Complete Works.* V. *1946–1952.*

Speech, "That Human Being Called the Client." American Institute of Architects Central State District Conference, October, 1953. Quoted briefly in *Architectural Forum,* XCIX (November, 1953), p. 58, and *Time* magazine, LXII (December 14, 1953), p. 84.

With Pietro Belluschi, Louis Kahn, Vincent Scully, and Paul Weiss: "On the Responsibility of the Architect." *Perspecta 2* (1953), pp. 45–57. Based on tape recordings of Yale University "studio discussions." Excerpted in John M. Jacobus, Jr., *Philip Johnson.* New York: Braziller, 1962, p. 113.

1954

Speech, Minneapolis Institute of Arts, May 4, 1954.

"School at Hunstanton." *Architectural Review,* CXVI (September, 1954), pp. 148, 152.

1955

Speech, "Style and the International Style." New York, Barnard College, April 30, 1955.

Informal talk to students, School of Architectural Design, "Part I: The Seven Crutches of Modern Architecture." "Part II: Taliesin West: An Appreciation." Cambridge (Mass.), Harvard University, December 7, 1954. Part I published in *Perspecta 3* (1955), pp. 40–44; excerpted in Jacobus, *Philip Johnson,* pp. 113–18.

"The Wiley House," *Perspecta 3* (1955), p. 45.

Foreword to Rachel Wischnitzer, *Synagogue Architecture in the United States: History and Interpretation.* Philadelphia: The Jewish Publication Society of America, 5716/1955. p. VII.

"The Town and the Automobile, or The Pride of Elm Street." Unpublished article.

1956

Remarks on Mies van der Rohe, June 26, 1956.

With others: "One Hundred Years of Significant Building. I. Office Buildings." *Architectural Record,* CXX (June, 1956), pp. 149, 151. Statements on the Wainwright Building and Philadelphia Saving Fund Society. "II. Administration and Research Buildings." Statements on Minerals & Metals Research Building, I.I.T., p. 206.

"Is Sullivan the Father of Functionalism?" *Art News,* LV (December, 1956), pp. 44–46, 56–57.

1957

With John Peter: "Conversations Regarding the Future of Architecture." *Print,* XI (February–March, 1957), pp. 37–39. Excerpts from L.P. record with statements by Philip Johnson and Eero Saarinen on Le Corbusier, Frank Lloyd Wright, and Mies van der Rohe, and by Mies on his own work.

"100 Years, Frank Lloyd Wright and Us." *Pacific Architect and Builder* (March, 1957), pp. 13, 35–36. Digest of speech to Washington State Chapter, A.I.A., Seattle, on the occasion of the centennial of the Institute's founding.

"The University of St. Thomas, Houston." *Architectural Record,* CXXII (August, 1957), pp. 138–39.

Speech, "The Twentieth-Century Art Museum." Utica (New York), Munson-Williams-Proctor Institute, November 8, 1957.

Interviews, "Philip Johnson (I)" and "Philip Johnson (II)," in Selden Rodman, *Conversations with Artists.* New York: Devin-Adair, 1957, pp. 52–56, 60–70.

1958

With others: "Historical Labor Museum for CIO–AFL." *National Institute for Architectural Education Bulletin,* XXXIV (February, 1958), pp. 8–9. Philip Johnson wrote the program for the competition sponsored by the Marble Institute of America and made a brief statement on the formulation of the requirements as printed.

"A New Design for Sarah Lawrence." *Sarah Lawrence Alumnae Magazine* (February, 1958), pp. 6–7.

Series of lectures for Vincent Scully's course at Yale University: "International Style," April 25, 1958; "Post-War Frank Lloyd Wright and Le Corbusier," May 2, 1958; "Retreat from the International Style to the Present Scene," May 9, 1958.

"The Work of Mies van der Rohe," in Alexandre Persitz and Danielle Valeix, "L'Oeuvre de Mies van der Rohe." Boulogne/Seine: L'Architecture d'Aujourd'hui, 1958, pp. 101–03. Excerpted from *Mies van der Rohe.*

Introduction to *The Collected Writings of Alvin Lustig,* edited and published by Holland R. Melson, Jr. New Haven (Conn.), 1958. pp. 9–10.

1959

"Architekten und ihr erster Auftrag." *Baukunst und Werkform,* XII (January, 1959), pp. 3–6.

Speech, "Whither Away—Non-Miesian Directions." New Haven (Conn.), Yale University, February 5, 1959.

"Parthenon, Perfection and All That." *Art News,* LVIII (March, 1959), pp. 43, 66. Review of A. W. Lawrence, *Greek Architecture.*

Speech, American Association of Museums, Pittsburgh (Penna.), June 4, 1959.

1960

Statement, with others: "Fairest Cities of Them All." *New York Times Magazine,* January 24, 1960, p. 15.

"Letter to the Museum Director." *Museum News,* XXXVIII (January, 1960), pp. 22–25.

"Great Reputations in the Making: Three Architects." *Art in America,* XLVIII (Spring, 1960), pp. 70–75.

"Where Are We At?" *Architectural Review,* CXXVII (September, 1960), pp. 173–75. Review of Reyner Banham, *Theory and Design in the First Machine Age.* Excerpted in Jacobus, *Philip Johnson,* p. 118.

Informal talk. London, Architectural Association, School of Architecture, November 28, 1960.

Interview, "Architectural Student Jonathan Barnett Interviews Architect Philip Johnson." *Architectural Record,* CXXVIII (December, 1960), pp. 16, 238.

American Museum Architecture. The Voice of America Forum Lectures. Architecture Series, 8. Washington (D.C.): Voice of America, 1960. Originally broadcast by the Voice of America.

1961

With others: "Jury Discussion: Eighth Annual Design Awards." *Progressive Architecture,* XLII (January, 1961), pp. 154–56.

Statement in catalogue of "Inaugural Exhibition, Amon Carter Museum of Western Art." Fort Worth (Texas), January, 1961. Reprinted in *Kentiku* (May, 1962), p. 21.

"Moderne Theaterarchitektur." *Bühnentechnische Rundschau,* I (February, 1961), pp. 15–16, 21–24. Speech delivered at "Colloquiums über Theaterbau," Berlin, Deutsche Sektion des Internationalen Theater-Instituts, November 21, 1960. Reprinted in English: "9 Actual Theatre Designs." *Musical America,* annual issue, LXXXI (January, 1961), pp. 12–14; "Actual Theatre Designs." *Annual of Architecture, Structure & Townplanning* (India), 1962, pp. C 26–33.

Speech Honoring Mies van der Rohe on His 75th Birthday. Chicago, February 7, 1961.

Statement in "The Sixties: A P/A Symposium on the State of Architecture. Part I: The Period of Chaoticism." *Progressive Architecture,* XLII (March, 1961), pp. 122–33.

Speech, "The International Style—Death or Metamorphosis." New York, Architectural League Forum, The Metropolitan Museum of Art, March 30, 1961. Excerpted in *Architectural Forum,* CXIV (June, 1961), p. 87, and in Jacobus, *Philip Johnson,* pp. 119–20.

Letter to the editor, "The F. D. R. Memorial Competition—Pro and Con." *Architectural Forum,* CXIV (April, 1961), p. 187.

Speech, "If I Were President for a Day . . ." Washington (D.C.), Women's National Democratic Club, April 27, 1961.

Statement, with others: "What Is Your Favorite Building?" *New York Times Magazine,* May 21, 1961, pp. 34–35.

With others: "International Council of Museums Congress." *Architectural Design,* XXXI (August, 1961), pp. 340–42. Speech delivered at Turin, International Council of Museums Congress, May 25, 1961.

"Theater Query." *Performing Arts,* III (June 30, 1961), p. 5. Reply to letter by Theodore H. Kenworthy.

"Architect Replies to *Dance News* Suggestion." *Dance News,* XXXIX (December, 1961), p. 6.

Letter to Dr. Jürgen Joedicke, December 6, 1961. Published in Jacobus, *Philip Johnson,* pp. 120–22.

"Johnson." *Perspecta* 7 (1961), pp. 3–8.

Karl Friedrich Schinkel im zwanzigsten Jahrhundert. Schriftenreihe des Architekten- und Ingenieurs-Verein zu Berlin, Heft 13. Berlin, 1961. 24 pp. Delivered as a speech in Berlin, March 13, 1961. Reprinted in English, "Schinkel and Mies." *Program,* New York, Columbia School of Architecture (Spring, 1962), pp. 14–34.

1962

With others: "Modern Architecture and the Rebuilding of Cities." *Arts and Architecture,* LXXIX (February, 1962), pp. 16–17, 30–32. Abridged report of panel discussion sponsored by the Graham Foundation for Advanced Studies in the Fine Arts, Chicago, Illinois Institute of Technology, November, 1961.

"The Architectural New Look." *Yale Scientific Magazine,* XXXVI (March, 1962), pp. 32, 33, and cover.

"Article for *The Kentiku* by Philip Johnson." Introduction to Philip Johnson issue, *Kentiku,* 5 (May, 1962); also, architect's statements on the Glass House; Amon Carter Museum of Western Art; Museum of Modern Art Garden; Campus, University of St. Thomas, Houston; Dormitories for Sarah Lawrence College; Brown University Computing Center; Wiley House; Robert Leonhardt House; House for Mr. and Mrs. Eric Boissonnas. English summary of Japanese text, pp. 1–6.

"Western Taste and Eastern Models." *Nation,* CXCIV (May 19, 1962), pp. 448–49. Review of Walter Gropius, Kenzo Tange, Yasuhiro Ishimoto, Herbert Bayer, *Katsura.*

Statement concerning the Franklin Delano Roosevelt Memorial written for the Fine Arts Commission, Washington, D.C., submitted June 8, 1962. Published in U.S. Congress, House. Subcommittee on Enrolled Bills and Library of the Committee on House Administration, *Franklin Delano Roosevelt: Hearings on H. J. Resolution 712 and H. J. Resolution 713 to Authorize and Direct the Franklin Delano Roosevelt Memorial Commission to Raise Funds for the Construction of a Memorial,* 87th Congress, 1st session. Washington (D.C.): Government Printing Office, 1962, pp. 34–37.

"Recent Work of Philip Johnson." *Architectural Record,* CXXXII (July, 1962), pp. 113–28. Includes Johnson's own comments on Kline Science Center, St. Anselm's Abbey, and Brown University Computing Center.

Speech, "The Art of Building—The Seven Shibboleths of Our Profession." Oceanlake, Oregon, 11th Annual Northwest Regional A.I.A. Conference, October 12, 1962.

"Selected Writings of Philip Johnson," in John M. Jacobus, Jr., *Philip Johnson.* New York: Braziller, 1962. pp. 113–22 (see under respective items, above).

1963

Speech, Yale University, February 13, 1963.

"Crisis in Architecture." *Response* (April, 1963), pp. 5–6. Transcript of statement, Princeton Symposium on World Affairs, Princeton University, April 20, 1963.

Dedication speech, Sheldon Memorial Art Gallery. Lincoln (Neb.), University of Nebraska, May 16, 1963.

"Full Scale False Scale," *Show,* III (June, 1963), pp. 72–75.

"The Art of Architecture and the Capital of a World." *Historic Preservation,* XV (July–September, 1963), pp. 94–99. Speech delivered at Washington (D.C.), Corcoran Gallery of Art, April 3, 1963. Excerpted in "Even Sainted L'Enfant Helped Make D.C. Ugly," *Washington Post,* April 28, 1963, p. E5.

"An Art Gallery for a University Campus (Sheldon Memorial Art Gallery)." *Architectural Record,* CXXXIV (August, 1963), pp. 129–31.

"Art Gallery by Philip Johnson, Architect." *Arts and Architecture,* LXXX (August, 1963), pp. 18–21, 30, 31. Transcript of a televised discussion and tour of the Sheldon Memorial Art Gallery with Sybil Moholy-Nagy.

"You Cannot Plan Campuses . . . They Grow Like Topsy." *Yale Architectural Magazine,* I (Fall, 1963), pp. 6–10 and cover.

"Commencement Address, Pratt Institue, 1963." *Pratt Alumnus,* LXX (Fall, 1963), pp. 10–13. Excerpts in "Abstracts," *Architectural and Engineering News* (September, 1963), pp. 101–02, 118, and in Emerson Goble, "Behind the Record: A Bad Bad World." *Architectural Record,* CXXXIV (October, 1963), p. 9.

With others: "Statements by Architects on the Architecture of the Synagogue," in catalogue of the exhibition "Recent American Synagogue Architecture." New York, The Jewish Museum, November, 1963, p. 22.

"A Personal Statement," in *Four Great Makers of Modern Architecture.* New York: Columbia University Press, 1963. pp. 109–12. Speech on Mies van der Rohe given during symposium at the Columbia University School of Architecture, April 3, 1961.

1964

"Architect's Statement," in *The Sheldon Memorial Art Gallery, University of Nebraska, Lincoln,* 1964.

"Architectural Details: 3. Philip Johnson." *Architectural Record,* CXXXV (April, 1964), pp. 137–52.

"Kline Geology Laboratory; Kline Science Centre, Yale." *Architectural Design,* XXXIV (April, 1964), pp. 174–77.

Statement on the New York State Theater in "Theater Glamour Again." *Architectural Record,* CXXXV (May, 1964), pp. 137–44.

Interview, "The Role of the Architect." *Progressive Architecture,* XLV (June, 1964), pp. 166–67.

"Young Artists at the Fair and at Lincoln Center." *Art in America,* LII (August, 1964), pp. 112, 123.

1965

Speech, Yale University, April 19, 1965.

With others: "Structure and Design." *Fortune* Bahamas Conference, "The Future. The New Markets–II." Eleuthera, The Bahamas, May 4, 1965.

Speech, Architectural League dinner, New York, May 26, 1965. *News Bulletin,* The Architectural League of New York, pp. 1–4.

With others: Interview with J(an) C. R(owan), "The Major Space." *Progressive Architecture,* special issue, XLVI (June, 1965), pp. 144–45, 173.

Statement in "Le Corbusier: A Preliminary Assessment." *Progressive Architecture,* XLVI (October, 1965), p. 236.

Speech, "Our Ugly Cities Are Getting Uglier." Austin, Texas Conference on Our Environmental Crisis, organized by the School of Architecture, The University of Texas, November 21–23, 1965. Transcript printed in *Texas Conference on Our Environmental Crisis.* Austin: University of Texas, 1966. pp. 80–90.

"Whence and Whither: The Processional Element in Architecture." *Perspecta 9/10* (1965), pp. 167–78. Excerpted in Robert A. M. Stern, *New Directions in American Architecture.* New York: Braziller, 1969. pp. 42–47.

1966

Statement in catalogue of the exhibiton "40 under 40." New York, The Architectural League of New York, Spring, 1966. p. 34.

Speech to the Governor's Council on Natural Beauty. New York, Hilton Hotel, February 25, 1966. Published as "Report of the Panel on Townscape (Philip Johnson, Chairman) to the Governor's Council on Natural Beauty," *Summary Report of the Governor's Conference on Natural Beauty,* pp. 19–21.

Address at banquet honoring him as Building Stone Institute's Architect of the Year. Atlanta (Georgia), Building Stone Institute's 47th Annual Convention, March 9, 1966.

Speech in honor of Kenzo Tange. New York, Architectural League dinner, March 24, 1966.

"Philip Johnson Explains His Remarkable Underground Museum." *Vogue,* CXLVII (May, 1966), pp. 200–201.

"Statement on Mies van der Rohe on the Occasion of His 80th Birthday." *Bauen und Wohnen,* V (May, 1966), p. 192. Text in German, French, and English.

Commencement address, "Our Ugly Cities." South Hadley (Mass.), Mount Holyoke College, June 5, 1966. Published in *Mount Holyoke Alumnae Quarterly,* L (Summer, 1966), pp. 86–88. Reprinted in *Stone Magazine,* LXXXVI (September, 1966), pp. 13–14, 21. Excerpted in *Fortune,* LXXIV (July 1, 1966), p. 68; excerpt reprinted in *Terrazzo-Tile and Modern Flooring,* II (September, 1966), pp. 7, 24.

Review of Robin Boyd, *The Puzzle of Architecture. Architectural Forum,* CXXIV (June, 1966), pp. 72–73, 93.

"Projekt für die neue Kunsthalle der Stadt Bielefeld." *Bauen + Wohnen,* XX (September, 1966), pp. 334–36.

Interview by Francine du Plessix, "Philip Johnson Goes Underground." *Art in America,* LIV (July–August, 1966), pp. 88–97.

Philip Johnson: Architecture 1949–1965. Introduction by Henry-Russell Hitchcock. New York: Holt, Rinehart and Winston, 1966. 116 pp.

Review of *Philip Johnson: Architecture 1949–1965. Architectural Forum,* CXXV (October, 1966), pp. 52–53.

Interview with Paul Heyer, in Paul Heyer, *Architects on Architecture: New Directions in America.* New York: Walker, 1966. pp. 279–92. Excerpts reprinted in *Architectural Forum,* CXXV (November, 1966), pp. 66, 67, 68, and 97.

". . . A Grain of Salt." *Image 4* (1966), pp. 48–49. Excerpts, in student publication of University of Texas School of Architecture, of question-and-answer session following Johnson's address at Texas Conference on Our Environmental Crisis, November, 1965 (see above).

1967
Comment on report by Commissioner of Parks August Heckscher on New York City Park System, American Institute of Architects Third Theme Session. New York, Hilton Hotel, June, 1967. Quotations in *F. W. Dodge Construction News,* June 2, 1967, p. 8.

Statement on "The Problem of Religious Content in Contemporary Art." First International Congress on Religion, Architecture and the Visual Arts. New York, August 29, 1967. Published in *Revolution, Place and Symbol. Journal of the First International Congress on Religion, Architecture and the Visual Arts.* New York City and Montreal, August 26–September 4, 1967. pp. 137–40.

1968
"Architecture: A Twentieth Century Flop." *Look,* XXXII (January 9, 1968), p. 30.

"Why We Want Our Cities Ugly," in *The Fitness of Man's Environment.* Smithsonian Annual II. New York: Harper & Row, 1968. pp. 145–60. Speech delivered at Smithsonian Institution Annual Symposium, February 17, 1968; excerpt in *Sunday Washington Star,* February 19, 1967, p. 29.

"Jury's Report," letter of March 12, 1968, by Philip Johnson, Chairman, to the Hon. Jason R. Nathan, Administrator, Housing and Development Administration, in *Record of Submissions and Awards: Competition for Middle-Income Housing at Brighton Beach, Brooklyn, 1968,* pp. 9–11. Quoted in part in Robert A.M. Stern, *New Directions in American Architecture.* New York: Braziller, 1969, p. 10, and in Robert Venturi, Denise Scott-Brown, and Steven Izenour, *Learning from Las Vegas.* Cambridge (Mass.): MIT Press, 1972, pp. 134–35.

Speech, *Esquire* Seminar, 1968.

1969
Speech, "Tribute to the Late Mies van der Rohe." New York, annual meeting of the American Institute of Arts and Letters, December 5, 1969.

With John Burgee: *The Island Nobody Knows.* New York State Urban Development
Corporation, Welfare Island Planning and Development Committee, 1969. 20 pp.

1970
Statement on the John F. Kennedy Memorial, Dallas, Texas, 1970.

"Philip Johnson on the Art of Architecture." *Building Design,* no. 23 (August 10,
1970), pp. 6–7.

Statement on Pop Art, in *American Painting 1900–1970.* New York: Time-Life Books,
1970, p. 164.

1971
"A Charleston Critique." *Historic Preservation,* XXIII (January–March, 1971), p. 17.
Transcript of speech delivered at the 24th Annual Meeting and Preservation
Conference, National Trust for Historic Preservation. Charleston (South Carolina),
November 7, 1970.

"An Open Letter to Mayor Kollek." *New York Times,* February 26, 1971, p. 33.

1972
"The Addition to the Boston Public Library," November 9, 1972. 2 pp., offset.

1973
"Beyond Monuments." *Architectural Forum,* CXXXVIII (January–February, 1973), pp.
54–68, 70, 72, and 74. Adapted from "Monuments for the Masses," Graham
Foundation Lecture, Chicago Chapter, American Institute of Architects, December 15,
1972.

"The Design of the Bobst Library and the State of the Art Today." March, 1973, 5
pp., mimeographed. Reprinted in Program of the Fifteenth Anniversary Party of the
Women's Architectural Auxiliary of the New York Chapter, American Institute of
Architects, January 30, 1974.

"The Architectural Aspect of the I. D. S. Center in Minneapolis." October, 1973.
Published as "A There, There." *Architectural Forum,* CXL (November, 1973), p. 38.

Interview with John W. Cook and Heinrich Klotz in *Conversations with Architects.* New
York: Praeger, 1973. pp. 11–51.

1974
"The Design of the Museum: Johnson/Burgee," statement on the Neuberger Museum,
March 8, 1974. Published in *The Making of a Museum: 1.* Neuberger Museum, State
University of New York College at Purchase, May, 1974.

Interview with Lee Radziwill, "Fancy Speaking." *Esquire,* LXXXII (December, 1974),
pp. 159–61, 220–24.

1975
"Commemorative Tribute of the American Academy of Arts and Letters to Louis I.
Kahn." Joint Ceremonial of the American Academy of Arts and Letters and the
National Institute of Arts and Letters. New York, May 22, 1974. Published in
*Proceedings of the American Academy of Arts and Letters and the National Institute of Arts and
Letters,* Second series, Number 25 (1975), pp. 79–80.

"Presentation to Saul Steinberg of the Gold Medal for Graphic Art," Joint Ceremonial
of the American Academy of Arts and Letters and the National Institute of Arts and
Letters, May 22, 1974. In *ibid.,* p. 21.

With Richard Lippold and Robert Motherwell: "Architecture vis-à-vis Painting and
Sculpture—A Trialogue," dinner meeting of the Institute, April 3, 1974. In *ibid.,* pp.
47–61.

Speech, "A New Day Dawns," delivered at the convention of the International Union of Bricklayers and Allied Craftsmen on the occasion of Johnson's acceptance of the 1975 Louis Sullivan Award for Architecture, September 15, 1975. Published in a booklet by the International Masonry Institute: Washington (D. C.), 1975.

Lecture, "What Makes Me Tick." Columbia University, September 24, 1975.

"Postscript" (dated April 1, 1974), in *Five Architects: Eisenman, Graves, Gwathmey, Hejduk, Meier.* New York: Oxford University Press, 1975. p. 138.

Selected Writings by Philip Johnson, edited by David Whitney. Translated into Japanese by Tadashi Yokoyama. Tokyo, A.D.A. Edita, 1975. 314 pp.

1976
Interview on James Stirling, in "Interviews with Craig Hodgetts." *Design Quarterly 100.* Special issue: *Inside James Stirling.* Issues in Architecture, II (1976), p. 22.

"The Shape of the Office Building." Unpublished manuscript, 1976.

1977
"Notes on Gwathmey/Siegel" (written April 18, 1976). Introduction for *Charles Gwathmey and Robert Siegel: Residential Works 1966–1977.* Tokyo, A. D. A. Edita, 1977. p. 6.

Index

Page numbers in italics refer to illustrations. Buildings are listed under architects' names when these are identified in the text, otherwise under locality. Chronology and Bibliography are not indexed.

Index prepared by Helen M. Franc.